H

Zed Titles on Globalization

Globalization has become the new buzzword of the late 1990s. Despite the very different meanings attached to the term and even more divergent evaluations of its likely impacts, it is clear nevertheless that we are in an accelerated process of transition to a new period in world history. Zed Books' titles on globalization pay special attention to what it means for the South, for women, for workers and for other vulnerable groups.

Nassau Adams, *Worlds Apart: The North-South Divide and the International System*

Samir Amin, *Capitalism in the Age of Globalization: The Management of Contemporary Society*

Asoka Bandarage, *Women, Population and Global Crisis: A Political-Economic Analysis*

Michel Chossudovsky, *The Globalisation of Poverty: Impacts of IMF and World Bank Reforms*

Peter Custers, *Capital Accumulation and Women's Labour in Asian Economies*

Bhagirath Lal Das, *An Introduction to the WTO Agreements*

Bhagirath Lal Das, *The WTO Agreements: Deficiencies, Imbalances and Required Changes*

Bhagirath Lal Das, *The World Trade Organization: A Guide to the New Framework for International Trade*

Diplab Dasgupta, *Structural Adjustment, Global Trade and the New Political Economy of Development*

Graham Dunkley, *The Free Trade Adventure: The WTO, GATT and Globalism: A Critique*

Bjorn Hettne et al, *International Political Economy: Understanding Global Disorder*

Terence Hopkins and Immanuel Wallerstein et al., *The Age of Transition: Trajectory of the World-System, 1945–2025*

Jomo, K. S. (ed.), *Tigers in Trouble: Financial Governance, Liberalisation and the Economic Crises in East Asia*

Hans-Peter Martin and Harald Schumann, *The Global Trap: Globalization and the Assault on Prosperity and Democracy*

Harry Shutt, *The Trouble with Capitalism: An Enquiry into the Causes of Global Economic Failure*

Kavaljit Singh, *The Globalisation of Finance: a Citizen's Guide*

Henk Thomas (ed.), *Globalization and Third World Trade Unions*

Christa Wichterich, *The Globalized Woman: Reports from a Future of Inequality*

David Woodward, *Foreign Direct and Equity Investment in Developing Countries: The Next Crisis?*

For full details of this list and Zed's other subject and general catalogues, please write to: The Marketing Department, Zed Books, 7 Cynthia Street, London N1 9JF UK or e-mail: sales@zedbooks.demon.co.uk

Global Futures: Shaping Globalization

edited by

JAN NEDERVEEN
PIETERSE

Zed Books

LONDON · NEW YORK

Global Futures: Shaping Globalization was first published by Zed Books Ltd,
7 Cynthia Street, London N1 9JF, UK and Room 400, 175 Fifth Avenue,
New York, NY 10010, USA in 2000.

Distributed in the USA exclusively by St Martin's Press, Inc.,
175 Fifth Avenue, New York, NY 10010, USA.

Second impression, 2001

Cover designed by Andrew Corbett
Set in Monotype Garamond by Ewan Smith
Printed and bound in Malaysia

A catalogue record for this book is available from the British Library.

Library of Congress Cataloging-in-Publication-Data

Global futures: shaping globalization / edited by Nederveen Pieterse, Jan
   p. cm.
   Includes bibliographical references and index.
   ISBN 1-85649-801-8 – ISBN 1-85649-802-6
      1. Social prediction. 2. Economic forecasting. 3. Progress.
   I. Nederveen Pieterse, Jan.

HM901.G58 2000
303.49–dc21

99-054579

ISBN 1 85649 801 8 cased
ISBN 1 85649 802 6 limp

Contents

Acknowledgements

In October 1997, the Institute of Social Studies celebrated its forty-fifth anniversary as the oldest development studies institute in Europe. Asked to organize a conference to celebrate the occasion, I chose the theme of global futures. This was implemented through a public lecture series that ran from September 1996 – featuring Richard Falk, David Held, Riccardo Petrella, Hazel Henderson, Martin Khor, Tariq Banuri and Mike Featherstone – building up to a conference on 8–10 October 1997. I am in great debt to the colleagues who took the initiative, in particular Professor Hans Opschoor, Rector of the Institute of Social Studies, and the working group that helped bring it about, consisting of Jim Björkman, Hans van Dommele, Matty Klatter, András Kráhl, John Sinjorgo and Thanh-dam Truong.

Besides the contributors to this volume, many scholars and policy-makers contributed to the public lectures and the conference and, for the usual reasons, not all their contributions can be represented in this volume. I should like to express my profound thanks for their distinguished contributions: Tariq Banuri, Gustavo Esteva, Steve Fuller, Reginald Green, David Held, Martin Khor, Ruth Pearson, Riccardo Petrella, Jan Aart Scholte, Boaventura de Sousa Santos and Rebecca Tsosie. Many other colleagues offered advice and help and I should like to express my cordial thanks to them. They include Karamat Ali, James Anaya, Daniel Chavez, Noam Chomsky, Jeff Cohen, Fiona Dove, Louis Emmerij, Gustavo Esteva, Richard Falk, John Kenneth Galbraith, Keith Griffin, Alexander Haridi, Deniz Kandiyoti, Martin Khor, David Korten, W. D. Lakshman, Soileh Padilla Mayer, Edward Said, Zia Sardar, Jai Sen, Noordin Sopiee, Bart van Steenbergen, Hasmet Uluorta and Howard Wachtel. I also cordially thank colleagues at the Institute of Social Studies who contributed as discussants or in other capacities. They include Jim Björkman, Ranjit Dwivedi, Valpy Fitzgerald, Des Gasper, Jeffrey Harrod, Bert Helmsing, Joost Kuitenbrouwer, Guillermo Lathrop, Hans Opschoor, Graham Pyatt, Mohamed Salih, Ashwani Saith, Thanh-dam Truong, Peter Waterman and Saskia Wieringa. Numerous colleagues from institutions and universities abroad attended the conference – there are too many to mention, but their contribution is gratefully acknowledged. I am grateful to

Lisa Chason, who has copy-edited the original papers in this collection. On behalf of the ISS I would like to express appreciation to the institutions that sponsored the conference and the Institute's Dies Natalis: the Netherlands Ministry of Foreign Affairs, the European Commission (Directorate General VIII Development), NCDO (National Committee for International Co-operation and Sustainable Development), WOTRO (Netherlands Foundation for the Advancement of Research in the Tropics), FMO (Finance for Development), Unilever, Euroconsult, the Levi Lassen Foundation, Stork, and Van Hecke Catering.

The Institute of Social Studies is a graduate school in development studies located in The Hague. A university in its own right, it offers MA, diploma and PhD degrees. Most students are from Asia, Africa and Latin America and increasingly also from Eastern Europe. No doubt it will long continue to make its contribution to constructive global futures.

Chapter 7 is also being published in *Alternatives*. Chapters 2, 6, 8 and 9 are also being published in the *Review of International Political Economy*. An earlier version of Chapter 1 appeared in Ziauddin Sardar (ed.) (1999), *Rescuing All Our Futures: The Future of Future Studies* (Twickenham/Westport, CT: Adamantine Press/Praeger, pp. 146–62).

Jan Nederveen Pieterse

About the Contributors

Fantu Cheru is professor of African and Development Studies, School of International Service, American University, Washington, DC.

Louis Emmerij is special advisor to the president, Inter-American Development Bank, Washington, DC and a member of the Group of Lisbon. He was formerly director of the ILO and the OECD Development Centre, and rector of the Institute of Social Studies.

Richard Falk is Albert G. Milbank professor of International Law and Practice, Princeton University and is affiliated with the World Order Models Project, Washington, DC.

Mike Featherstone is professor of sociology and communication and director of the TCS Centre, Nottingham Trent University. He is the editor of *Theory, Culture & Society* and co-editor of *Body & Society*.

Keith Griffin is professor of economics, University of California at Riverside. He is a member of the World Commission on Culture and Development.

Hazel Henderson is a futurist based in St Augustine, Florida. She is chair of the Commission to Fund the United Nations.

Azza Karam is a member of the Politics Department, Queen's University, Belfast and was formerly with International IDEA, Stockholm.

Anthony King is professor of art history and sociology, State University of New York at Binghamton, NY.

Joan Martinez-Alier is professor of economics, Universita Autonoma, Barcelona.

Jan Nederveen Pieterse is associate professor, Institute of Social Studies, The Hague.

Jan Pronk is minister of environment, The Netherlands. At the time of writing, he was minister for development cooperation. He is a former director of UNCTAD.

Howard Wachtel is professor of economics and acting dean of College of

Arts and Sciences, American University, Washington, DC. He is a fellow of the Transnational Institute.

Sakamoto Yoshikazu is professor emeritus, University of Tokyo and senior research fellow, Peace Research Institute, International Christian University, Tokyo.

Michael Watts is professor of geography, University of California at Berkeley.

Abbreviations and Acronyms

ARM-PC	Anticipatory Risk Mitigation Peace-building Contingents
ASEAN	Association of South East Asian Nations
BSE	bovine spongiform encepalopathy
CAPM	capital asset pricing model
CEO	chief executive officer
COPORA	Congressional Office for Public Opinion Research and Assessment
DC	developed country
DFI	direct foreign investment
EC	European Commission
ECOSOC	Economic and Social Council (EU)
EU	European Union
FAO	Food and Agriculture Organization
FDI	foreign direct investment
GATT	General Agreement on Tariffs and Trade
GDP	gross domestic product
GNP	gross national product
HANPP	human appropriation of the products of photosynthesis
HIPC	heavily indebted poor country
ICIDI	Independent Commission on International Development Issues (the Brandt Commission)
IDB	International Development Bank
ILO	International Labour Organization
IMF	International Monetary Fund
INTELSAT	International Telecommunications Satellite Consortium
IPCC	Intergovernmental Panel on Climate Change
ISS	Institute of Social Studies
LDC	less developed country

LETS	local exchange trading system
Mercosur	Common market of the Southern Cone (Latin America, comprising Argentina, Brazil, Uruguay and Paraguay)
MIPS	material input per unit service
MUDS	multi-user domains
NAFTA	North American Free Trade Agreement
NCDO	National Committee for International Cooperation and Sustainable Development
NGO	non-governmental organizations
NIC	newly industrializing country
NIE	newly industrializing economy
OPEC	Organization of Petroleum Exporting Countries
ppm	parts per million
R&D	research and development
RRG	rural regional government
OECD	Organization for Economic Cooperation and Development
SDN	Sustainable Development Network (of the UNDP)
SEATO	South East Asia Treaty Organization
TNC	transnational corporation
UNCED	United Nations Conference on Environment and Development
UNDP	United Nations Development Programme
UNCTAD	United Nations Conference on Trade and Development
UNEP	United Nations Environment Programme
UNESCO	United Nations Educational, Scientific and Cultural Organization
UNICEF	United Nations Children's Fund
UNRISD	United Nations Research Institute for Social Development
UNSIA	United Nations Security Insurance Agency
WBCSD	World Business Council for Sustainable Development
WCED	World Commission on Environment and Development (the Brundtland Commission)
WOTRO	Netherlands Foundation for the Advancement of Research in the Tropics
WTO	World Trade Organization

Introduction

Is there life after globalization? At the cusp of the millennium, there is a growing global reform movement, involving international NGOs and civic associations, labour organizations, the UN and other international organizations, governments and regional bodies, and to some extent also corporations. It concerns global governance and democratization, international finance and macroeconomic reform, environment and development, and social and cultural change. This collection is a one-stop overview of global reform thinking. In a single volume, it brings together different concerns, approaches and thinkers. While the concerns addressed are by no means exhaustive, it represents a wide angle on global futures.

Close your eyes, imagine that we are in the year 2020 and tell us what you think the world should look like. This is what I asked contributors to Global Futures to do. This invitation clashes with deeply ingrained principles in social science – thou shalt not be prescriptive, thou shalt be normative only accidentally, thou shalt not offer recipes and thou shalt not predict. Some of the points made in the original proposal are the following.

From Critique to Affirmation

There are many critiques but few constructive proposals. Critique, critique of critique, critique of critique of critique, and so on, or deconstruction, deconstruction of deconstruction, and so on, make up much of the intellectual fare, with 'resistance' and 'opposition' as further options. To some extent, this reflects the political and ideological malaise that has existed since the 1980s. Of course, negation implies affirmation – for what is critique without alternatives? – but whether affirmation is implicit or explicit makes a difference. Explicit affirmation, saying what we want and not just what we don't want, generally means being holistic, normative, programmatic. Imagining and setting forth what an inclusive and emancipatory future would be like evokes a politics of construction, a shift to mid- and long-term perspectives, a style of communication different from critique, an education of desire.

Constructivism

Structuralist and deterministic perspectives of various kinds used to prevail, but conventional wisdom in social science now has it that social realities are constructed – traditions are invented, nations are imagined, identities are constructed and institutions exist because and as long as people believe in them. Processes of construction are shaped by historical conditions, are framed by language and epistemology, and are in part voluntary and deliberative; both structure and agency therefore play a part in construction. If social realities are constructed, then, to the extent that agency plays a part – and this itself is probably a frontier that can be pushed – well, let us construct them. At the very least, navigation is easier in the presence of beacons.

Futures

Obviously, there are many kinds of futures. Insurance, business and economics, planning, environmental studies and strategic thinking involve sophisticated techniques of forecasting and risk analysis. Through credit, securities, options, forwards and other instruments, futures form part of markets. Cybernetics, simulation and game theory have long since entered social science. Utopianism, another kind of futures thinking, often involved blueprints, at times of complete social arrangements, which led to the classic criticisms of Karl Popper and Ralf Dahrendorf that Utopias do not open but close futures and reflect totalitarian imaginations; they opted instead for piecemeal social engineering. Laclau (1990) argues against parachuting in political goals that do not arise out of social struggles themselves. All the same, various forms of 'realistic' or 'hard-nosed' Utopianism are as current as ever, though not necessarily as prominent. Here futures are used in a conversational sense: programmes presented for discussion, scenarios developed for clarification and setting directions for constructive political imagination and action. Scenarios and programmes are the common currency of political and policy debates, and in one sense this project is also about bridging the gaps between intellectual and policy cultures – between critique and construction, deconstruction and reconstruction.

Global Futures

The primary concern is with futures of world-scale relevance or resonance, rather than local, national or regional futures *per se*, although obviously these are mutually implicated in many ways. Arguably, one reason reports such as those of the Brandt, Brundtland and South Commissions have been ignored in wider circles is that they focus on North–South relations (ICIDI 1980; WCED 1987; South Commission 1990). They could pass largely unnoticed in public climates in the North, such as the USA, in part because they seem to address 'their', not 'our' future. No doubt North–South relations are central to global futures, but it may be wise, and not merely expedient, to broaden the imagery of 'development' towards concerns not merely of the South but of the North as well. This goes beyond the usual 'mutual interest' formula. There are now several 'Souths' and many problems are being shared North and South – problems of competitiveness, trade and investment, innovation-driven growth, jobless growth, ecological hazard, multiculturalism, mega-urbanization, crime. In the process 'development', including global development, takes on new meanings.

Critical Utopias

It would be exciting to see an ensemble of forward-looking and affirmative programmes for futures of social policy, gender, culture, human rights, cities, in a context of proposals for transformation of the world economy, global politics, development policies, international financial institutions and ecological economics. This of course includes obstacles and resistance in the way of emancipatory futures. Scenarios of political circumstances, coalition building and implementation should be part of such a discussion. This may involve multiple time-frames, such as 20 years for mid-term and 50 or more for long-term futures (as in Held 1995). Taking a cue from Malaysia's Vision 2020, the project may be characterized as a Global Vision 2020. It may be argued that there are many progressive proposals around and that what is in short supply is political will, but that is a little too easy. Programmes have often been institutional (e.g. UN reform), bureaucratic in language (commission reports), narrow in terms of target audience (government, academia, social movements, business), or concern (single issue). Even so, there is plenty to build on. What is envisaged here is reflexive and wide-ranging in terms of concerns and audience.

By bringing together different domains of transformation and disciplines, this volume offers an interactive perspective on global transformation. Several contributors – futurists and policy makers – have long been active in this field. In addition, the volume includes academics whose regular concern is analysis and critique, for the objective is also to widen the radius of debate.

Richard Falk has been writing about global reform for many years. Louis Emmerij, formerly with the ILO and OECD, has been responsible for placing the question of employment on the map of international policy. He contributed to the human development approach and is now a member of the Lisbon Group. In the 1970s, Jan Pronk was associated with the Nobel prize-winning economist Jan Tinbergen and his work on the New International Economic Order; he was a director of UNCTAD and is presently minister of the environment of the Netherlands; at the time of writing, he was minister for development cooperation. Hazel Henderson, an iconoclastic economist, has long been active in alternative futures. In the 1980s, Joan Martinez-Alier published the first study to introduce the discipline of ecological economics. Keith Griffin is a founding contributor to the human development approach and has recently been a member of the World Commission on Culture and Development. In this volume they update their positions and offer their latest views. Other contributors have long been active in global studies. Yoshikazu Sakamoto is one of Japan's well-known scholars of international relations. Howard Wachtel is well known as a labour economist and for his work on international finance. Anthony King is known for his comparative work on colonial architecture, cities in the South and global culture. Fantu Cheru has done significant work on social movements in Africa. Michael Watts is known for his innovative research in development studies and Mike Featherstone for his work on global culture and social theory. Azza Karam has recently published a study of Islam, women and the state in Egypt.

The chapters take a big-picture approach to global conditions and shuttle between global and local circumstances. By combining chapters a variety of interactive concerns can be addressed (global reform and international political economy, environment and development, globalization and feminism, technology and cultural change, etc.), which contributes to a dynamic and complex perspective on ongoing transformations and global reform. One of the objectives of this project is to make broad-ranging conversations on futures normal – an acceptable and, in time, regular part of social science. In part, this involves a shift from paradigm politics to scenario politics. Paradigm politics tends to be ideological, static, divisive, while scenario politics brings us, to some degree at least, into the stream of reality. Another objective is to adopt a big-picture approach to development questions. If development studies are to be holistic, then let us see the whole. Even piecemeal change, in an interconnected world, needs the whole picture, and so Karl Popper and Karl Marx meet up. Critical holism might be a heading for this agenda (Nederveen Pieterse 1999).

The general remit has been to set forth desirable and plausible proposals for global conditions in 2020. This forces us to think of what we actually want, and thus to make conscious (and therefore subject to debate) the unconscious desire that directs our analysis and criticism. In the process, global futures function as an intellectual and political Rorschach test. A global 2020 vision reveals fundamental premises and sensibilities, shows a particular angle on the present and reflects back on the project itself. The remit triggers agency and evokes subjectivity, and so there is a moral passion to the contributions, which is not usually the case in such edited volumes. Dimensions of global futures are *principles* (of analysis or policy, methodologies, or general sensibilities in approaching global futures), *proposals* and *implementation*. What follows is only a brief précis, because a detailed discussion would lead too far.

Richard Falk in Chapter 2 formulates an agenda for the democratization of global governance centred on the renunciation of force in international relations, human rights, sustainable development, the global commons and accountability. According to Jan Pronk in Chapter 3, globalization is unstoppable but needs to be given a political direction. He advocates taking a developmental approach to globalization or 'steering globalization', particularly international finance. He proposes strengthening existing international organizations and agreements, while at the same time strengthening civil society in a framework of cultural pluralism. According to Louis Emmerij in Chapter 4, necessary reforms to address world economic problems are redefining the economic responsibility of the state and redefining the social responsibility of the private sector, along with stricter surveillance of banking and finance, and regional and global social contracts. Hazel Henderson's general framework, outlined in Chapter 5, is a paradigm shift from zero-sum to win-win economics. Part of this is the role of citizen groups and socially responsible enterprise. Her global reform proposals include the regulation of global finance, global taxes, reform of the IMF and World Bank, and a UN security insurance agency. While general presuppositions vary (from Emmerij's dialectics of disaster to Henderson's paradigm shift) and institutional scenarios differ (from strengthening existing institutions to creating new ones), Falk, Pronk, Emmerij and Henderson broadly concur on steering globalization, the reform of international institutions, and regulating international finance as a priority.

Others probe further within this general remit. In Chapter 6 Howard Wachtel counsels that reform proposals must make sound economic sense: 'Scarce reformist political capital is not to be squandered on quixotic schemes'. Wachtel critically reviews the Tobin tax on foreign exchange transactions, taxes on fixed capital and a unitary profit tax, and makes a case for a tax on foreign direct investment, to be discounted if core labour laws are upheld. Yoshikazu Sakamoto in Chapter 7 views domestic democratization as a condition for the democratization of international relations, which matches Falk and Pronk's approaches and David Held's 'double democratization'. According to Sakamoto, 'Interstate cooperation will not ensure the protection and promotion of the rights and interests of citizens unless states are under the democratic control of civil society, which is sufficiently powerful to counteract the impact of the globalized market and the corresponding tendency of the state to turn into a subservient "market state".' Sakamoto introduces the concept of 'civic states' and inserts a regional dimension. Regional cooperation (the case in point is cooperation in East Asia) can be 'an alternative to global marketization' if it takes place based on democratic principles.

In Chapter 8 Fantu Cheru gives a sober perspective on what global reform would mean concretely from the point of view of sub-Saharan African countries, in particular for peasants. To strengthen democratic movements in Africa, Cheru proposes inclusive cross-movement coalitions, South-South cooperation and improved access to information. Michael Watts's general framework, described in Chapter 9, is 'structural constraints and conjunctural opportunities' in reworking modernity. Poverty eradication is a question of capacities and citizenship. The struggles of those entering global capitalism during this second Great Transformation (a recurring theme through several contributions) have the capacity to change its shape, as did the struggles of the first Great Transformation in the nineteenth century. Joan Martinez-Alier in Chapter 10 brings together ecological economics and collective action. He questions technical solutions to ecological problems, or ecological modernization, and draws attention to social movements for environmental justice as enabling forces in bringing about ecological equity. Cheru, Watts and Martinez-Alier all question narrow economistic views on development and see the way forward in socially re-embedding development and ecology through social movements. Perhaps a limitation of social movements in this context is that they are more effective in relation to local than global concerns. In Chapter 11 Azza Karam takes stock of feminist achievements and questions feminist conventional wisdom. Thinking ahead, she sees plural feminisms that are inclusive of differences among women also in the South and of the needs of men.

The closing section centres on cultural dynamics. In Chapter 12 Keith Griffin presents a challenging argument on the relationship between culture and economic growth according to which cultural diversity past and present stimulates economic development and innovation. Griffin proposes the reconstruction of states on a multicultural foundation reflecting 'the recognition that pluralism is a collective asset, a public good that can yield benefit to all'. Mike Featherstone takes issue in Chapter 13 with both Utopian and dystopian views of technology, treats technology as mediated through social and cultural practices, contrasts reflexive modernity and human development perspectives and points to the potential of new information technologies such as the Internet to enable global citizenship. This addresses the question of access to information, raised by among others Cheru. For Anthony King, in Chapter 14, the global is a sphere of hegemonic, managerial representations, which he counters through a vista of urban global governance in 2020, which might be achieved through a United Cities Organization, on the premise that the grassroots now are in the cities.

These are reflective, wide-ranging conversations on futures, so they do not go deeply into the specifics of implementing future proposals, an approach usually reserved for single-issue treatments or analyses from the point of view of a single institution. Nederveen Pieterse advocates postmodern regulation, while Emmerij evokes a Bismarck to redefine the economic responsibility of the state. Martinez-Alier and King take a science fiction angle, looking back from the 2020s at the twentieth century.

Arguably, one of the weaknesses of global futures thinking follows from the theme of global futures itself (a point made by Cheru and King). Such an exercise runs the risk of leading to global glibness rather than global futures. The present surfeit of globality, the excess of the global, is a reason for caution. A remedy would be local rather than global futures, in other words, careful and meticulous attention to local processes and institutions.

Is the global a new managerial dream? No doubt it is. No doubt it is also a new social science fad that produces a stream of glibness (like post-modernism some years earlier, and cyberspace or some other theme five years from now). But there are counter-trends. Refugees from Rwanda and Burundi in camps in Tanzania write letters to the secretary-general of the United Nations in the name of humanity (Malkki 1993). The global is not *only* an elite domain, it is also a popular domain – witness its role in popular culture. It is a political and economic rendezvous that reaches everywhere, a fateful turn in human history, which calls for engagement, and not only in global terms. The interaction between globalization and localization, or 'glocalization', is familiar enough. Global futures presuppose local futures, for there is no space without place. But local futures also require global futures as enabling environment and echo-chamber, as incubator of sub-jectivities that can make for viable local futures. This interplay is addressed in anthropological perspectives on futures thinking (see Wallman 1992). Dimensions of global futures that are *not* considered in this collection are, to mention a few, the retasking of the military and the growing role of peacekeeping and conflict prevention (cf. Nederveen Pieterse 1998); the role of media; religion, interreligious dialogue and forms of spirituality; the role of art, taking into account rapidly changing aesthetics; and indigenous peoples.

Futures are a wild-card subject. Risk and appeal are closely related. To global futures, there is a price. Any future comes with a price-tag. But we should also consider the price of *no* constructive futures. Whenever futures go out of the window, a collective agenda falls to pieces; life doesn't stop, however, it just flees in all directions. People turn to individual solutions and improvisations. People need futures like they need air. Without an enabling future people disperse to islands of individual experience. Whenever futures break down – as they did in Palestine, Northern Ireland and during times of war in former Yugoslavia, Rwanda, Burundi – there is a breakdown in social cohesion, with all its social and psychological ramifications. Without meaning-ful futures, people migrate out, and we all know of 'inner migration' as well. Globally, moreover, people need hospitable futures to inhabit and nourish the imagination. At a time when globalization generates so much anxiety, insecurity and 'resistance', a forward-looking volume of critical and constructive per-spectives on global transformation may provide a welcome change.

References

Held, D. (1995) *Democracy and Global Order*, Polity, Cambridge.

ICIDI (1980) *North–South: A Programme for Survival* (the Brandt Report), ICIDI, London.

Laclau, E. (1990) *New Reflections on the Revolution of our Time*, Verso, London.

Malkki, L. (1993) 'Citizens of humanity: internationalism and the imagined community of nations', unpublished paper.

Martinez-Alier, J. (1987) *Ecological Economics*, Blackwell, Oxford.

Nederveen Pieterse, J. (ed.) (1998) *World Orders in the Making: Humanitarian Intervention and Beyond*, Macmillan/St. Martin's Press, London/New York.

— (1999) 'Critical holism and the Tao of development', *European Journal of Development Research*, 11 (1): 75–100.

South Commission (1990) *The Challenge of the South*, Oxford University Press, New York.

Wallman, S. (ed.) (1992) *Contemporary Futures: Perspectives from Social Anthropology*, Routledge, London.

WCED (1987) *Our Common Future* (the Brundtland Report), Oxford University Press, New York.

1

Shaping Globalization

JAN NEDERVEEN PIETERSE

These brief reflections on shaping globalization and global futures address three types of question. One, why should global futures be addressed? Two, in what fashion can they be addressed, according to what kind of premises or principles? Three, what forms can global reform and global futures take?

Why Global Futures?

Why would global futures figure on the agenda? The answer to this question centres on the ramifications of globalization, technological change, and the emergence of global citizenship. Globalization refers to the accelerated worldwide intermeshing of economies, and cross-border traffic and communication becoming ever denser. Technological change is speeding up. Risks and opportunities are globalizing. All this belongs to everyday experience. Accordingly, globalization means global effect and global awareness, and therefore increasingly it also means global engagement.

Citizenship under these circumstances is no longer simply national, or, more precisely, the national domain is now one among several relevant organizational spheres, and citizenship is becoming increasingly national *and* local, regional, global at the same time. In addition, citizenship is no longer as state-centred as it used to be. The point of democracy is no longer simply influencing the actions of government. National governance has become one institutional sphere among several. Citizenship is not simply 'international' either, because the concerns at issue are not simply a multiplication of nation-state or intergovernmental structures. Governance is increasingly a matter of international politics, supranational institutions, international treaties and law, in the process involving macro-regional bodies, transnational corporations, transnational citizen groups, and media – interacting in complex, turbulent, multi-centric ways.

Considered in an evolutionary context, humanity has been growing in capacity, technological accomplishment and reflexivity. Collective awareness of concerns that affect the species and the planet – such as the environment, population, development – has been growing, and so has its public articulation, notably in UN global conferences, so that arguably a global public sphere is emerging. At the same time, technological and political accomplishment and awareness do not 'line up' to add up to a condition of collective capacity. Interests are widely dispersed, subjectivities and agendas are diverse, and institutional capacities are relatively feeble.

WHY FUTURES? Anticipation and planning used to be a prerogative and defining feature of government – 'gouverner, ç'est prévoir'. It extended to business and finance in tandem with the development of instruments of credit (banking, securities, options, derivatives) and insurance, which hinge fundamentally on the capacity to estimate, calculate and hedge outcomes. In both governance and business, forecasting has achieved considerable technical sophistication.

Recently the World Business Council for Sustainable Development initiated a project on Global Scenarios with the following justification:

> Planning for a sustainable future requires business to be able to anticipate and not just react to change. This is the rationale underlying our project on Global Scenarios. This project is designed to help business people reach a shared view of the future and challenge the 'mental maps' they hold about sustainable development. This will allow them to anticipate, not react to, the exposures facing their corporations and ensure that they are fostering sustainable development.

Here the capacity to anticipate is presented as enabling for business people: it puts them ahead in relation to circumstances, technologies, and presumably also public criticism, and enables them to develop a shared agenda.

Capacities to anticipate and plan are crucial to business and financial markets, to governments and international institutions. Accordingly, some futures have already been planned and negotiated, bought and sold several times over before citizens have even begun to think about them. This implies that the horizons and agendas according to which futures are planned and designed reflect limited interests and agendas. Should such capacities to anticipate be reserved to business and government, or should they be a matter of broad public awareness? If they did not become part of civic reflection it would mean that citizen groups would be relegated to a back seat, forever *reacting* to the futures designed, prepared and communicated piecemeal by governments and corporations.

At the same time, both government and business planning are constrained. Governments increasingly deal with many political and social forces and variables. Corporations are exposed to such flux in the market that they operate with limited time horizons. In the marketplace, contingency is a fact of life: 'there is absolutely no way, in the evolving marketplace, that you can know exactly who the suppliers, customers, competitors and collaborators are' (C. K. Prahalad in Gibson 1997: 66). A standard quip in business management is: look at how many companies of the Fortune 500 still figure on the list five or ten years hence. It also follows that in government and business planning the command-and-control model no longer applies.

The 'colonization of the life world' – commodification, bureaucratization – is a familiar metaphor (although, with the reconfiguration of the state, bureaucratization is to an extent being replaced by informalization). This includes a routinized process of the colonization of futures, because of the concentration of forecasting and planning capabilities in government and corporate hands. The organization of public space, as in urban and infrastructure planning, is an example. What is needed, then, is a decolonization of futures or, to use more general language, a democratization of futures. Gradually it is becoming a common understanding that not only the end stage of public planning but also the design stage needs to be participatory.

There are many forums in which governments, international institutions, banks and corporations compare notes, set agendas and build coalitions. This happens less among citizen groups. 'Alternative forums' take place on the periphery of intergovernmental conferences, regional meetings of social organizations, sectoral conferences and academic conferences. Both joint agenda-setting and anticipation are less developed among citizen groups than among corporations and governments. They are not as well endowed with think-tanks, nor do they organize forums aligning their views and agendas. This is happening even less *across* areas of concern – for example, human rights groups comparing notes with environmental groups, environmental organizations comparing notes with women's groups and indigenous peoples – except locally. Citizen groups concerned with human rights, ecology, women's or community issues, all have their values and preferred futures. But where do they intersect, interconnect? How and to what extent do these various single-issue concerns and futures line up? Thus for citizen groups a preoccupation with futures, local and global, would involve several functions: dialogue across groups; aligning normative concerns; developing a proactive stance and anticipatory sensibilities and capabilities; making futures a matter of public concern.

Another reason why futures thinking is taking on a new relevance is that several modes of anticipation that were available in the past have lost their appeal. Futures used to be packaged and delivered as part of the grand ideologies that framed the social and political movements of the past, particularly nationalism and socialism. The 'national question' and the 'social question' of the nineteenth century reconverged in twentieth-century social movements, such as the anti-colonial national liberation movements. The ideologies bequeathed by the nineteenth century followed positivist epistemologies and structuralist modes of thinking, relating to macro processes such as imperialism, capitalism and dependency. The future scenarios that emerged from these are now no longer viable or attractive. Nationalism is making place for postnationalism, or at least the reconfiguration of energies in various directions – local, regional, macro-regional, international, global. Delinking or dissocation from capitalism has little meaning in a real world where localities scramble to attract foreign investment. The expectation of a world-scale crisis of capitalism followed by an opening towards socialism has now very few adherents (among the last are the original world-system theorists; e.g. Wallerstein 1994 and Amin 1997).

REGIONAL FUTURES Samuel Huntington's 'clash of civilizations' seems so hopelessly static and antiquated that even arguing against it feels like a waste of time. If civilizational destinies or regional projects still seemed relevant a few decades ago, they now sound increasingly quaint. Calls for 'the West' to be concerned with this or that (as in Huntington) are outdated at a time when business is eyeing 'emerging markets' across the seas.

Evocations of an 'Asian Century' sound outdated even before it has begun. One, the dynamics are Pacific rather than Asian, witness the intercontinental sprawl of the Chinese diaspora. Two, while there is an 'Asian Renaissance' (Ibrahim 1996), its lineages are not purely Asian (just as the makings of the European Renaissance extended well beyond Europe). Three, much of the talk of 'Asian values' is authoritarian in intent, and is often laughed at inside the region. Four, Asian industries, those of Japan included, depend on technology from outside the region, particularly the United States (McRae 1995). Five, because of their export orientation, East and Southeast Asian economies depend on markets in the West. Complementarities among Asian economies, while considerable and growing, would not be sufficient to sustain the countries' exports. Five, intercultural exchange between East and West is so far advanced and so deeply historically layered that in many ways the two can no longer be meaningfully separated. Six, in a 1996 speech in Beijing Prime Minister Mahathir of Malaysia declared the twenty-first century a 'Global Century' rather than an 'Asian Century'. This was a sensible gesture of diplomacy – Western markets would not react well to an upsurge of inward-looking Asian chauvinism; it may also be taken as an expression of an Asian humanism that sets forth a global engagement. Seven, the recent 'Asian crisis' shows the frailty of the Tiger economies.

Similar considerations apply to other regional and civilizational projects. Thus interpretations of India centred on 'Indic civilization' have historical purchase and thus inform futures, but would they be sufficient to generate relevant future scenarios, or would they rather feed neo-chauvinist Hindutva ideology? This also applies to Islamist projects. The wide world of Islam represents an alternative globalism with considerable historical and civilizational depth, geographical scope and growing economic opportunities. At the cusp of the millennium, however, the Islamic world is dependent in the fields of science and technology, in investments and growth opportunities, armaments and security. Financially and economically, culturally and politically, it is profoundly wired to global centres.

Regional and civilizational projects are most intelligently viewed not as contradictory to but as part of global dynamics. In 2020 Islam will be the second major religion in most of Western Europe (in some countries it already is). Some parts of Europe have been reindustrializing thanks to Korean and Taiwanese investments. Japanese management techniques offer a model to overcome the Taylor model of standardized mass production, from the Pacific to Ireland (Walley 1995: 150–1). Accordingly, regional projects should both inform and be informed by global futures. This is not an argument for going global *tout court*. Rather, it is to argue for an interdependence and balance of local, national, regional and global engagements.

How Global Futures?

The mainstream managerial approach to futures is forecasting and risk analysis, which tend to reflect institutional vested interests. Another approach is to criticize dominant futures in order to keep futures 'open' and forestall the 'standardization of dissent' – see, for instance, Ashis Nandy and Zia Sardar (Sardar 1999). Alternative futures is a third approach. Like critical approaches this seeks to be inclusive of interests excluded in the managerial approach, but rather than ringing the alarm bell it seeks to inform futures by placing beacons or attractors that, like magnets, channel collective energies. This approach comes in the form of Utopian and postmodern variations.

Utopias in the sense of blueprints of desirable societies no longer match contemporary mentalities. Critique of Utopianism is now part of contemporary reflexivity. Nineteenth-century Utopias tend to reflect a similar positivist epistemology, authoritarian design and command-and-control outlook as the ideologies of the epoch, which they extrapolate forward. At the turn of the millennium, there is an upsurge in apocalyptic mentalities rather than classical Utopias – witness the Branch Davidians in Waco, Texas and the Aum Shinrikyo cult in Japan (Thompson 1996).

Over time discourse has shifted from 'the future' to 'futures'. Forecasting implies a future that already exists 'out there'. The main problem is its visibility, which may be approximated by means of extrapolation and trend analysis. Currently the understanding is more of futures as options and opportunities. The main preoccupation in future thinking, certainly in business management, is no longer forecasting but *imagining* and secondly *creating* futures.

> The big challenge in creating the future is not predicting the future. It's not as if there is only one future out there that is going to happen, and that the only challenge is trying to predict which of the potential futures will actually be the right one. Instead, the goal is to try to imagine a future that is plausible – the future that you can create. (Gary Hamel in Gibson 1997: 81)

This implies that futures are *open*: 'there is no proprietary data about the future', 'nobody owns the twenty-first century' (Gibson 1997: 81, 6). A corollary to this understanding of multiple futures is the now common technique of devising *scenarios* or schematic representations of clusters of future options (first implemented in the Interfutures project of the Organization for Economic Cooperation and Development (OECD 1979).

The openness of futures implies that they are premised on human fallibility. Following Popper, this is what George Soros (1998) sees as fundamental to an open society. This also means open in terms of their view of human nature. Gillian Slovo (1996) concludes a book about her parents, Ruth First and Joe Slovo, on this note: 'I'd realised that memory, experience, interpretation could never be fixed or frozen into one, unchanging truth. They kept on moving, relentlessly metamorphosing into something other so that the jagged edges of each fragment would never, ever slot together.' This articulates a sensibility that is much closer to our contemporary everyday sense of social experience than the deterministic and reductionist thinking of the past.

> Linearity is an artificial way of viewing the world. Real life isn't a series of interconnected events occurring one after another like beads strung on a necklace. Life is actually a series of encounters in which one event may change those that follow in a wholly unpredictable, even devastating way. (Michael Crichton, quoted in Gibson 1997: 6)

George Soros accepts part of the logic of *laissez-faire* thinking: 'if our understandings are imperfect, regulations are bound to be defective', but he disputes the conclusion: 'since regulations are faulty, unregulated markets are perfect' (1997: 6). Flawed regulation that is reflexive in relation to its flaws, then, is better than no regulation at all. We might term this 'postmodern regulation'. It refers to an approach to regulation that is flexible in understanding the necessary though limited status of regulation in relation to social life, which is multi-dimensional, messy and reflexive. Regulation alters the field it seeks to regulate and generates loopholes, avoidance behaviour, resistance. Full transparency is an illusion – it was illusory in relation to societies (as communist bloc countries showed) and it would be so in relation to global conditions. Accordingly, global regulation must be bold in acknowledging the importance of setting global standards, and modest in recognizing that the importance of regulation lies in part˙ in the avoidance it creates. Thus regulation should follow fuzzy logic rather than linear thinking.

WHAT DO FUTURES FEEL LIKE? Futures are many. Every epoch has its futures. Every place has its futures. And within each place and period, different groups perceive different futures as they experience different hopes and fears. Futures are not only rational projects but also emotional experiences. Futures are not simply a matter of rational choice: they are made up of images, aspirations and anxieties, some of which are unconscious, and escape or resist rationalization. To futures, there are both explicit and implicit dimensions, above and below the waterline, and not all that is implicit can be made explicit. Logic and plausibility play a part in choosing futures but so do emotional, aesthetic and imponderable considerations. So a relevant question to ask is: What do futures feel like?

RECENT FUTURES PAST Generalizations are superficial, but at least we can review the dominant, hegemonic futures during the recent past. Thus in the 1950s futures felt *modern* – modern furniture, Le Corbusier architecture. A mainstream future was the American Dream, broadcast by means of Hollywood movies. Dissident futures such as George Orwell's *1984* and Aldous Huxley's *Brave New World* served as counterpoints. Futures thinking at the time – the birth time of 'futurology' – was centred on technology, such as space technology, armaments, robotics and artificial intelligence, and was modernist in spirit. Some of these trends had been in evidence well before that – as in the science fiction novels of Jules Verne and H. G. Wells, Italian Futurism, Soviet Taylorism, and Gramsci's 'Americanism'.

The backdrop of the Cold War provided a duopoly of futures – the Free World of mass consumption and the Worker State of socialism. The rift between them intensified with the Vietnam War and '1968'. Mainstream futures were shaken and a wide array of dissident futures emerged, images of struggle and liberation – such as *tiers mondisme*, the civil rights movement, 'protracted people's war', the Great Cultural Revolution, Che Guevara's *focismo*, liberation theology.

Major concerns during the Cold War were peace and security. Security issues and strategic thinking played a large part in mainstream future thinking (for instance, domino theory) and in dissident futures on the part of the peace movement. The nuclear age and collective security, cheerfully premised on 'Mutually Assured Destruction', provided an aura of threat and doom, of 'exterminism'. In the course of the 1980s, this took different turns and 1989 sealed the demise of state socialism:

> I grew up in the everyday fear of this implosion and the real possibility that I and everyone I knew might not survive. The fear, a fact of life for more than three decades, has receded. I, my family, and my friends will probably live into the next century – a time with its own dangers, known and unknown, but at least without the threat of imminent extermination. All at once, the millennium feels like a beginning. (Clifford 1997: 344)

Those who grew up during the Cold War have grown accustomed to polarized world views. Does not everything have a colour and does not every colour figure somewhere on the spectrum? If now, however, we consider the everyday practices lived and advocated by diverse circles, they are almost without exception based on synergies between state, market and social forces. The terms and forms of cooperation vary, but the old antagonisms and antinomies – between capital and labour, state and society – no longer survive as such. The middle ground, long shunned as tainted and suspect, is coming to its own. For instance, in the words of George Soros: 'Instead of there being a dichotomy between open and closed, I see the open society as occupying a middle ground, where the rights of the individual are safeguarded but where there are some shared values that hold society together' (1997: 9).

From the 1970s, a new range of futures emerged. Earlier studies of population growth had offered doomsday scenarios, neo-Malthusian premonitions of limits to population growth. Now environmental scenarios predicted *Limits to Growth*, as in the title of the Club of Rome report (Meadows et al. 1972). It was followed by a host of studies such as *Mankind at the Turning Point* (1974), and *Building a Sustainable Society* (Brown 1981). Also economists turned to futures thinking, such as Herman Kahn and the Hudson Institute (*The Next 200 Years*, 1976), the UN-sponsored project of Wassily Leontieff and associates (1977), the OECD's Interfutures project (1979) and the US government-sponsored study *The Global 2000 Report to the President* (1981) (discussed in Hughes 1985: 13–24.) Sociological futures typically addressed the relationship between technological change and socioeconomic, political and cultural transformation, in particular how the 'third industrial revolution' of information technology is changing social practices. Examples are Daniel Bell's postindustrial society, Alvin Toffler's *Future Shock* and *Third Wave*, Naisbitt's *Megatrends* (1996), and Kenneth and Elise Boulding's work (1995). A pioneer work in alternative futures was Hazel Henderson's *Creating Alternative Futures* (1978). Other futures studies focused on North–South differences (Kothari 1974; Falk 1975), built on New International Economic Order thinking (Bedjaoui 1979), or attempted a synthesis (Masini 1983). Gradually these futures – based on technology, developed by demographers, security analysts, environmental studies, economists, sociologists – have become part of general futures thinking. In the 1990s, different tensions and futures have come to the fore. Identity politics and new social movements came in the place of national and social struggles. All these have come into a new focus in opposition to free market politics. Globalization became the new arena. The new terrain of contestation became neoliberalism, with structural adjustment in the South and the erosion of welfare states in the North.

Which Global Futures?

NEOLIBERAL FUTURES As an ideology, neoliberalism is probably past its peak. The trust in the 'magic of the marketplace' that characterized the era of Ronald Reagan and Margaret Thatcher has run its course. The criticisms of 'the market rules OK', common and widespread, are gradually crystallizing into an alternative perspective. However, while a reform perspective is gradually taking shape, the alternatives to neoliberalism reflect a variety of interests and positions that have not been able to cohere ideologically or institutionally.

Meanwhile 'pragmatism rules OK', which in effect means muddling through. Under the circumstances, monetarism is the default ideology and policy. Institutionally, in the WTO and IMF, neoliberalism remains the conventional wisdom. In development politics, it prevails through the remnants of the 'Washington consensus'. In NAFTA, it prevails in principle. In Euroland, it prevails through the European Monetary Union. Financial and monetarist regimentation is ironing out the actual varieties of capitalism (Albert 1993).

This reflects the continuing hegemony of finance capital and the central position of financial institutions. The core of the neoliberal powerhouse is finance capital. Money and finance function as the central arbiter and regulator of regional and global development. Ironically so, since finance itself is the most unregulated of all economic spheres – witness the volatility of international financial hyperspace that has been at the source of most of the recent crises. While monetarism serves as the default discipline and ideology of the neoliberal world, the financial world itself is out of control. The nexus between international trade and finance has been severed, so that speculation on currency fluctuations and other financial instruments have become quantitatively more important than production and commerce. Twenty-four-hour trading and electronic triggers have increased volatility and risk. The relationship between profit and taxation is being eroded or reversed. Corporate tax rates are shrinking. Government subsidies and incentives take the place of taxes. Deregulation and access to hyperspace enable corporations to register headquarters and record profits at offshore tax havens.

Among the neoliberal futures of the 1990s is Kenichi Ohmae's *The Borderless World,* or the world as a duty-free store. This is a global extension of Walt Rostow's 'stage of high-mass consumerism' and a replay of the American Dream (which in the United States, because of workloads and chronic poverty, is a dream no longer attainable). Ohmae's former position as director of McKinsey Japan accounts for the signature of his 'Pacific' ideology – American marketing and mass consumerism coming to Asia, and Japanese corporate strategies boomeranging westward. Techno-futures receive a new boost from cyberspace hype, which is supposed to ensure a long boom, brainwaves, a civilization of civilizations and a wired global society: 'We're facing twenty-five years of prosperity, freedom, and a better environment for the whole world. You got a problem with that?' (Schwartz and Leyden 1997: 115). This kind of future *à la* Bill Gates glosses over poverty and inequality within the United States, let alone worldwide, and also ignores that cyberspace is a zone in which conflicts are being reproduced (Sardar and Ravetz 1996).

The future of a borderless world for capital is gradually becoming a self-fulfilling prophecy through the structural reform policies initiated by the IMF and World Bank. The WTO and the attempts to arrange the free movement not only of commodities but of capital as well are translating it into a global dynamic. This is a world viewed from a Northern window, seen through Western and Japanese eyes. It fills in the blanks in Francis Fukuyama's

The End of History, which predicts indefinite political stability in the advanced world while small wars and skirmishes splutter on in the periphery. Daniel Moinyhan's *Pandemonium* of ethnic conflicts (1992) and Robert Kaplan's (1996) slide into anarchy in the periphery, from Africa to the Balkans, supplement this prognosis, whose regional effects are to be contained by means of selective 'humanitarian intervention'.

Neoliberal futures are being contested on many grounds – labour, the right to development, the environment, local interests, and cultural diversity.[1] Looking back on the 1992 Rio conference on the global environment and development, Martin Khor sees a 'clash of paradigms'. 'The free market paradigm ... represented by the Bretton Woods institutions, which persisted in promoting structural adjustment programmes based on market liberalisation, and by the GATT/WTO which was dominated by the Northern governments advocating the opening up of markets (especially of developing countries)' and the 'paradigm of partnership and cooperation ... represented by the United Nations series of world conferences' (1997: 9).

This kind of characterization, though not without plausibility, may be misleading. One, the concept of paradigm is derived from the natural sciences and either does not apply or would have a much looser meaning outside it. Two, it homogenizes positions and suggests more coherence in positions than actually exists. It conceals the improvised and patchwork character of actual policy frameworks. Three, it sidelines the question whether the 'paradigm' would be capable of reproducing itself – in other words, whether it has a future at all. Four, juxtaposing the two policy frameworks as paradigms gives a mistaken impression that they are somehow of equal status. Five, the image of a clash ignores the overlap in positions, eliminates the middle ground, and overlooks actual and possible cooperation.

The question is whether the neoliberal regime is capable of reproducing itself. Major elements of instability in the neoliberal scenario are:

- Financial instability: witness the series of financial crises in emerging markets.
- Unemployment, automation and 'jobless growth' (Rifkin 1995).
- Inequality and poverty within and between societies, and their nexus to conflict and security risk.
- Environmental risk (Daly and Cobb 1994).
- The downward trend of corporate taxes and the inability to finance common goods, nationally and globally.
- The risk of global oversupply (Greider 1997).
- Tensions between the market and democracy (Attali 1997).

For such hazards, deregulation, liberalization and privatization provide no remedy. Accordingly, some form of regulation is in the interest of parties both large and small. Without taxation, no infrastructure. Without taxation, no proper education, no affordable health care. Without taxation, no public sphere. Without a public sphere, no legitimacy. Without legitimacy, no security. This in itself is a familiar future scenario. It could take the form of global 'Californianization' while California is being 'Brazilianized'. A world of gated communities, high barbed-wire fences, steep hierarchies, robots on the work-floor and at the gate, and automated surveillance all round. A world of creeping privatization of public space, as in Los Angeles (cf. Mike Davis' *City of Quartz* (1990)). A 'post-human' world (see Chapter 13), of which we see one face in *Blade Runner* and other cinematic dystopias.

This world, however, cannot reproduce itself. The neoliberal scenario, if all the padding of state support really is removed, is not coherent, is self-contradictory and self-defeating. *Laissez-faire* and the 'self-regulating market' have been critical positions (i.e. Manchester school criticism of mercantilism, supply-side criticism of Keynesianism) and a corrective of excessive state intervention, but they are not a stand-alone self-sustaining model.

Regulation in order to function must be of global scope, for anything short of global regulation invites evasion and 'dumping'. At the same time the gap between countries at different levels of development makes a straight-forward global consensus quite unlikely – not for lack of trying, witness numerous sensible commission reports; witness the recurrent stalemates in global conferences on virtually any issue: the environment, population, trade. The real world stretches all the way from Palaeolithic hunters and gatherers (Amerindians in the Amazon, Aboriginals in the Australian outback, Khoisan in the Kalahari) to the high-tech worlds of information technology. In world music, cinema (John Boorman's *Emerald Forest*, Peter Weir's *Last Wave*, Jamie Uys's *The Gods Must be Crazy*) and science fiction, in indigenous peoples' networks and human rights fora these worlds meet, but where else? The scope and the limitations of global rendezvous have been demonstrated in the conferences in Rio, Vienna, Copenhagen, Cairo, Beijing, Istanbul. These have been exemplary in the range of parties represented – international institutions, governments, TNCs, NGOs, labour unions, professional associations, media. But participation has hardly been on equal terms and outcomes, on the surface at least, have been uneven and meagre.

A familiar friction runs between the 'Washington consensus' that used to embrace the IMF and World Bank, and the UN institutions and their agenda of human development (UNDP, UNCTAD, UNICEF, UNESCO), social development (the Copenhagen Social Summit, UNRISD) and sustainable development (UNEP). This rift goes back to the divergence between the Bretton Woods institutions and the UN system that emerged after the Second World War and took the form of different voting systems. One set of institutions would deal with the 'hard' issues of finance and economics, and the other with the 'soft' issues of social welfare, entitlements and human rights (Singer 1995).

Such a division of labour is now out of synch with current insights into how economics works – the hard and the soft are deeply interwoven. *Soft* elements such as education, health care, housing, income distribution, cultural exchange, social capital, civic trust and institutional density translate into *hard* economic data of productivity and growth. Cultural diversity has been an engine of economic growth (see Chapter 12). Without community participation, development projects don't work. Facilities such as micro credit – popularized by the Grameen Bank in Bangladesh and now being applied in the USA and UK – typically bridge the two spheres of concern. In relation to environmental concerns, the distinction between soft and hard does not make sense. In sustainable development, the common denominator in the 1990s, the hard and the soft cannot be separated. Over the years the World Bank has been incorporating 'soft' elements as part of its brief – gender, participation, NGOs, environment – and has now begun to transform itself to a 'knowledge bank'.

GLOBAL GOVERNANCE Slow progress with regard to global governance should not conceal the fact that we inhabit a world shaped by over a hundred years of international regulation and institution-building. This includes arrangements with regard to time zones (Universal Standard Time), the International Red Cross, regulation of the conduct of war, UN treaties from the Declaration of Human Rights to the Law of the Sea, and the International Court of Justice. An international public sector already *de facto* exists. In this context, sovereignty need no longer be thought of as a zero-sum game. Sharing it does not reduce sovereignty. Another stepping-stone in the process of global governance is regional governance (as in the European Union). Trade-offs of pooling sovereignty include security and stability, reduced anxiety and conflict, reduced military spending, and economic and technological cooperation.

The Commission on Global Governance (1995) is at pains to point out that global *governance* is not global *government*. It is not about creating a superstate but about strengthening the international order and international law. If we combine this with current ideas about politics, interactive decision-making and the state (e.g. Mulgan 1994), one can think of facilitative governance, or governance as management of networks and the coordination of synergies across sectors.

Progressive agendas include 'double democratization' simultaneously within societies and in international relations, 'cosmopolitan democracy', including the formation of regional parliaments (Held 1995), and substantive UN reform – 'redefining the United Nations as an organization not of governments but, in the final analysis, of "the people"' (Sakamoto 1997: 8). Another option is the formation of world parties (Kreml and Kegley 1996). What is at stake in global governance, besides its institutional design, is the question of global reform.

GLOBAL REFORM There is now a growing consensus in favour of managing, steering or shaping globalization. The leading industrial nations are considering new global rules on investment, banking and trade. Global *laissez-faire* involves more risk than even the privileged few can afford. The collapse of Long-Term Capital Management was the writing on the wall of Wall Street (Soros 1998). Planning globalization, the position at the other end of the spectrum, has takers only among the adherents of world socialism. There is, then, a broad middle ground in favour of managing globalization, but the question is what is the content of this consensus. Two major positions within this middle ground are for global reform within the existing structures or through new institutions.

A case in point is the architecture of the financial system and whether it requires modest adjustments in the present system or a new financial architecture. Within the broad consensus that the world financial system is in need of reform, a loose sketch of positions may run as follows. A minimum position is in favour of 'transparency' and the standardization of accounting systems (held by the IMF, World Bank, WTO, US Treasury). A midway position considers imposing restrictions such as higher reserve requirements, higher thresholds of access to offshore banks and modest reform of international institutions (World Bank, OECD). A stronger reform position favours new international institutions such as a global central bank that should impose restrictions on hot money and international taxes (UN agencies).

TABLE 1.1 Global reform perspectives

Globalization	Frameworks	Institutions
Technical adjustments	Neoliberalism	IMF, WTO
Reform within structures	Social liberalism	World Bank, OECD
Reform through new structures	Social democracy, global New Deal	Labour, ILO, UN system

Proposals for new institutions include recombining the Bretton Woods institutions and the UN system, with a view to realigning economic and financial regimes and social development. One proposal is for the adjustment of voting systems (Green 1995); another is for an Economic Security Council that would take over the role of the international financial institutions under UN auspices (Commission on Global Governance 1995; Haq 1995; Henderson 1996; Chapter 5 of this volume). What matters, beyond these institutional arrangements, is the alignment of international financial regimes and social development. What is at issue is the role of central banks, particularly in the North, and their relationship with the IMF. The broader issue is the restoration of banking as a public utility, which ultimately involves a new mode of regulation.

The 1999 *Human Development Report* (UNDP 1999) proposes a 'global architecture' that would include:

- A global central bank to act as a lender of last resort to strapped countries and to help regulate finance markets.
- A global investment trust to moderate flows of foreign capital in and out of Third World countries and to raise development funds by taxing global pollution or short-term investments.
- New rules for the WTO, including anti-monopoly powers to enable it to keep global corporations from dominating industries.
- New rules on global patents that would keep the patent system from blocking the access of Third World countries to development, knowledge or health care.
- New talks on a global investment treaty that would include developing countries and respect local laws.
- More flexible monetary rules that would enable developing countries to impose capital controls to protect their economies.
- A global code of conduct for multinational corporations, to encourage them to follow the kind of labour and environmental laws that exist in their home countries.

Regulation, in order to succeed, must be global in scope – anything else invites evasion. In order to achieve global scope, regulation must be acceptable across North–South differences. It must encompass a politics of development that addresses the interests and agendas of advanced countries, NIEs and LDCs. In effect, this means an agenda of global development. Advocating global reform on moral and ethical grounds, or purely political grounds, has no more appeal than the reach of ethical and political consensus. It is probably more sensible to treat global reform primarily as a form of global risk management. Partnership develops when its advantages outweigh its costs. 'Mutual interest' then remains the guiding principle, but this should now encompass wider concerns, such as environmental and security hazards.

If straightforward negotiations do not deliver because the parties are unequal and have diverse interests, *widening* the terrain of negotiation to broader fields of common concern may open up new opportunities for give-and-take. Areas that come to mind are ecology, natural resources, regional security, migration, cultural diversity and indigenous knowledge. Exploring the rainforest for medicinal herbs while granting intellectual property rights to local inhabitants and contracts for revenue sharing is an example (Van der Vlist 1994).

Not only must fields of negotiation be wider than they are at present, but future proposals must also be interactive multidimensionally: global governance must heed the global economy; global taxes must interact with policies regarding development, ecology, population, gender and cultural diversity. In other words, global reform must turn on intersectoral synergies. This goes against the grain of the *sectoral* structure of institutions, ministries and agendas. Sectoral barriers contribute to the stalemate in negotiations. In bureaucracies as well as in the disciplinary structure of academia, they separate finance, development, welfare, ecology, and so forth, as part of the legacy of eighteenth- and nineteenth-century rationalism and its classificatory spirit. By definition, they exclude from view, and from discussion, questions of global reform – such as global governance and global taxes – that have profound multiplier effects across many spheres. These fences and boundaries are out of step with the current increasingly holistic and interdisciplinary under-standings of development and politics.

At the same time, many conflicts of interest cannot be resolved within narrow frameworks. An example is the friction between the labour standards movement and the right to development. In the North labour standards (labour rights, no child labour, no sweatshops, minimum wage, job safety, etc.) are widely viewed as a major terrain of progressive intervention. This position is shared by a broad coalition from labour unions to social organizations, from the ILO to Democrats in the US Congress. In the South, this position is much more controversial. Many view it as undermining the competitiveness of the South, which is based on labour flexibility. For late industrializers the competitive edge of low labour standards and minimal environmental regulation offers a slim chance to step into the industrialization process.

Positions in the North are inconsistent in that for all the attention bestowed on labour, measures are taken to free the movement of capital. Freeing capital while regulating labour may not be a particularly even-handed way of going about things. Positions in the South are one-sided in that industrial-ization on the basis of 'primitive Taylorization' and environmental devastation does not add up to a sustainable development path. The problem is that two cases and levels of argument are intertwined. One is a general case for labour standards as a protection for labour at a time when capital mobility is growing; the other is a particularist case on the part of labour unions and governments in the North facing capital flight and job loss, to counter capital flight by reducing the advantages of relocation. A level playing field for labour is one question; regulating capital movement is another; comparative competitiveness is a third; the right to development is a fourth. Considering each in its own sphere, these conflicts of interest are insoluble. They could only be addressed within a wider, comprehensive approach.

One framework for addressing wide-ranging issues is new social contracts (e.g. Commission on Population 1996; Rifkin 1995). An advantage of the contract approach is that contracts are compatible with market standards as well as bureaucratic procedures; they cut across spheres of government, market and society. Contracts can be comprehensive and address multi-dimensional issues, while avoiding unwieldy and politically unrealistic options such as a 'new constitutionalism'. According to the Group of Lisbon, 'A contract is the appropriate choice when the parties involved are numerous, the problems are complex and multidimensional, and the solutions are of a long-term structural nature' (1995: 110). The Group of Lisbon proposes global social contracts on basic needs, democracy, culture and the environment. To serve as settlements across domains, they could take the form of specific targeted negotiating platforms, such as Tobin taxes for restraining international financial speculation, global taxes for global information structure and ecotaxes for planetary survival.[2] However, it is not easy to think of such wide-ranging arrangements within the existing structures.

In business, the talk is not simply about imagining the future but also about implementation or 'building the future' (Prahalad in Gibson 1997: 67). Governments and international institutions do not simply imagine futures either. Malaysia's Vision 2020 (catch up with advanced countries) and other developing country future visions serve as government policy targets. A forward-looking approach would be welcome also on the part of citizen groups. Avenues out of the global stalemate include the following:

- A stock-taking of socially progressive best practices and future proposals, and cross-referencing them across domains and geographies. This refers to innovation not simply in a technological sense, but in social practices, institutions, values and expectations.
- The development of global public opinion concerning not only planetary predicaments but also future options.
- The development of multidimensional relations of negotiation, i.e. across different sectors and dimensions, along with institutional reform.

The development of global public opinion is necessary for the generation and articulation of political will. Besides, if the objective of progressive futures is democratization, the means toward their realization must be democratic as well. First, the infrastructure is increasingly available. This is the upside of 'CNN culture' and planetary satellite wiring. Second, there have been breakthroughs in recent years, for instance concerning the environment, human rights and women's rights. In a fairly short time-span the environment has become recognized as a planetary concern and institutionalized in the notion of sustainable development as the yardstick of all economic and technological initiatives. Human rights and women's rights are other fields in which considerable social progress has been set in motion. Another area of profound change in recent years is international security, brought about by unanticipated changes in international relations – the break-up of the Soviet bloc and the end of the Cold War – as well as collective action. No matter then the range of complexities, political sensitivities and cultural differences, social progress can be achieved.

These avenues may be obstacle-courses of complexity, but what we may now find unimaginable may be common sense and common practice a few years or decades hence. Various future options are interdependent. Global reform and global taxes cannot be implemented without further progress in global governance. Global governance depends on global public opinion and political will. One way of seeing this is as a stalemate in which progress in any sphere cannot proceed without change in other domains. Another view is that this is a virtuous circle in which progress in one sphere opens opportunities for progress in all.

Notes

1. Critical future-oriented studies that have taken on globalization and inequality have centred on alternative economics (Henderson 1991; Ekins 1992), civic actors (Korten 1990), the world economy and international relations (Makhijani 1992; Brecher et al. 1993; Cavanagh et al. 1994; Falk 1994; Gurtov 1994), North–South relations (South Commission 1990; Muzaffar 1993), ecology (Lipietz 1995), poverty (Townsend 1996).

2. On Tobin taxes see Haq et al. 1996, on global taxes see Chapter 6 of this volume. On 'infostructure' see Connors 1997.

References

Albert, M. (1993) *Capitalism against Capitalism*, Whurr, London.

Amin, S. (1997) *Capitalism in the Age of Globalization*, Zed, London.

Attali, J. (1997) 'The crash of Western civilization: the limits of the market and democracy', *Foreign Policy*, 107: 54–64.

Bedjaoui, M. (1979) *Towards a New International Economic Order*, Holmes and Meier, New York.

Boulding, K. and E. (1995) *The Future*, Sage, London.

Brecher, J. et al. (eds) (1993) *Global Visions: Beyond the New World Order*, South End, Boston, MA.

Cavanagh, J., D. Wysham and M. Arruda (eds) (1994) *Beyond Bretton Woods: Alternatives to the Global Economic Order*, Pluto, London.

Cleveland, H., H. Henderson and I. Kaul (eds) (1995) *The United Nations: Policy and Financing Alternatives*, Apex Press, New York.

Clifford, J. (1997) *Routes: Travel And Translation in the Late Twentieth Century*, Harvard University Press, Cambridge, MA.

Commission on Global Governance (1995) *Our Global Neighbourhood*, Oxford University Press, New York.

Connors, M. (1997) *The Race to the Intelligent State: Charting the Global Information Economy in the 21st Century*, Capstone, Oxford.

Daly, H. E. and J. B. Cobb Jr (1994) *For the Common Good* (2nd edn), Beacon Press, Boston, MA.

Davis, M. (1990) *City of Quartz*, Verso, London.

Ekins, P. (1992) *A New World Order: Grassroots Movements for Global Change*, Routledge, London.

Falk, R. (1975) *A Study of Future Worlds*, Free Press, New York.

— (1994) *On Humane Governance: Towards a New Global Politics*, Polity, Cambridge.

Galbraith, J. K. (1996) *The Good Society*, Houghton Mifflin, Boston, MA.

Gibson, R. (ed.) (1997) *Rethinking the Future*, Nicholas Brealey, London.

Green, R (1995) 'Reflections on attainable trajectories: reforming global economic institutions', in Griesgraber and Gunter (eds) (1995), pp. 38–81.

Greider, W. (1997) *One World, Ready or Not: The Manic Logic of Global Capitalism*, Simon and Schuster, New York.

Group of Lisbon (1995) *Limits to Competition*, MIT Press, Cambridge, MA.

Griesgraber, M. J. and B. G. Gunter (eds) (1995) *Promoting Development: Effective Global Institutions for the 21st Century*, Pluto, London.

Gurtov, M. (1994) *Global Politics in the Human Interest* (3rd rev. edn), Lynne Rienner, Boulder, CO.

Haq, M ul (1995) *Reflections on Human Development*, Oxford University Press, New York.

Haq, M. ul, I. Kaul and I. Grunberg (1996) *The Tobin Tax: Coping with Financial Volatility*, Oxford University Press, New York.

Held, D. (1995) *Democracy and Global Order*, Polity, Cambridge.

Henderson, H. (1978) *Creating Alternative Futures: The End of Economics*, Kumarian Press, West Hartford, CT.

— (1991) *Paradigms in Progress*, Knowledge Systems, Indianapolis.

— (1996) *Building a Win-Win World*, Berrett-Koehler, San Francisco.

Hughes, B. B. (1985) *World Futures: A Critical Analysis of Alternatives*, Johns Hopkins University Press, Baltimore, MD.

Ibrahim, A. (1996) *The Asian Renaissance*, Times Books, Singapore.

Independent Commission on Population and Quality of Life, Report of the (1996) *Caring for the Future*, Oxford University Press, New York.

Kahn, H., W. Brown and L. Martel (1976) *The Next 200 Years*, Morrow, New York.

Kaplan, R. D. (1996) *The Ends of the Earth*, Random House, New York.

Khor, M. (1997) 'Effects of globalisation on sustainable development after UNCED', *Third World Resurgence*, 81/82: 5–11.

Korten, D. C. (1990) *Getting to the 21st Century: Voluntary Action and the Global Agenda*, Kumarian Press, West Hartford, CT.

Kothari, R. (1974) *Footsteps into the Future*, Free Press, New York.

Kreml, W. P. and C. W. Kegley, Jr (1996) 'A global political party: the next step', *Alternatives*, 21: 123–34.

Lipietz, A. (1995) *Green Hopes: The Future of Political Ecology*, Polity, Cambridge.

McRae, H. (1995) *The World in 2020*, HarperCollins, London.

Makhijani, A. (1992) *From Global Capitalism to Economic Justice*, Apex, New York.

Masini, E. (ed.) (1983) *Visions of Desirable Societies*, Pergamon, Oxford.

Meadows, D. H. et al. (1972) *The Limits to Growth*, Basic Books, New York.

Moinyhan, D. P. (1992) *Pandemonium*, Random House, New York.

Mulgan, G. (1994) *Politics in an Antipolitical Age*, Polity, Cambridge.

Muzaffar, C. (1993) *Human Rights and the New World Order*, Just World Trust, Penang.

Naisbitt, J. (1996) *Megatrends Asia*, Nicholas Brealey, London.

Nandy, A. (1999) 'Futures and dissent', in Ziauddin Sardar (ed.), *Rescuing All Our Futures: The Future of Future Studies*, Twickenham/Westport, CT, Adamantine Press/Praeger, pp. 227–33.

OECD (1979) *Interfutures: Facing the Future*, OECD, Paris.

Ohmae, K. (1992) *The Borderless World*, Collins, London.

Rifkin, J. (1995) *The End of Work*, Tarcher/Putnam, New York.

Rostow, W. W. (1960) *The Stages of Economic Growth*, Cambridge University Press, Cambridge.

Sakamoto, Y. (ed.) (1994) *Global Transformation*, UN University Press, Tokyo.

— (1997) 'Civil society and democratic world order', in S. Gill and J. H. Mittelman (eds), *Innovation and Transformation in International Studies*, Cambridge University Press, New York.

Sardar, Z. (1999) 'The problem of futures studies', in Ziauddin Sardar (ed.), *Rescuing All Our Futures: The Future of Future Studies*, CT, Adamantine Press/Praeger, Twickenham/Westport, pp. 9–18.

Sardar, Z. and J. R. Ravetz (eds) (1996) *Cyberfutures: Culture and Politics on the Information Superhighway*, Pluto, London.

Schwartz, P. and P. Leyden (1997) 'The long boom: a history of the future 1980–2020', *Wired*, July: 115–29, 168–73.

Singer, H. W. (1995) 'Rethinking Bretton Woods: from an historical perspective', in Griesgraber and Gunter (eds), (1995), pp. 1–22.

Slovo, G. (1996) *Every Secret Thing: My Family, My Country*, Little, Brown, New York.

Soros, G. (1997) 'The capitalist threat', *The Atlantic Monthly*, February.

— (1998) *The Crisis of Global Capitalism*, Public Affairs, New York.

South Commission (1990) *The Challenge to the South*, Oxford University Press, New York.

Thompson, D. (1996) *The End of Time: Faith and Fear in the Shadow of the Millennium*, Sinclair-Stevenson, London.

Townsend, P. (1996) *A Poor Future*, Lemos & Crane, London.

UNDP (1999) *Human Development Report 1999*, Oxford University Press, New York.

Van der Vlist, L. (ed.) (1994) *Voices of the Earth: Indigenous Peoples, New Partners and the Right to Self-determination in Practice*, International Books, Utrecht.

Wallerstein, I. (1994) 'Peace, stability, and legitimacy 1990–2025/2050', in G Lundestad (ed.), *The Fall of Great Powers*, Oxford University Press, New York.

Walley, P. (1995) *Ireland in the 21st Century*, Mercier Press, Dublin.

I

Global Reform

2

Humane Governance for the World: Reviving the Quest

RICHARD FALK

The Quest

Both world wars in the twentieth century encouraged world leaders to embark on a deliberate effort to reform world order in fundamental respects. The League of Nations, and then the United Nations, emerged from this. Both of these experiments in the restructuring of relations between states have been impressive if compared to what had previously existed in international political life. However, such steps are deeply disappointing if appraised from the perspective of what is needed to create on a global scale a mode of governance that corresponds in normative stature (widely shared ethical standards and societal goals) to the most humane public order systems that have been operating at the level of the sovereign state.

The proximate goal of humane governance, then, seems relatively modest, at least at the outset. It is true that the idea of humane governance on any level of social complexity is conceived of as a process, with horizons of aspiration being continuously re-established with an eye to the improvement of the existing social, economic and political order from the perspective of a democratically established agenda. Such a quest should not be confused with the Western tendency towards linearity of expectations, which in recent centuries has been realized in technological innovation and in relation to consumerist satisfactions. It may be that in some circumstances normative horizons reflect the ebb and flow of history, with the emphasis placed on sustainability of past achievements or even the restoration of prior levels of humane governance after periods of regression. The idea of progress that has reigned in the West for many years is a misleading invention by optimists (as is its sibling, the idea of decline and fall leading to inevitable doom, the work of pessimists). The future is inherently obscure, too complex to fathom and too dependent on the vagaries of human action for good or ill. Such uncertainty underscores human responsibility in achieving the normative potential that is currently perceived; almost everything necessary for human well-being is sufficiently achievable to be worth pursuing. At the same time, there can be no assurances of success given the existence of countervailing projects and pressures.

Delimiting the idea of humane governance on behalf of the peoples of the world is itself a daunting and inconclusive undertaking. The unevenness of material circumstance, cultural orientation and resource endowment makes it especially difficult, and even suspect, to universalize aspirations and set forth some image of humane governance that can be affirmed by all. It seems appropriate to be tentative, inviting dialogue across civilizational and class boundaries as to the nature of humane governance. From such a bottom-up process, areas of overlapping consensus can begin to be identified, and the negotiation of differences in values and priorities facilitated. If successful, this interactive dynamic could in time produce a coherent project, democratically conceived, to establish humane governance for all peoples.

At present, there are ingredients of humane governance present that seem to reflect widely endorsed aspirational principles, but so far no legitimation of an overarching project has taken place. And there are factors at work obstructing the effort to establish such a project as a viable undertaking. There is, first of all, the anti-Utopian mood that has emerged from the perceived failure of Marxism-Leninism as the leading modern experiment in applied Utopics. Second, the potency of market forces seems mainly organized around the energies of greed and self-interest, and these have come to dominate policy-forming arenas at all levels of social organization. Third, this potency has been embodied in regional and global structures that have sapped the normative creativity of states, especially by imposing the discipline of global capital on existing structures of governance, as further reinforced through the ideas of neoliberal economics. Fourth, this economistic world picture has acquired added force, having been embraced by the leaders of the most powerful states and adopted by the most influential global actors, including the IMF, World Bank and WTO. And fifth, the new assertiveness of non-Western civilizations has challenged the assumption that Western normative projects deserve universal acceptance (Falk 1996).

The focus on humane governance is not meant as a repudiation of economic and cultural globalization or of market forces. These powerful elements in the existing global setting provide many beneficial opportunities for improving the material, social and cultural experience of peoples through-out the world. Beyond this, the tides of history have swept neoliberal ideas into such a commanding position in this early period of globalization that it would be disheartening to mount a frontal challenge, especially given the absence of viable alternatives. What is being proposed is more limited. It recognizes that *within* globalization there exists the potential for humane governance, but only if activated by the mobilization of diverse, democratic forces, what I have elsewhere identified as a process that can be associated with 'globalization-from-below' (Falk 1993 and 1997).

The Approach

Without entering into a complex discussion of successful projects of social change, it seems useful to consider two positive examples: decolonization and human rights. Actually, of course, each of these narratives if fully related would involve an elaborate and controversial exposition that provided an interpretation of specific as well as general context. Here, my purpose is to show how unlikely aspirations were realized given supportive changes in underlying historical conditions.

In the case of decolonization, the values of self-determination and the ideology of nationalism had long challenged the legitimacy and stability of the colonial order. The moment Woodrow Wilson's ambiguous programme of global reform was launched in the aftermath of the First World War, ideas subversive to the colonial order were validated, inspiring individuals who had been caught up as subjects of colonial masters, even though this appears not to have been Wilson's intention. The outcome of the Russian Revolution also provided colonized peoples with a powerful, if dangerous and opportunistic, geopolitical ally in the form of the Soviet Union. The Second World War both weakened the morale and diminished the capabilities of the main colonial powers. It also created a fluid situation in which nationalist movements perceived opportunities for success that had not previously existed. The story of decolonization is, of course, many stories. Each struggle was distinct, but there were general conditions that resulted in an overall shift in the relation of forces within the wider colonial reality. A new flow of history ensued that could not have been reasonably anticipated even a few decades before it occurred.

The second example involves internationally protected human rights. The legitimacy of human rights as a core aspect of humane governance owes its main modern origins to the French Revolution, but this is quite different from endowing the world community with the capacity to pass judgement on the internal processes of governance of a sovereign state. Indeed, the social contract that forms the basis of the United Nations is explicit about its refraining from interventions in matters 'essentially within the domestic jurisdiction' of states. (This understanding is, of course, written into the UN Charter in the form of Article 2(7), although with limiting conditions. The word 'essentially' provides much room for political interpretation and changing attitudes towards sovereign rights. Additionally, deference to internal sovereignty is overridden by UN action taken to uphold international peace and security.) The modern Westphalian system of world order is premised on the idea of territorial sovereignty, which is inconsistent with the sort of external accountability that is implied by the acceptance of an obligation to uphold international human rights standards. So why would states voluntarily agree to a pattern of obligation that erodes their own sovereignty?

The short answer to a complex inquiry is that states generally have not taken seriously a formal commitment to uphold human rights obligations, undoubtedly feeling secure by resisting moves to establish implementing procedures and enforcement mechanisms. These expectations of governments were disturbed by several unanticipated developments: the rise of transnational human rights civil society organizations (that is, human rights NGOs); the invocation of human rights by the West as a major dimension of the Cold War; the success of the anti-apartheid campaign; the internal reliance on international human rights demands by movements of domestic opposition, especially in Eastern Europe during the 1980s; the conjoining of support for political and civil rights with the advocacy of economic liberalization in the new geopolitics of globalization.[1] The relevant point here is that the normative idea associated with the establishment of human rights has gathered political momentum over the years. The implementation of the idea is still far from complete, but its contribution to humane governance is one of the most impressive achievements of the late twentieth century.

In the next section, several normative ideas are identified that seem crucial to the project of seeking to promote humane governance on a global scale. These ideas are selected, in part, because they are *already* embodied in the normative order (that is, validated by international law and morality, which now includes what might be called an environmental ethos).[2] As such, their realization has some claim to inter-civilizational support, and the aspirational element relates only to various degrees of implementation. The enumeration that follows makes no claim to comprehensiveness. It does seek to set forth normative ideas that have been globally though perhaps insufficiently validated, and that seem central to the promotion of humane global governance.

Dimensions of Normative Potential

Mainly as a result of social struggle, many normative goals have been acknowledged in recent decades, which, if fully realized, would both neutralize the negative aspects of globalization and create positive momentum for progress towards the attainment of humane governance in the decades ahead.[3] But the task is not a simple one. The normative goals have in many instances been reduced by practice and neglect to a rhetorical affirmation, lacking in substance and political conviction, and inducing widespread cynicism as to their relevance. The ideas of neoliberalism that have been attached to the implementation of globalization are generally opposed to any direct undertakings that subordinate economistic considerations to those of human well-being. And as is argued in the prior section, the political strength of regional and global market forces has been manifested partly through a reorientation of outlook on the part of leaders at the level of the state, infusing them with a sense of mission based on non-territorial priorities and the world picture of globalization. As a result, territorial priorities and identities of many citizens are subordinated. This divergence of outlook was evident in the grassroots reluctance of the peoples of Europe in response to the Maastricht Treaty as compared with elites who were generally much more comfortable than their citizens with the loss of economic sovereignty. This divergence has narrowed somewhat in a number of countries as a result of backlash politics, including widespread strikes, the rise of right-wing chauvinistic populism, and the efforts of leaders to reassure citizens about their social and economic prospects within a more regionalized political setting.

With these considerations in mind, it seems important to revisit some normative breakthroughs in law and morality that have been made during this century, which could, if more seriously implemented, contribute dramatically to humane governance for the peoples of the planet. Taken as a whole these nine normative initiatives provide 'a plan of action' for global civil society in relation to the goal of humane governance on a global scale.

RENUNCIATION OF FORCE IN INTERNATIONAL RELATIONS Even prior to the United Nations Charter, international law in the Pact of Paris had in 1928 already codified the idea that states had no legal right to use force except in self-defence. This idea was carried forward in the UN Charter as a central element, the prohibition included in Article 2(4), and the exception for self-defence delimited in seemingly more restrictive language in Article 51. The right of self-defence was limited to responses to a prior armed attack, and a claim of self-defence was required to be immediately reported for action to the Security Council. The text of Article 51 gives the impression that even in a situation of self-defence the primary responsibility rests with the Security Council, not with the victim of an attack. If implemented as written, the role of force in international political life would be radically changed, especially to the extent that these ideas about force are linked to the obligation of states in Article 33 to seek peaceful settlement of disputes endangering world peace and security.

As is widely appreciated, this normative promise was never consistently fulfilled. For one thing the UN was unable to provide the sort of collective security arrangements that would protect a state against threats of aggression. It was unrealistic to expect a threatened state, especially if vulnerable to attack, to wait until an armed attack occurred before exercising its right of self-defence. The circumstance of Israel is illustrative: surrounded by hostile states, small in size, and convinced that its security rests on the option to strike pre-emptively as it did most spectacularly in the 1967 Six Day War.

A second obstacle to implementation was the extent to which the UN scheme depended on a continuing commitment by the permanent members of the Security Council to base their responses to uses of force on Charter considerations rather than ideological alignments and geopolitical considerations.[4] With the East/West split dominating the political scene, the conditions were almost never present in the Security Council for the sort of response pattern envisioned by the Charter. Furthermore, geopolitical tensions meant that the collaborative arrangements relating to collective security called for in Chapter VII of the Charter were never put into practice except ritualistically, such as the operation of the Military Staff Committee consisting of military representatives of the permanent members.

It has been evident since the end of the Cold War that the reasons for non-implementation cannot be explained by geopolitical tensions alone. An additional element is the unwillingness of major states to transfer political control to the UN in situations involving the use of force. The attitude of the US government is both decisive and revealing in these respects. More than ever, its leaders are unwilling to entrust its soldiers or its foreign policy to a UN command structure, or to a collective process over which it lacks full control.

And finally, serious threats to the security of states could not be confined to armed attacks. Claims to use force have been associated over the years with responses to state-sponsored terroristic attacks (US attack on Libya in 1986 and support for the Contras in the war against the Sandinistas in Nicaragua, Israeli attacks on Lebanon), to threatened proliferation of nuclear weaponry (Israeli attack on Osirak, Iraq in 1981), to acute suppression of human rights and genocidal conduct (Tanzania against Uganda, Vietnam against Cambodia in 1979, USA against Panama in 1989).

In some respects, the current situation is very supportive of this long effort to curtail war. Territoriality is far less significant in the new geopolitics, and the role of war is less relevant to the success and failure of many states (Mueller 1990). The practical rationale for peaceful settlement is stronger than ever. Most political violence in the present world is of an intra-state variety associated with claims of self-determination. The economistic view of state policy exerts pressure to minimize public expenditure, including that on defence. The threats associated with the further proliferation of weaponry of mass destruction, including chemical and biological weaponry, are unlikely to be eliminated unless all states, including nuclear weapons states, join in their renunciation.

Despite these reasons for seeking a warless world, the obstacles remain formidable: entrenched economic and bureaucratic interests in military establishments; distrust of the capacity and objectivity of the UN system; inertia associated with reliance on the state to provide security against adversaries; and persisting, unresolved regional conflicts, border disputes and territorial conflicts involving offshore islands. In addition, geopolitical actors, especially the US government, insist on the relevance of force to deter and contain so-called 'rogue states' and to prevent the further fraying of the nuclear non-proliferation regime.

In these regards, only a transnational peace movement is likely to be able to revitalize the long and crucial struggle to minimize war and preparations for war. At the moment, there is no effort in this direction except in relation to transnational initiatives to abolish nuclear weaponry and some intergovernmental efforts to control the spread of nuclear weaponry and to encourage regimes of prohibition with respect to chemical and biological weaponry.

HUMAN RIGHTS As earlier argued, one of the most dramatic normative developments during the last half-century has involved the universal recognition by governments of the binding nature of international human rights obligations. The human rights framework has been set forth in the Universal Declaration of Human Rights; the Covenant on Civil and Political Rights; and the Covenant on Economic, Social, and Cultural Rights. In some sense, the embodiment of human rights' standards in international law was quite a dramatic acceptance by governments of encroachments on their claims of supremacy over sovereign territory and sensitive state–society relations. The initial acceptance of such an encroachment was either cynical (authoritarian governments feeling free to disregard external obligations of a general aspirational nature) or superficial (giving lip-service to widely endorsed standards of behaviour, but without enforcement or procedures for external accountability).

There was no indication that the governments who joined in endorsing the Universal Declaration 50 years ago thought that they were engaged in a fundamental process of global reform of the sort that would result from an effective process of implementation. The radical nature of the norms agreed upon, and periodically affirmed, can be appreciated by reference to Article 25 of the Universal Declaration, which promises every person 'the right to a standard of living' sufficient to satisfy basic human needs, and Article 28, which insists that everyone 'is entitled to a social and international order in which the rights and freedoms set forth in this Declaration can be fully realized'. Of course, realizing such rights fully would by itself satisfy many of the core expectations of humane governance, and seems more Utopian than ever in its current remoteness to the realities and outlook of neo-liberalism. At the same time, the obligations have been clearly expressed and endorsed as forming part of international law.

Unlike the situation pertaining to the renunciation of force, geopolitical and transnational democratic factors encouraged the implementation, although unevenly and incompletely, of agreed standards of human rights. First of all, civil society organizations (often still called NGOs, which is quite misleading) arose to gather information about human rights violations, and exerted pressure on governments to alter their practices; media exposure also turned out to be an important instrument to induce compliance.[5] Second, the ideological divisions in the Cold War led the West in particular to emphasize human rights violations of Soviet bloc countries. What started as hostile propaganda turned in the direction of potent politics subsequent to the Helsinki Accords of 1975, with the rise of opposition movements in East Europe and with the change of leadership style in Moscow during the

Gorbachev years. Third, under the aegis of the United Nations, and with the backing of grassroots efforts, especially in the United Kingdom and the United States, the anti-apartheid movement seemed to be an important factor in pushing the white leadership in South Africa to abandon apartheid by voluntary action. Fourth, the unevenness of working conditions within the context of economic globalization encouraged adversely affected social forces, such as organized labour, to call for the furtherance of human rights, as in relation to China or Indonesia. Many of these supportive moves were partially or totally opportunistic, but their effect has been to put human rights firmly on the global political agenda.

These developments are momentous, but many rights remained unfulfilled almost everywhere, and many peoples remained exposed to oppressive patterns of governance. In addition, cultural patterns in several regions of the world are at odds with basic ideas about human rights in circumstances that leave even governments that sincerely accept international standards virtually helpless (Kothari and Sethi 1991). The will to implementation is insufficient to influence larger states even when the international community is strongly mobilized at grassroots levels, as has been the case with respect to Tibet and East Timor. And then there are the complex claims about Asian Values or Islamic Civilization as being not adequately incorporated in the process or substance of international human rights, giving governments increased discretion to interpret standards in accordance with particular cultural outlooks. From such perspectives also emerges the view that the implementation of human rights, as distinct from the authority of the norms, is a matter for the sovereign state, and that intervention on behalf of human rights is never justified unless under the auspices of the United Nations, and then is rarely effective in light of the experience in Bosnia and Rwanda in the 1990s. There is also the contention that the assertion of human rights is filtered through the prism of geopolitics in a manner that gives rise to double standards, with some violators being subjected to severe sanctions while others are shielded from scrutiny despite their horrifying practices. And finally, there is the argument that the West, including civil society organizations, is only interested in civil and political rights, and gives no serious attention to economic and social rights, which are of paramount importance to the majority of people in the world.

Taken as a whole, the record of achievement with respect to human rights is impressive, yet cruelty and abuse remain widespread, and the task ahead on the road to fuller compliance remains formidable. The undertaking is additionally complicated by the inter-civilizational agenda associated with the recent assertion of non-Western ideas and values. The challenge of humane governance involves closing further the gap between promise and performance, which includes taking increased account of those whose victimization has a special character, as is the case with indigenous peoples. What will achieve further gains for human rights is the continuing convergence and spread of civil society initiatives with reinforcing geopolitical trends. There is a danger here that human rights becomes discredited to the extent that it is used insensitively as an instrument of inter-civilizational pressure, intensifying conflict and engendering misunderstanding. The institutionalization of protection for human rights within the European Union suggests that a shared political community committed to liberal democratic values is more likely to accept real accountability to external review of compliance than are more heterogeneous and less democratic states. And possibly, more generally, it suggests that the most promising means under current global conditions to advance humane governance with respect to human rights is at regional levels of interaction, while leaving the way open for further incremental developments within the UN system. The UN has steadily upgraded its concern for human rights, holding a high-profile global conference on the subject in 1993, and shortly thereafter adding to its formal make-up a High Commissioner for Human Rights.

From the perspective of this chapter the main point is that within the standard-setting, fact-finding, monitoring and reporting efforts of both intergovernmental and civil society, there has emerged a framework for the achievement of the sort of human rights culture that is presupposed by the goal of humane governance. Much needs to be done, but the tensions between universality of approach and diversity of cultural values and political outlook are likely to bring disappointment in the near future to both universalists and relativists. At this stage it would be useful to identify overlapping and convergent ideas about advancing human rights through extensive inter-civilizational and inter-religious dialogue. It would also improve the overall context for the promotion of human rights if major states, in particular the United States, refrained from relying on human rights rationales as pretexts for sanctions being imposed on states with whom it had strong ideological differences (e.g. Cuba).

COMMON HERITAGE OF HUMANKIND The Maltese ambassador, Arvid Pardo, in the course of a celebrated 1967 speech in the United Nations, made one of the most idealistic suggestions for global reform. Pardo proposed treating seabed resources of the high seas as belonging to the common heritage of humankind rather than being subject to appropriation by states with the technological and entrepreneurial capabilities. This proposal evoked a strong positive response throughout the international community. The common heritage principle carried within itself the possibility of a more equitable distribution of resources situated beyond the limits of territorial authority. It was also capable of extension to the polar regions and to the potential wealth of space. Its potential relevance to the transfer of technology, especially relating to health and food, is obvious. This relevance is reinforced by the treatment of knowledge and information associated with the Internet as a global public good, although combined with commercial control over various forms of data and the classification of other material as secret. The idea of common heritage could also be used, in part, to raise revenues for the UN system, weakening thereby the organization's bondage to the priorities of its most powerful members.

And yet the substantive outcomes have been so far disappointing. The language of common heritage, while retained as a goal, has been virtually emptied of substantive content in the Law of the Seas context as a result of heavy lobbying by the private sector and the gradual adoption of a neoliberal outlook by Western states, led by the United States and Thatcherite Britain. This is a process of 'normative co-option' whereby a progressive idea is introduced with great fanfare, but then applied in such a way as to deprive it of substantive content. In this instance, it is making common heritage subordinate to the operation of global market forces. Such a process contributes to a kind of complacency in which there is the illusion of commitment to human well-being, but without any tangible results. This pattern invites cynicism, and leads to widespread despair.

It is important at this stage to view the idea of common heritage critically, but with an appreciation of its potential role in a future world order based on humane governance. It is a normative idea that could be extended in many directions, ranging from relations to a variety of areas outside of sovereign territory to the protection of cultural and natural heritage even within the territory of a state to the status of knowledge and technological innovation relevant for human well-being, including the results of bio-genetic research. The politics of co-option in relation to common heritage is illustrative of the policy outcome in settings where global civil society is relatively passive and global market forces are mobilized in defence of their interests.

SUSTAINABLE DEVELOPMENT   One of the most creative and influential normative ideas of the 1980s has been that of 'sustainable development'. It was initially articulated in the report of the World Commission on Environment and Development published under the title *Our Common Future* (WCED 1987), and seemed to merge and reconcile in an organic and practical way the environmental concerns of the North with the developmental preoccupations of the South. The idea of sustainable development underpinned the discourse of the Earth Summit (UNCED) held at Rio in 1992, avoiding the divisive North–South view of the environmental challenge that had been evident in Stockholm 20 years earlier. It also reinforced the tendency of the North to accept the main burden of subsidizing adjustment costs in the South associated with environmental protection, a pattern that had been initiated in relation to efforts to persuade poorer countries to forego technologies that had serious ozone-depleting effects. At Rio a multi-billion dollar Global Environmental Facility was agreed upon and established to promote sustainable development in several main sectors of activity by facilitating North–South resource transfers (see *Agenda 21* Plan of Action (UNCED 1992)). In addition, more than 150 national councils of sustainable development have been established throughout the world since 1992. The UN has created a Commission on Sustainable Development, which meets twice a year to follow up on the sustainable development approach adopted at Rio.

But sustainable development, like common heritage, was a slogan, as well as a substantive principle with dramatic normative implications for behavioural adjustment. It was easy to invoke the language without making the changes in practices that would be required if sustainability were to be given appropriate weight. George Bush, then president of the United States, famously announced prior to Rio that the American standard of living was 'not negotiable'. In effect, if the rich countries were not even prepared to consider some limitations on affluent lifestyles, it would be impossible to induce poorer countries to forego short-term developmental opportunities even if they were environmentally damaging, as in relation to timber production and slash-and-burn forest clearance.

Experience to date has suggested both the importance of the idea of sustainable development in framing the global debate on policy, and the limited capacity to ensure tangible results to the sustainability commitment. Neoliberal ideas, as elsewhere, tend to prevail, and the funds pledged to support sustainability, inadequate to begin with, have not materialized. As a result, many have questioned whether there is any serious effort being made in relation to sustainability, given the strength of global capital and its insistence on the efficient use of resources, as measured by relatively short-term gains, as well as its visceral resistance to all forms of regulatory restraint imposed on private-sector activities.

Sustainable development is a crucial idea in relation to reconciling policy responses to the environment and poverty in a world of very uneven economic and social circumstances. There is a series of other normative ideas associated with this perspective, perhaps best summarized in the Rio Declaration on Environment and Development (UNCED 1992). However, for the normative reconciliation to be genuine and behaviourally significant it needs to be balanced and seriously implemented. Otherwise the political language becomes a trap that disguises policy failure. A major challenge for advocates of humane governance is to identify the means by which to implement sustainable development practically and concretely on a state, regional and world scale.

GLOBAL COMMONS Another closely related normative idea that is generally accepted, and underlies many of the initiatives taken to advance international environmental goals, has been associated with the notion of a 'global commons'. In essence, affirming the existence of a global commons acknowledges the growing insufficiency of relying on states to achieve an acceptable form of global governance by acting on their own. With reference to oceans, polar regions, ozone depletion, climate and biodiversity there is the awareness that only global cooperative regimes with longer-term perspectives can avoid disaster befalling the global commons. Impressive results have been achieved through the medium of 'law-making treaties' that seek to bind the entire world to act within an agreed framework of rights and duties. These results owe a great deal to pressures mounted by transnational civic initiatives.

As elsewhere, the results are incomplete, and do not engender hope that enough is being currently done to protect the global commons from further dangerous types of deterioration. A major difficulty, evident in efforts to impose limits on the emission of greenhouse gases, has been the unwillingness of the rich countries to bear all the burdens of high adjustment costs and the refusal of poorer countries to divert resources from their roles of achieving economic growth as rapidly as possible. This difficulty is compounded by domestic political pressures that are less sensitive to the importance of the global commons, and thus are opposed to taking steps for their protection if the result is higher costs and restrictions on behaviour.

FUTURE GENERATIONS   The acceleration of history, coupled with concerns about carrying capacity, catastrophic warfare, biodiversity, global warming and overpopulation, has given rise to growing concerns about the responsibility of present generations to the future. Such concerns reverse centuries of Western optimism about the future based on a theory of progress that rests on scientific discovery giving rise to a continuous flow of life-enhancing technological innovations and increases in economic productivity. One effect of such hopeful expectations has been the virtual guarantee that those born in the future would enjoy a better life on the average than their forebears, thereby relieving the present generation of any responsibility. This normative move to endow the future generation with rights has been incorporated into several important international treaties, and enjoys some support as an emergent principle of international law (Macdonald 1997; Sands 1997). The General Conference of UNESCO formulated the overall ethos as a Declaration on the Responsibilities of the Present Generations to Future Generations on 12 November 1997.[6]

Of course, the commitment to future generations remains a rather empty commitment with no tangible impact on the behavioural patterns of the present, but it is a normative idea that has been validated and widely endorsed. As such, it provides the basis for fulfilling the temporal dimension of humane governance, that is, the assurance that future generations enjoy life prospects equivalent or superior to those enjoyed by present generations. In this manner, the normative idea of sustainability is linked with the human rights of the unborn.

ACCOUNTABILITY: THE RULE OF LAW AND PERSONAL RESPONSIBILITY   A widely endorsed normative idea is the duty of all governments and their officials to uphold international law, which includes the obligation to conduct foreign policy within the constraints of law. Such a legalist orientation subordinates sovereign discretion to a framework of agreed-upon constraints and procedures. The constitutional structure for this framework is codified in the UN Charter, and elaborated in some crucial resolutions of the General Assembly such as that of the Declaration on Principles of International Law and Friendly Relations Among States.[7]

The extension of these ideas to wartime conditions occurred after the Second World War in the form of war crimes trials against surviving leaders in Germany and Japan. Both were applauded for the effort to hold individual leaders responsible even if they had acted under the colour of sovereign authority, and criticized as arbitrary expressions of 'victors' justice'. This principle of accountability in relation to the humanitarian law of war has been revived during the 1990s in response to atrocities and genocidal conduct in former Yugoslavia and Rwanda. In addition, war crimes trials have been recently proposed in relation to a series of earlier occurrences, including the reign of terror in Cambodia during the years of Pol Pot's rule and with respect to the crimes attributed to the regime of Saddam Hussein in Iraq. These initiatives have given rise to a strong movement in global civil society, a coalition of hundreds of organizations, to establish a permanent international criminal court, with pressure being mounted on governments to take formal action.

Again, as with earlier normative innovations, the record of achievement is not satisfactory. Geopolitical factors still guide the foreign policy of almost all states, with law and morality used as self-serving rationalizations or as the basis of propaganda attacks on adversaries. Legal standards are not applied uniformly by the United Nations, leading to accusations of double standards. Major states reserve for themselves discretionary control over recourse to force. Even in constitutional democracies, such as the United States, it is exceedingly rare to be able to challenge foreign policy as violative of international law: the courts are reluctant to override the executive branch in the setting of external relations, and the authority of Congress is limited to initial authorizations of war and subsequent withholding of appropriations in relation to contested foreign policy, especially in wartime. More fundamentally, the ethos of government in most countries continues to be that a great power is animated by interests and a mission, and is sovereign in relation to law when it comes to matters of such vital concerns as security.

REDRESS OF GRIEVANCES In recent years there have occurred a myriad of claims associated with events long past. To mention a few: the inquiry into the Nazi origins of Swiss gold during the Second World War; the abuses by imperial Japan of 'comfort women' in Korea, the Philippines and elsewhere; the effort by Afro-Americans and by Africa to receive reparations for the injustices of slavery and the slave trade; the Armenian effort to exert pressure on the government of Turkey to acknowledge genocidal policies in

1915; the struggle of indigenous peoples in the United States and elsewhere to obtain an apology for past wrongs and receive some specific forms of relief. What these various undertakings have in common is their insistence that the past, even the distant past, contains unresolved issues of equity that remain open wounds. The call for redress involves various attitudes, including opportunistic efforts to receive monetary rewards, and each initiative must be evaluated.

What is evident, however, is that the surfacing of claims for redress of past grievances reflects a search for inter-generational equity that complements in many ways the rise of support for obligations to future generations. The acceleration of history seems to be causing a greater sense of time-consciousness with respect to past and future, making such inter-generational concerns part of the subject matter of justice, and hence of humane governance.

GLOBAL DEMOCRACY   Rooted in the Preamble to the UN Charter is an affirmation of the populist foundations of international institutional authority: those oft-repeated opening words, 'We the Peoples of the United Nations determined to save succeeding generations from the scourge of war' through the action of representatives acting on behalf of governments 'do hereby establish an international organization to be known as the United Nations.' From this democratic seedling, almost a fortuitous element in the statist world of 1945, the UN has evolved over time and increasingly presents itself in various formulations as the emergent ideology of global civil society (Archibugi and Held 1995).

The pursuit of global democracy is taking many forms, ranging from the participatory activism of transnational citizens' groups around the world to global conferences under UN auspices that have served as places of conflict and cooperation in the relations between peoples and governments. Proposals for the creation of the Global Peoples' Assembly within the United Nations system is one element of the effort of transnational democratic forces to enhance their role in the global authority structure. The secretary-general of the UN, Kofi Annan, has given his endorsement to democratizing moves, and has even suggested holding a millennial peoples' assembly in the year 2000.

This focus on global democracy remains almost totally a project to be realized in the future. In fact, its ideological emergence and the activism evident in several global settings have caused a statist backlash, a reluctance to extend the consensus supportive of democracy to the global level, including within the United Nations system. Europe is currently a testing ground for the extension of democratic forms to a regional undertaking, with the European Parliament already offering some insight into some aspects of 'regional democracy' as the foundation of regional humane governance. It seems evident that a coalition of global market forces and geopolitical actors are resistant to all efforts to give coherent political form to the strivings of global civil society. The prospect for global democracy remains the over-arching goal of those committed to the pursuit of humane governance for the peoples of the world.

Moving Forward

This enumeration of normative ideas incorporates an interpretation of both the functional challenges facing humanity and a view of human betterment that includes leaving room for the expression of cultural and ideological difference. The political prospects for realizing these ideas in practice depend on the strengthening of global civil society and its continuing orientation along these normative lines. Global civil society should not be romanticized as necessarily aligned with the project for humane global governance. There are tensions evident throughout global civil society, as in any other political arena. My contention is that up to this point, and seemingly into the future, those perspectives that have supported the normative ideas being affirmed here have dominated global civil society. But such a conclusion cannot be taken for granted. There are also regressive normative ideas at the grassroots level that are being organized transnationally, including coalitions associated with anti-immigrant, fascist and cyber-libertarian positions. In addition, there is a range of what might be called visionary ideas being promoted by individuals, groups and segments of global civil society. These ideas are radical in content and claim, and are not embedded in the operational codes of international law and morality. Illustrative of visionary ideas would be 'the ethos of non-violence' as the foundation for security or of the 'citizen pilgrim' as orienting political loyalty in an imagined political community of the future (see also Falk 1995).

A hopeful outlook regarding the future depends on sustaining and deepening the influence of global civil society, and collaborating where possible with other political actors, including states and agents of the private sector. Such collaboration in the past has been very effective in promoting such general goals as the furtherance of human rights and environmental protection, and more particular undertakings such as the prevention of mining in Antarctica or the movement in support of a regime of prohibition on land-mines. Often the collaborative process takes the form of a law-making treaty that establishes an appropriate regime. Two such collaborations that are now in process involve the campaign to abolish nuclear weapons (an alternative to the geopolitical project to enforce the non-proliferation regime) and the effort to establish a permanent international criminal court.

Another aspect of a hopeful stance toward the future arises from the assumption that there exists widespread human support on a trans-civilizational basis for species survival and for the betterment of material circumstances. The validation of the normative ideas mentioned above lends credibility to the assertion of this shared sensibility, although disappointments with implementation also need to be taken into account. Implementation will involve encounters with opposing ideas and interests often linked to powerful social forces in control of influential states and shaping private sector outlooks, particularly the ideas bound up with the economistic world picture as expounded by the proponents of economic neoliberalism. Underlying this concern about these normative ideas is the central Hegelian conviction that ideas matter, and that in the fluid historical circumstances of the present (with states losing some of their control and dominance and other actors arising in various settings), ideas matter greatly.

And finally, in commentating on global trends and future arrangements, the context is too complex to yield the sort of understanding that could support meaningful predictions as to what will happen. This uncertainty is an encouragement for those in favour of the normative ideas being advocated. The current perception that overwhelmingly powerful political forces and countervailing ideas block their realization should not be converted into a sense of resignation or cynicism. The future remains open to a wide spectrum of possibilities, including those directly associated with humane global govern-ance. Recent international history, associated with the peaceful ending of the Cold War and the successful struggle against colonialism, has confirmed that desirable outcomes occur even when most instruments of assessment have concluded that such results are virtually impossible. In this sense, political and societal miracles happen, but not by waiting. They happen only as a result of commitment and struggle dedicated to the attainment of such goals. The framework of normative ideas that have been depicted, and enjoy widespread support throughout global civil society, give some political struc-ture to such striving as we near the end of this millennium.

Notes

1. This element is generally described under the rubric of 'human rights' as an element of foreign policy, but that is a selective and somewhat contradictory notion. Economic and social rights are not only excluded, but are in practice curtailed or opposed as part of the neoliberal programme.

2. The various aspects of the international environmental ethos are best summarized in the Rio Declaration on Environment and Development. For text see Weston 1990.

3. My own effort to clarify this overall quest is Falk 1995; see also Falk 1975.

4. The 1956 Suez Operation was the only time that geopolitics was somewhat sub-ordinated by the superpowers. This occurred also during the Korean War, but in this instance the explanation is procedural, a fortuitous result of the Soviet boycott of the Security Council at the time for the unrelated issue of protesting the refusal to adjust Chinese representation after 1949 to the outcome of the civil war.

5. I have been persuaded to abandon NGO as a term of art by the analysis and arguments of Liszt Vierira, 'Civil society and globalization,' an undated paper summarizing her book *Cidadania e Globalizacao* 1997.

6. For text see *Future Generations Journal*, 1998, no. 24, 15–17.

7. G.A. Res. 2625 (XXV), 24 October 1970.

References

Agius, E. and S. Busuttil (eds) (1997) *Future Generations and International Law*, Earthscan, London.

Archibugi, D. and D. Held (eds) (1995) *Cosmopolitan Democracy*, Polity, Cambridge.

Falk, R. (1975) *A Study of Future Worlds*, Free Press, New York.

— (1993) 'The making of global citizenship', in J. Beecher, J. Brown Childs and J. Cutler (eds), *Global Visions: Beyond the New World Order*, South End Press, Boston.

— (1995) *On Humane Governance: Toward a New Global Politics*, Polity, Cambridge.

— (1996) 'False universalism and human rights: the case of Islam', *Third World Quarterly*

— (1997) 'Resisting "Globalisation-from-above" through "Globalisation-from-below"', *New Political Economy*, 1 (2): 17–24.

Kothari, S. and H. Sethi (1991) *Rethinking Human Rights: Challenges for Theory and Culture*, Lokayan, Delhi.

Macdonald, R. (1997) 'Future generations: searching for a system of protection', in Agius and Busuttil (eds) (1997).

Mueller, J. (1990) *Retreat from Doomsday: The Obsolescence of Major War*, Doubleday, New York

Sands, P. (1997) 'Protecting future generations: precedents and practicalities', in Agius and Busuttil (eds) (1997).

UNCED (1992) *Agenda 21*.

Vierira, L. (1997) *Cidadania e Globalizacao*, Rio de Janeiro: Editora Record.

Weston, B. H. (ed.) (1990) *Basic Documents in International Law and World Order*, West Publishers, St. Paul.

WCED (1987) *Our Common Future* (the Brundtland Report), Oxford University Press, New York.

3

Globalization: A Developmental Approach

JAN PRONK

In 1992, at a conference entitled 'Agenda 2000', I addressed the issue of whether or not development cooperation was out of date.[1] My answer to that question was no, development cooperation is not a thing of the past, but it is not a thing of the present either, because there exists neither unequivocal development nor a strong desire for international cooperation. After the decade of adjustment of the 1980s and after the end of the Cold War in 1989, I said that the 1990s would be a decade of transition: transition from adjustment to development, transition from authoritarian regimes to economic and political democracy, transition from postcolonial and post-Cold War societies to new international configurations better able to cope with the major problems of the forthcoming century. The transition period would be characterized more by international conflict management than by cooperation to guarantee a sustainable society.

The main reason for my pessimism was that although a new spirit was emerging in favour of sustainable growth and development, and although there was a will to translate this new consciousness into concrete action, the world lacked the capacity to do so. Even if we were to agree that the new technological and ecological reality required a new political agenda, the capacity to implement this agenda would have been eroded by that same reality. In my view, the turn of the decade had been characterized by a crisis not only in development policies but also in the theory and the concept of development itself, because some fundamental questions had been side-stepped: questions of power and inequality and questions regarding the ecological sustainability and the physical limits of economic growth. Addressing these questions would require a strong democratic public authority, but because of the prevailing market ideology such an authority was much less effective and much more contested than before.

It was not only the widespread shift from the state to the market that had produced this result, but also the inherent erosion of nation-states themselves.

Nation-states had been weakened by transnational economic forces on the one hand, and by domestic conflicts on the other. These conflicts were rooted not only in economic inequalities but also in cultural differences between religious, ethnic or other identity groupings. Addressing these conflicts would require economic development policies to eliminate injustices for which strong public authorities were needed. However, these capabilities were being eroded. Moreover, the non-economic or cultural dimensions of these conflicts were only very dimly understood after a period during which the main ideological conflict had centred on questions regarding the relationship between the individual and the state or concerning economic welfare. The new questions focused on the role of tradition and on the relationship between the individual and self-defined social groups and their identities. The conflicts between such groups were often fought regardless of public norms and rules – for instance, human rights or the rule of law – because the authority of the state itself was in dispute.

So, I concluded, transitional policies would have to focus on conflict management, on adopting a new agenda, on the integration of development and peace, on the acceptance of the role of culture in politics, and on establishing new public institutions able to cope with this agenda. When all this had been accomplished a solid basis would have been established upon which development cooperation could flourish: development cooperation is not out of date, it is not a thing of the past, but neither is it of today. However, development cooperation will be very necessary and hopefully possible in the future.

Development Cooperation Revisited

Was I overly pessimistic in my considerations back in 1992? Yes and no. First, even since 1992, quite a few nations have suffered from disruptive domestic conflicts. Some have been contained or resolved, for instance the apartheid conflict in South Africa or the civil wars in Mozambique, Mali and Guatemala. Others have continued or worsened, such as the Israeli–Palestinian conflict, or the civil wars in Sudan and Afghanistan. In other societies, violent wars have commenced or restarted: genocide in Rwanda, massacres in Algeria, violence in Sri Lanka, Sierra Leone and Kenya. Simply counting the number of civil wars fought in a specific year does not answer the question of whether or not the overall trend is upward or downward. Anyway, at present, there are more violent conflicts within nations than during the Cold War. The potential for such conflicts is growing and surfacing more easily, and violence between identity groups within nations and across borders is increasing. One tendency is very clear: such conflicts are not on the international agenda, or only in exceptional cases. And when they are, the international community finds itself at a loss: rather than contributing to the containment of the conflict, it becomes itself a party to it or affected – divided or paralysed – by it.

So, I consider my pessimism at the time justified in that violent conflicts have remained a very substantive hallmark of the 1990s. However, I may have been too gloomy concerning the potential for economic and social development. The fears I expressed in 1992 have not been realized: remarkable economic development did take place in the early 1990s, partly made possible by rigorous adjustment policies in the decade before, which resulted in a fair degree of macroeconomic stability as a necessary prerequisite for lasting economic growth. During the past decade, there has been a great deal of macroeconomic growth. Remarkable progress has been made in terms of life expectancy, food security and levels of literacy and education, though the number of income-poor people is still increasing – currently at nearly 1.5 billion. This is true of nearly all parts of the world: Africa, Latin America, Eastern Europe and most industrialized countries. As a matter of fact, most countries are better at stimulating economic growth than at equitable distribution of affluence. This failure directly contributes to the increasingly sharp economic and social polarization within societies. The income ratio of the wealthiest 20 per cent of the world population as against the poorest 20 per cent has grown from 30:1 in 1960 to nearly 80:1 at present. Hence, in many parts of the world, macroeconomic growth continues to go hand in hand with the grossest social abuses.

But there is growth and this was also expressed in the growth of world trade. The volume of world trade is presently expanding at roughly twice the pace experienced at the beginning of the decade. And the value of world trade has expanded faster than world production for the seventh year in a row. The growth of international investment is even more striking. Foreign direct investment currently amounts to some US$350 billion, a fivefold increase since the mid-1980s. And in both trade and investment flows the share of developing countries is increasing rapidly. A major change is thus under way in the world economy. In the past the global economy was primarily driven by trade, a role now being assumed by FDI. It is the multinational corporations that are responsible for this.

During the first part of the 1990s international economic cooperation intensified as well. The conclusion of the GATT Uruguay Round substantially cut down trade barriers. After the establishment of the World Trade Organization new elements were added to the agenda, such as services, investments and the financial sector. At the same time, regional trade cooperation was strengthened by means of regional trade agreements (NAFTA, for example, and ASEAN). In Europe, far-reaching decisions were taken concerning the establishment of an Economic and Monetary Union and the introduction of a single currency, explicitly to improve Europe's international competitiveness in the global market.

The liberalization of capital transactions has been taken up by the IMF, whose resources have been recently enlarged by raising the quotas and by a new allocation of Special Drawing Rights. The Paris Club dealt with an increasing number of indebted countries and welcomed the Republic of Russia, an important former creditor as well as a new debtor, as a member. This, together with the highly indebted poor countries (HIPC) initiative, will also help these countries to participate in the world economy.

The common characteristic of these international agreements is that they all concern the same field: international economic development resulting from an interplay between market forces. These agreements have been effective and have resulted in decisions and in the build-up of new rules, new international policy measures and the strengthening of institutions. However, international cooperation did not proceed in other fields: social policy, poverty reduction, climate change, desertification, forest conservation, water resources management and migration. International conferences were held on these issues too, but they were seminars, mere talking shops, taking no decisions. And there was no progress at all in the international management of conflicts.

The international and inter-governmental consultations that did produce results in fact helped market forces to interact globally and to meet and compete with each other, by allocating investment, increasing production, facilitating transportation and trade, providing worldwide access to technology, pushing and attracting capital across borders, opening up new markets, and fostering global information and communication. Indeed, during this decade the globalization of markets has been greatly facilitated by inter-governmental decisions. What international cooperation there was facilitated globalization. The 1990s have become the decade of a breakthrough in the globalization process.

Globalization

One development that was difficult to assess in 1992 was the impact of the globalization process. We can now say that it is a revolution. As with all revolutions, globalization is irreversible and uncheckable, transforming whole societies. Technological advances, the driving force behind globalization, continually enhance our potential to communicate with anybody, anywhere at any time. Technological progress enables us to process, store, retrieve and communicate information in whatever form, unrestrained by distance, time and volume. It is communications and information technology that intensify economic interdependence on a world scale. This revolution is adding immense new capacities to human intelligence and constitutes a resource that fundamentally changes the economy and our way of life, as soon as we are affected by it.

The world's financial markets have taken advantage in every way possible of the deregulated and uncontrolled financial environment created during the past decade. Global currency transactions increased threefold between 1986 and 1992. As long as enormous profits can be made from wild swings in the exchange value between currencies, the volume of international capital transactions will continue to grow. The extreme volatility of the global financial markets is obvious. They are also dangerous, since the frantic intensity of their activities leads to unpredictability and thus contains all the seeds of economic instability. Recent history provides many examples of what can ensue. In 1982, Argentina, Brazil, Mexico and other developing nations defaulted on their debts to foreign banks. A decade later, the external indebtedness of all developing countries more than doubled. In 1989, Japan's 'bubble economy' of inflated financial values collapsed. In 1992, the British pound and the Italian lira came under successful attack, forcing them to devalue. The following year, it was the turn of the French franc and other European currencies. In 1995, Mexico collapsed anew and Japan was engulfed in a crisis of falling prices and failing debts. Ironically, the one bulwark against these disasters is government – ironically, because government is anathema to the advocates of the globalized economy. Yet, time and again, it has been government that has had to intervene in order to extinguish the fires inadvertently lit by the marketplace's misguided enthusiasm. Incidentally, government has had to play this role at great cost to the taxpayer.

Recently the debate on the pros and cons of globalization has intensified as a result of the unexpected instabilities in the economies of Southeast Asia, the heroes of the world economy during the last two decades. To a certain extent, these instabilities were of their own making: too much reliance on real estate leading to real estate speculation; a hasty expansion of financial service industries, leading to uncontrolled excess bank credits and weaknesses in the financial systems; a waste of savings on unproductive investment; an increasing imbalance between the expansion of the wealth-creating machine and socially productive investment; insider profiteering; undisciplined monetary policies; inadequate fiscal policies; and overvalued currencies.

These imbalances have been sharpened by reactions from international markets. The market responses could be considered excessive and, in part, exacerbated by unscrupulous speculators, who had their way in a free-for-all, without suspension of markets and without agreed rules and principles or agreed professional, ethical and behavioural standards and without clear disclosure requirements.

International Pressure

During the recent annual meeting of the IMF and the World Bank in Hong Kong this market crisis caused Prime Minister Mahathir of Malaysia to accuse the great powers of conspiring against Asian countries by pressing them to open up their markets and then manipulating their currencies to knock them off as competitors. Most forms of currency trading, according to Mahathir, are 'unnecessary, unproductive and immoral'. In his view, currency trading should be limited to financing real commodity trade, and other forms of currency trading should be made illegal. This was considered an extreme position but quite a few other Asian politicians made it clear that they are planning to slow, or even reverse, the liberalizations that have opened their economies to global forces, because that process has given too much room to a tendency for markets to overreact and to speculate. There was a recognition that sound policies and domestic reforms would be required, but there was also a fear that these would not be a guarantee against shifts in international market sentiment, which could lead to a withdrawal of the capital that has underpinned development so far and to the manipulation of currencies. There are many reasons to judge markets as undependable, arbitrary or even manipulated. No wonder that many developing countries resist pressure to further open their markets.

I do not believe in a conspiracy theory as put forward by Prime Minister Mahathir. But international pressure exists. The US, for instance, is calling for further liberalization of the Chinese economy before China is admitted to the World Trade Organization. As US Deputy Treasury Secretary Larry Summers recently declared, this can only take place if China accepts the norms of openness in the international system. This would also include agreement to roll back barriers in financial services: 'The process of market opening is like peeling an onion,' Summers said, 'it happens slowly, layer by layer, and there are plenty of tears involved.'

These tears would be worthwhile according to advocates of globalization. Opening up markets to foreign banks, securities and insurance companies and money managers would not enlarge the financial sector problems in developing countries but would lead to a more uniform and transparent framework, increasing global investment flows and decreasing volatility in emerging markets. In the post-communist, post-statist world of the 1990s, it is said that deregulation and market liberalization, after an initial transition period, will only produce positive results for national economies and for ordinary people. This would not only be true for transport and communication, including telecommunication and information technology and for trade in general but also for finance. 'Financial markets don't just oil the wheels of economic growth. They are the wheels,' in the words of Lawrence Summers. And the US Treasury Secretary Robert Rubin in Hong Kong referred to the agglomeration of liberal trading and investment activities as the emblems of a 'new economy'. For, if you limit the flow of capital, you run the risk of stopping the flow of technology and that would put you out of business in this knowledge-based global society characterized both by life-long learning, which is not for fun but for survival, and creative destruction, not only of enterprises but of knowledge bodies, data banks and information flows, too.

Within the framework of the IMF and WTO, developing countries are bullied into the open, integrated global economy. The more the demands of the global economy are met, the stronger the world financial system will be.

That would benefit the providers of money and capital, who can then make decisions on the direction and allocation of money, in the short as well as the long run, on a daily, and, as a matter of fact, minute-to-minute basis, 24 hours a day, without having to bother about different rules and regulations in different countries. Will it benefit those countries, too? It remains to be seen. Economically weaker nations are quite concerned that they will become easy targets for international financial speculation, in particular because the international rules themselves set by governments in international meetings and conferences on the world economy – from Singapore to Hong Kong – still seem to be dictated by the G7 and are not aimed at any form of protection for national economies against fluctuations or for people against poverty and unemployment. There are no rules or even codes of conduct for banks and other financial institutions, other than 'feel free, compete and get bigger, at any cost'. The only rule next to 'open up your economy to international competition' is 'get your fundamentals right'. That is necessary indeed, but those fundamentals themselves are defined in terms of macro-finance – the gap in the government budget and the rate of inflation – and not in terms of a fundamental equilibrium between haves and have-nots, which is not only an economic but also a social, political and human imperative for the survival of nations.

Is there an alternative? Globalization is inevitable. It is also believed to be unmanageable. In the words of Thomas Friedman:

> Globalization isn't a choice. It's a reality ... and no one is in charge – not George Soros, not 'great powers' ... [They] didn't start it, [they] can't stop it ... You keep looking for someone to complain to, someone to take the heat off your markets. Well guess what ... there's no one on the other end of the phone. The global market today is an electronic herd of anonymous stock, bond and currency traders sitting behind computer screens. The members of this herd live everywhere where there is a trading floor ... everywhere that someone with a computer screen and modem can buy and sell currencies, stocks and bonds. ... The electronic herd cuts no one any slack. It does not recognize anyone's unique circumstances. The herd only recognizes its own rules. ... [When] you [start] to break the rules ... the herd sells you out ... [stampedes] you and [leaves] you as electronic roadkill. ... [When] that happens you don't ask the herd for mercy, you don't denounce the herd, you just get up, dust yourself off and get back with the flow of the herd. Sure, this is unfair ... [but] there's nobody to call.[2]

A Developmental Approach to Globalization

This may be true, but I still think that it is worthwhile to try to appoint someone to sit on the other end of the phone and to pick it up when it starts ringing – or, even better, someone or some institution, with the right not only to answer the phone but also to initiate calls, ask questions, issue timely warnings to potential victims of the herd, demarcate grazing areas for the herd and help to avoid stampedes. It's worth a try, because globalization is producing victims: by universalizing the market, advanced labour standards can be undermined, sophisticated environmental regulations can be avoided, forest and water resources can be pillaged and local artisanal production can be wrecked. As William Pfaff recently argued:

> The trade, labor and environmental regulations that globalization undermines were put there for a reason. Much of this regulation came about as a direct result of the rampant abuses and exploitation of the industrial and colonial systems of the 19th century. Do we really wish to restore the conditions for such abuses?[3]

The answer obviously has to be no. Globalization cannot imply a worldwide application of the minimal rules and regulations that the least advanced last entrant considers affordable. Neither would it be feasible to impose in one sweep on all countries alike all the rules and regulations applicable in the economically more advanced countries, since these have resulted from the democratic political action of free people. But there is a third way, which would consist of three elements. First, the strengthening of existing and the building up of other international organizations that could act as counter-vailing powers to transnational corporations and mega-banks, elaborating a framework of rules, guidelines and codes of conduct not only for governments but also for the transnationally acting private enterprises and conglomerates, and assisting governments of nation-states if they are in jeopardy of being overwhelmed by forces beyond their territorial control.

Second, an international agreement between governments monitored by such institutions, which would allow for a gradual integration of national economies into the global market. A smooth transition produces fewer victims than a big bang. Strengthened and reformed international institutions could help in formulating transparent conditions and time-paths, dictated not by a greedy or rampant herd of dealers in financial assets but by authorities with a public responsibility for broadly based, sustainable economic growth, social cohesion, a reasonable income distribution and preservation of the environment for future generations. The build-up of such international institutions would require a sharp deviation from the present trend: no weakening of the United Nations but a strengthening through radical reform that would enable this system to deal with the challenges of the global market and the demands of global civilization in the twenty-first century. These challenges and demands are different from and far greater than those existing after the Second World War, when the need for international cooperation led to the establishment of the UN. At that time, cooperation had to be institutionalized mainly at the inter-governmental level. Globalization today needs to be extended to two other levels: international cooperation to manage major instabilities and conflicts within countries, and international public action to try to stem excessive transnational private economic power. In order to achieve this objective, the basically economically oriented international institutions, such as the WTO, the IMF, the World Bank and also the EC, should be provided with a mandate that not only facilitates globalization but also guides and phases it. Facilitation, the present mode, is too passive and betrays public responsibilities. Planning globalization would be too ambitious an endeavour, because the market forces are too strong to be planned or controlled. But steering the process, countervailing these forces, giving weight to motives other than fast profit maximization, demarcating the spheres of life within which market forces can play, strengthening the voice of those who feel excluded or stampeded by these forces, constitute a public duty.

The third element of an alternative approach to globalization would be a strengthening of civil society within the nation-states to be integrated into the global market. This would involve strengthening laws, procedures and institutions guaranteeing human rights, fostering democratization and pluriformity, and inviting and welcoming the formally and informally organized demands of civil society, as well as enabling people in general to speak out and to communicate ideas, to voice their interests, feelings and desires without having to fear retaliation. All this is not a separate issue, unrelated to globalization, but a *sine qua non* if globalization is to have a chance of being not just the ultimate phase of pure capitalism, but a process serving the interests of all people, including those who consider their identity and dignity to be based on ideas and culture rather than on what they consume.

I want to emphasize strongly this third element of a 'developmental approach' to globalization. So far, the international financial community seems to be blind to the rest of the world in its obsessive greed while governments and the international organization system, which ought to have a broader and more far-sighted vision, keep silent. How else can we explain, for instance, that the IMF's conclusion in its most recent Article IV consultation on Algeria that 'Directors agree that Algeria's exemplary adjustment and reform efforts deserved continued support of the international financial community'? Algeria: where every week some one to two hundred people's throats have been cut, including women's and infants', for several years now. The Algerian government accuses the UN High Commissioner for Human Rights of intervention in domestic affairs when it dares to call for international attention to this systematic slaughtering of innocent people. But the global economy applauds: Algeria's exemplary adjustment and reform efforts deserve continued support of the international financial community. Money turns people blind, money silences, money kills.

How else can we explain that the bullying of countries into the global economy is not linked with efforts to bully them to respect basic human rights and values? I am not referring to the debate on Asian versus Western values accompanying the process of globalization, demonstrated in the heated exchange between Mahathir and George Soros, or the confrontation between Asian and Western countries at the UNCED Review Conference in 1997, when the EU and the United States were accused of urging the rest of the world to adopt a more modest economic lifestyle at a time when other countries were not yet in a position to compete with the West. Indeed, the credibility of the West is at stake when it looks as if advantages are being protected and denied to newcomers in the global economy, and to the citizens of these countries.

That debate should continue, with mutual respect, and Western countries have to understand that a debate consists of speaking and listening to the arguments of the other. A dialogue is not a sermon, and not all Western values can withstand criticism derived from other cultures and traditions, certainly not those Western values that are overly materialist and overly individualist. An open dialogue with other cultures, based on mutual respect, might even help the West to get rid of some of the distortions in the Western belief system, and encourage Western societies to value spiritual well-being and social relations as being at least as important as money and consumption. Mahathir's remarks on currency trading were a bit extreme, but he had a point. Money should not be an aim in itself; it is an instrument that helps to exchange goods and services in order to enhance people's welfare. There is some immorality in a system that puts money above welfare and declares the freedom to exchange money in all circumstances to be more important than the right to work, to feed, educate and house oneself and one's family, and to enjoy proper sanitation and health care. These rights and freedoms by definition do not collide with the market, but they are becoming increasingly incompatible with it, if only because basic human needs are seldom adequately provided for by the market only.

There is one value that should not be nuanced or de-emphasized. That is the value of liberty, the freedom not of capital but of the individual human being, the liberty not to trade money and goods but to exchange ideas. How is it possible that in the global economy all emphasis is laid on the former rather than on the latter? There are countries lured and bullied into a global economy that systematically and arbitrarily strip their citizens of their dignity. In Nigeria, all emphasis is laid on national security: political and military stability is enforced by troops who violently oppress minority groups that protest against the destruction of their physical environment by international oil companies and against the corruption of the ruling élites who consider their material interests best served by these agents of the global economy. In Burma, Kenya, China and Indonesia, pro-democracy advocates are thrown into prison, and dissent is effectively silenced by intimidation, exile, administrative detention or house arrest. Why only ask such governments to introduce capital account currency convertibility as a requirement to be integrated into the global economy, instead of insisting upon freedom of expression of opinion and freedom of exchange of ideas as the hallmark of belonging to global civilization? Why do we deliberately miss a chance to guarantee that globalization is not only in the interests of *haute finance* – the corporate managers, the megabanks and the Wall Street machos in the new old world of the West, the *nouveaux riches* in Asia and the Middle East and the robber barons in the chaotic capitalist states established on the ruins of communism in Eastern Europe and the ruins of colonialism in Africa – but also in the interest of those people who in earlier phases of capitalist growth were underpaid, underemployed and now feel not only exploited but also excluded, who are raising their voices and demanding access to the economy and a decent standard of living? Why, in our negotiations on the modalities of entry into the global market do we trust governments that do not trust their own people?

Global Market versus Global Civilization

Five years ago I said that the world seemingly lacked the capacity to deal with the major issues of sustainable development: poverty, ecology and conflict. In the post-Cold War, post-colonial, post-adjustment and post-North–South world of the 1990s a broader consciousness had arisen that these were the main issues to be addressed. However, we were even more aware that the development of our institutional and political capacity to confront these issues had not kept pace with the need. For this reason I forecast that the present period would be a decade not of development cooperation but of transition, during which we would not be able to do more than take stop-gap measures.

Looking back at the first half of this decade, we can say that there was stronger economic development and more intense international cooperation than I foresaw, but that this development was uneven and the cooperation unbalanced. The process of globalization, which has evolved faster than I anticipated in my address five years ago, has added to this unevenness and one-sidedness of development and international cooperation. It is technologically and economically, not politically, driven. Political decisions only seem to follow events and to aim at facilitating the workings of the global market.

This, in my view, is not sustainable. Globalization in its present form will sharpen inequalities. It will lead to ever-greater ecological distortions and physical scarcities. And by doing so it will enhance the conflict potential in the world. At the same time, the present globalization drive is further weakening the capacity of the polity, nationally as well as internationally, to deal with these three issues, which are major threats to the stability and the cohesion of global society. In *Jihad vs. McWorld*, Benjamin Barber describes Jihad as a dogmatic and violent particularism resulting from identity politics, partly as a reaction to a McWorld globalization:

Jihad and McWorld operate with equal strength in opposite directions ... the one recreating ancient subnational and ethnic borders from within, the other making national borders porous from without. ... [They] both make war on the sovereign nation state and thus undermine the nation state's democratic institutions. Each eschews civil society and belittles democratic citizenship, neither seeks alternative democratic institutions. Their common thread is indifference to civil liberty.[4]

I have tried to draft an agenda for an alternative approach to McWorld, a developmental approach to globalization consisting of four steps. First, to undertake efforts to phase and sequence full access of nations to the global market, using transparent criteria, which are formulated to protect nations and citizens. Second, to guide the process by strengthening public international institutions in order to countervail transnational economic power. Third, to strengthen the capacity of the world polity to deal with the so-called non-economic dimensions of the global market: ecology, climate, disease, poverty, and the prevention and management of identity conflicts. Fourth, to support movements within nations which enhance democracy, human rights, civil liberties and the cultural pluriformity of society. I would also urge that the last point be linked to the first in order to avoid a growing divergence between the global market and global civilization.

The present world is still characterized by an immense variety of peoples, societies, beliefs, traditions, languages and cultures. Globalization is threatening to annex them into a Western technological and economic monoculture. This threat is very real indeed, because the technologically modern channels of cultural communication – the media, advanced educational systems and information networks – are increasingly commercially financed and bring a uniform message, based on a Western materialist lifestyle. In so far as that lifestyle frees people from the bonds of religious or tribal oppression, this is a message worthwhile communicating anywhere in the world. In so far as it lures people into new dependencies by imposing cultural uniformity, the result is colonization of people rather than liberation. It would be a great pity if globalization were to have this effect. It would not only be the opposite of progress, but would also breed dissent and resistance, not so much from those who feel excluded by globalization but by those who feel overwhelmed by it. A cultural backlash against this form of proselytism is sure to follow. It will be very hard to counter the dislocation and degeneration of society that results.

There are endless problems to which we need answers. What is the relationship between ethnicity and violence? Is fundamentalism primarily a cultural phenomenon? How do we defeat the opposition to female empowerment? How do we deal with the confrontation between those who adhere to the universality of human rights and those who prefer culturally determined human rights? These questions are of existential importance to us all. They can only be tackled through inter-cultural dialogue. Such a dialogue, in order to be useful, must be based on a shared, deep, mutual respect. This means that we give others the benefit of the doubt, even on very vital questions on which we differ. We must, in all honesty, accept all that we can of the other's position.

Today, most of us live in a multicultural society or in societies that are rapidly acquiring a multicultural character. There are none that do not suffer from serious inter-cultural collisions. We can only overcome these situations through mutual respect and by bringing, as much as is still possible, the technologically and economically driven process of globalization back into the realm of democratic public political decision-making.[5]

Notes

1. The Agenda 2000 Conference was organized on the occasion of the fortieth anniversary of the Institute of Social Studies, The Hague, in 1992.

2. Thomas L. Friedman, 'Quit the whining. Globilization isn't a choice', *International Herald Tribune*, 30 September 1997.

3. William Pfaff, 'Globilization's depredations are real and brutal', *International Herald Tribune*, 25 September 1997.

4. Benjamin R. Barber (1996) *Jihad vs. McWorld*, Ballantine Books, New York, p. 6.

5. With thanks to Mr L. P. Ramondt for his assistance.

4

World Economic Changes at the Threshold of the Twenty-First Century

LOUIS EMMERIJ

The Current Orthodoxy

When studying recent reports published by prestigious organizations such as the World Bank (1997) and the OECD (1997), one cannot but be struck by an optimism beyond the bounds of empirical responsibility. These studies have a habit of extrapolating certain positive indicators and not the more problematic ones. The optimism about the future of the world economy exhibited in reports of this kind – and very much reflected in the international press – is irresponsible for at least two groups of reasons. The first is related to the choice of indicators. Present financial and economic policies are successful only if measured by their own 'abstract' indicators: rates of inflation, rates of interest, debt ratios, financial deficits – the Maastricht criteria, in short. They are *not* successful if measured by indicators of 'flesh and blood': rates of unemployment, individual incomes, income distribution, poverty, crime – the new social and urban questions.

Examples can easily be found. Individual incomes in the USA have actually decreased in real terms since 1973 and income distribution has worsened. In order for family income to remain at a decent level, more than one income-earner is now necessary. The European Union has an average rate of open unemployment of over 10 per cent, with countries like France and Germany reaching rates as high as 12 to 13 per cent. Real rates are even higher. And then there are the developing countries. In 1993 one hundred of these countries had a lower per capita income than five years earlier; 69 lower than in the 1970s; 35 lower than in the 1960s; and 19 lower than in 1960. Is this sustained economic growth? Until recently, one could always point to East and Southeast Asia for stupendous economic and social results. But it was rarely mentioned that these countries did *not* apply the current orthodoxy. They had their own way. If I were to believe in conspiracy theory – which

53

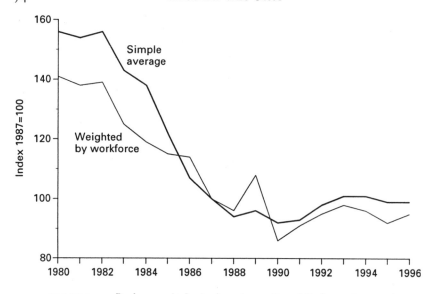

FIGURE 4.1   Real wages in Latin America, 1980–96 (index 1987 = 100)
Source: IDB, based on national data.

of course I do not – I would conclude that what has happened recently in that region is the revenge of the current orthodoxy. These countries are being urgently pressed by the IMF and others to mend their ways and do like everyone else.

The second group of reasons concerns characteristics of the current orthodoxy. The economic and financial policies that became fashionable some 15 years ago have three basic traits. They are crisis-prone; they are deflationary and anti-growth; and they encourage a spirit of speculation rather than entrepreneurship. That the current orthodoxy is crisis prone is obvious to anyone looking at the facts. We have experienced the 'lost decade' of the 1980s, as the Latin Americans call it. In the 1990s, we had the so-called Tequila crisis in Mexico and Argentina (1994–95). Since the middle of 1997, even the Asian Miracle countries have been severely hit, although their macro-economic fundamentals (so highly praised for so long) have not at all been weakened. Before and after these events we had the attack on the British pound ('the billion of Soros'), on the Italian lire and other currencies. Thus, there exists a tremendous volatility, including in the exuberant stock markets.

The current orthodoxy is deflationary and anti-growth. This may come as a surprise to some, but if we look at Table 4.1, which presents data on economic growth worldwide over the past 35 years, we observe a systematic slowing down of economic growth rates in all regions of the world, except in the Asian miracle economies (until 1995). Figure 4.1 also shows the evolution of real wages in Latin America between 1980 and 1996. The

TABLE 4.1 World economic growth (annual per cent)

	1961–70		1971–80		1981–90		1991–95	
	Simple	Weighted	Simple	Weighted	Simple	Weighted	Simple	Weighted
Latin America	5.0	5.5	4.3	6.0	1.1	1.3	3.1	2.8
Industrial economies	4.8	5.3	3.3	3.1	2.6	2.8	1.7	1.8
Asian miracle economies	6.9	4.3	7.5	5.7	7.0	8.1	7.8	10.2
World total	5.6	5.0	5.0	4.7	3.4	4.0	2.7	3.8

Note: Weighted by population; Latin America comprises 26 countries.
Source: IDB calculations, based on World Bank statistics.

cumulative average reduction during the 1980s was 50 per cent. Between 1990 and 1995 the average drop was 'modest', only a further 10 per cent. All this should not come as a surprise if it is remembered that the priority policy objectives of the current orthodoxy are the fight against inflation and the reduction of financial deficits, *not* the maximization of economic growth and employment creation.

The current orthodoxy encourages a spirit of speculation rather than entrepreneurship. All the incentives in the global system point to short-termism, easy gains, speculative gambling, partly forced by the uncertainties in the volatile marketplace. Even goods-producing enterprises now have purely financial units where fortunes are made and lost. Gradually the CEO (chief executive officer) is losing out to the CFO (chief financial officer). For all these reasons, I cannot share in the euphoria that I see around me. I am deeply concerned about the volatility and the high frequency of crises inherent in the current orthodoxy. But there is more. There are the serious social consequences of current economic policies that have given rise to a new social question.

Globalization and the New Social Question

I want to present the emergence of the New Social Question by advancing seven theses, noting that a thesis is not a certainty but a proposal that the author is willing to defend.

THESIS NUMBER 1   Globalization is private-sector-driven; regionalization is public-sector-driven. The growing globalization of financial and goods markets is being realized by private firms that function increasingly worldwide. They owe very little, if anything, to governments. On the contrary, when in March 1957 the Rome treaty was signed creating the European Common Market, there were six ministers of foreign affairs sitting around the table, with no private sector in sight. The same can be said about the creation of Mercosur and NAFTA. In a sense, these parallel activities demonstrate that the public sector is running several laps behind the private sector, in spite of having a head start.

THESIS NUMBER 2   The current orthodoxy, culminating more and more in globalization, has not solved the old, outstanding social problems like un-employment, poverty and income distribution, but has frequently intensified them. While it is true that life expectancy and enrolment rates have improved (look, however, at Eastern Europe and the quality of education) and that East and Southeast Asia have done better until recently (but see above), with respect to real-life indicators like those mentioned, the situation has further deteriorated in the bulk of cases.

THESIS NUMBER 3 A new social question has arisen that has two components. The first is the intensification of the old and existing social problems; the second is the emergence of new social problems like crime, a growing urban dualism and drugs, which itself has become a global industry. It is the combination of these two components that I call the new social question (UNRISD 1995).

THESIS NUMBER 4 Globalization is exacerbating the intensity of competition and the level of competitiveness. Competition is increasingly seen as the only solution for firms to survive, and the result is economic battles without mercy. Competition is also being seen as the miracle remedy for many social problems. You have high levels of unemployment, become more competitive; you have many poor, increased competition is the answer! But it will become clear that extreme competition diminishes the degree of diversity existing in a society and contributes to social exclusion: individuals, enterprises, cities and nations that are not competitive are marginalized and eliminated from the race. As systems lose their variety in this way, they lose the capacity to renew themselves. The Latin root of the verb compete is *competere,* which means 'to seek together'– a far cry from what competition is becoming in the global era (see Group of Lisbon 1995).

THESIS NUMBER 5 Technology has turned from a blessing into a curse. There was a time when futurologists proclaimed the wonders that technology had in store for us. We would be able to produce more with less labour and earn more by putting in fewer hours of work. Utopia, so we thought. But Utopia is here. We are producing more with less labour, but the 'less labour' is distributed by putting up to one-third of people out of work entirely. Societal restructuring has not kept pace with economic and technological restructuring. Labour markets, educational systems and pensions are structured in the same way as 50 years ago, while the economy and technology have changed beyond recognition.

THESIS NUMBER 6 We have entered a period that sees the creation of global wealth in the midst of increasing national and individual poverty. As mentioned, global enterprises are privately owned, they are in the business of profit making and they will, therefore, locate their multifarious activities in such a way as to minimize costs (including paying taxes) and maximize profits. At the same time, globalization is giving rise to a new social question. It follows that while enormous global wealth is being created in the globalizing economy, the income of many nation-states is declining at the very moment they need that income most because of the increased financial outlays necessitated by the new social question. Globalization can be a very positive factor. It does contribute to the creation of additional wealth. However, it is giving rise to a new distribution problem.

THESIS NUMBER 7 We urgently need the equivalent of the (welfare) state at the global level. At the end of the nineteenth century, capitalism had become an economic opportunity and a social problem at the national level. Extreme riches sided with appalling poverty. It took strong and imaginative people like Otto von Bismarck (hardly a radical) to start the building of a national welfare state to balance the raw power of the marketplace, to construct an income floor below which nobody could fall, and hence to ensure a more equitable distribution of income. Nation-states were strong and national decisions mattered in a world economy that was largely organized along national lines. The private sector became less free and more civilized.

Now, a century later, globalizing markets are gradually giving global private enterprises the freedom that their national predecessors had at the end of the nineteenth century. In a sense, one could call this the 'revenge' of the private sector in that, after almost a hundred years, it is increasingly successful in 'liberating' itself from the jaws of the nation-state. The global firm can locate itself in the best niches with respect to labour costs, taxes and social charges. Thus, on the threshold of the twenty-first century, a paradoxical situation again exists, but this time at the global level. We have a booming economy propelled by energetic and dynamic global enterprises coexisting with nation-states that are growing poorer and have to downsize the welfare fabric patiently constructed over the decades, particularly after the Second World War. What is now needed is a new Bismarck to redefine the economic responsibility of the state and the social responsibility of the business community, and to steer these two entities toward cooperation instead of cut-throat competition.

Major World Economic Challenges

The major challenges at the beginning of the twenty-first century follow logically from the diagnosis presented above. I should like to identify four principal tasks ahead of us: redefining the *economic* responsibility of the state in a global and regional era; redefining the *social* responsibility of the private sector in a global and regional era; moving from extreme competition to cooperation: towards global and regional social contracts; and Europe-wide regional cooperation.

ECONOMIC RESPONSIBILITY OF THE STATE Given the volatility and frequency of crises in the present economic and financial system (crises with serious income consequences for the majority of people in the countries concerned), it is an urgent responsibility of the state(s) to dampen this volatility, to minimize the frequency of crises, and to take care of the consequences of possible future crises that may affect individual people. After the Asian crisis began, more and more government officials realized that the current orthodoxy could not be left as free as it had been. There is a growing consensus that some sorts of capital control (like those in Chile and Colombia, for instance) are now becoming an urgent necessity, in order to maximize longer-term, productive capital inflows and to minimize hot money.

There must also be stricter surveillance of banking systems and financial markets in general. There was nothing wrong with the economic fundamentals in East and Southeast Asia, but there was a lot wrong with local banks and the way they handled national and international loans. In this regard it is important to review the exchange rate regimes and more particularly the costs and benefits of pegged currencies, linking the currency of a (small) country to the volatile currency of another (and much bigger) country. Governments must also take a much more active role in updating societal structures in order to make them more consistent with rapidly evolving economic and technological structures. Education, labour markets, pension systems and the organization of labour on the shop floor must be made much more flexible, to give people a chance to move more easily into and out of labour markets and education so that they get second and third chances in life.[1] Of course, there is no equivalent of the state at the international level. On the contrary, the relatively weak global institutions that do exist (UN, World Bank, IMF) are being attacked and weakened at precisely the moment they are needed most. This issue is discussed further below.

SOCIAL RESPONSIBILITY OF THE PRIVATE SECTOR Obviously the business community is not a charitable institution (although there does exist a tradition of charity) or a social workshop (although many captains of industry are concerned with the social situation around them). But entrepreneurs have always known that the investment climate depends to a large extent on the social and political stability of the country or the region in which they are operating. They therefore have a vested interest in social policies concerning employment, incomes, income distribution, education, health, and so on. Consequently, they are bound to favour countries and governments with progressive social policies. Take for example the German entrepreneur, a very large producer of soft drinks, who wanted to invest in orange plantations in Latin America. Although Costa Rica was more expensive for him than Brazil, he decided in favour of the former country precisely because of the (then) better social climate and much better income distribution.

FROM COMPETITION TO COOPERATION: TOWARDS GLOBAL AND REGIONAL SOCIAL CONTRACTS What we must now start to do is build the equivalent of the state at the global level, among other things in order to distribute the benefits of globalization more equitably in the public interest. In other words, we must start doing at the global level what was begun at the end of the nineteenth century at the national level.

An effective system of global governance is not only in the public interest, but also very much in the interest of the private sector. When a company becomes global, i.e. involved in ventures around the world, it needs the international system to provide security: international police to deter terrorists, bodies like the WTO to head off trade wars, institutions to assist emerging markets, an international human rights organization to protect its employees around the globe, etc. Without such an international public sector, international business would be lost – only pirates and criminals would flourish. Within such a framework, legitimate enterprise prospers. The key, therefore, is the recognition that a *contract* between nations and regions is required – a process of reaching public decisions among concerned parties along the lines of the common global good, including commonly defined objectives for coexistence and mutual development.

What is most urgently needed is a global social contract with special emphasis on meeting the basic needs of the world's population, including the poorest 20 per cent. Probably the most important challenge in the negotiations for such a contract is how to insert free and rapidly expanding global capitalism into a socially, environmentally and politically accountable system to benefit all citizens of the world. The inevitable second challenge then becomes how new socio-economic and political spaces can be organized at the world level within which regions and nation-states would lose a degree of sovereignty in exchange for new forms of free, representative and participatory democratic institutions.

Just as it was being recognized in the first half of the twentieth century in the industrial countries that national poverty could be tackled, so is it imperative that during the first half of the twenty-first century it be recognized that relieving the populations of the world is not an unrealistic target.[2] For instance, a fund can be set up (which may well precede the conclusion of the global social contract) to finance the global and regional social contracts. Global enterprises – the creators of global wealth – would have to contribute to this fund.[3] This would be a start in implementing the idea of a more equitable distribution of global wealth. Regional contracts should be introduced, although the extent is a matter for debate. Let us now consider this in the case of Europe.

REGIONAL COOPERATION IN EUROPE   I have always been and continue to be a fervent defender of One Europe, from the Atlantic to as far east as possible. In other words, I am as much in favour of widening as deepening, but in the case of conflict between these two approaches to the European Union, I would give priority to widening.[4]

The eastern enlargement of Europe poses a series of problems. Briefly:

(i)   it requires the integration of countries that are at a lower level of development than the European Union average. My comment here is that this was already the case, when Greece, Ireland and Portugal joined.

(ii)   The eleven aspiring 'eastern' countries are very different from economic, social and cultural points of view. Again, this is not new. Greece is very different from Sweden, and Finland does not have much in common with Portugal; nevertheless, they are all together in the European Union.

(iii) The eastern countries have been lacking in democratic traditions and market development. My comment is that this has also been the case in Germany, Spain, Portugal and Greece. So what?

A big step like the fifth enlargement of the European Union is, of course, a political step and cannot be judged by cost-benefit calculations only. Nothing of any importance has ever been decided by narrow economic considerations. What we need here is a grand design. The creation of Greater Europe can be realized only by setting up a European Social Contract. This would be a generalization of the Regional Fund (created at the first enlargement), the Structural Fund (created for the Mediterranean countries), and the Social Fund.

Unlike practically all contemporary decision-makers and most economists, I am convinced that present policies create opportunities for few and social problems for many. Current trends in the current orthodoxy and in globalization are not sustainable, because they lead to inequitable patterns culminating in the new social question. In order to remedy this situation we must think big, just as was done a century ago and again after the Second World War. We must create the equivalent of the state at the global level in order to repair the basic weakness of economic and financial globalization, namely the increasing dissociation between economic power organized on a world basis by global networks of industrial, financial and service enterprises, and political power that remains organized at the national and regional levels only. This dichotomy is rapidly leading to a situation where the world is governed, not only in the economic sphere but in other spheres as well, by groups of private networks of stateless and unaccountable firms. On the occasion of the eastern enlargement we could start with a European social contract before moving on to a global social contract. Because triumphant capitalism is *not* what we want or need. What we need is a set of balanced economic and social policies so that global wealth benefits everyone.

One must be careful in judging studies, also with respect to the time and period they were written. Look at the East Asian miracle study of the World Bank (1993) for instance, and look at the judgements about these economies today. Mind you, I continue to believe that there has been a miracle (by design). The same caution must be exercised in judging Bognar's 'bible'. In this 1968 study, the emphasis was very much on initiatives from above, which was normal in that time and that location (Africa). I believe that the European social contract and the global social contract must also be launched from above, although it will be obvious today that without the participation of civil society this whole idea is doomed to failure. In other words, social contracts must be accompanied by democratic contracts.

Notes

1. For more details see Emmerij 1997.
2. For more details concerning global contracts, see Group of Lisbon 1995.
3. I owe this idea to Dharam Ghai, the former director of UNRISD.
4. The following points are based on Working Paper No. 87 of the Institute of World Economics, written by the general director (Inotai 1997), except for the conclusions, which are my sole responsibility.

References

Bognar, J. (1968) *Economic Policy and Planning in Developing Countries*, Budapest.

Emmerij, L. (1997) 'Development thinking and practice: introductory essay and policy conclusions', in L. Emmerij (ed.), *Economic and Social Development into the 21st Century*, Johns Hopkins University Press, Baltimore, MD.

Group of Lisbon (1995) *Limits to Competition*, MIT Press, Boston, MA.

Inotai, A. (1997) 'What is novel about eastern enlargement of the European Union?' and 'The costs and benefits of eastern enlargement of the European Union', Working Paper No. 87, Institute for World Economics, Hungarian Academy of Sciences, Budapest.

OECD (1997) *Towards a New Global Age: Challenges and Opportunities*, OECD, Paris.

UNRISD (1995) *States of Disarray*, UNRISD, Geneva.

World Bank (1993) *The East Asian Miracle: Economic Growth and Public Policy*, World Bank, Washington, DC.

— (1997) *Global Economic Prospects and the Developing Countries*, World Bank, Washington, DC.

5

Life Beyond Global Economic Warfare

HAZEL HENDERSON

Current forces are now globalizing: industrial processes and technology; information and finance; work and migration; arms trafficking; human effects on the biosphere; and the patterns of Western culture. In these processes, more and more local borders and customs are overrun and the world's biodiversity and the richness of human cultural DNA codes are succumbing to global monoculture. Effects have included the loss of national sovereignty, the erosion of social contracts, retreats into fundamentalism and nationalism, inter-group rivalries and civic conflicts, secessionist movements, and the phenomenon of 'failed states'. Today's rapid globalization of human technological and economic systems is partly classic 'overshoot' – based on incorrect models and calculations and inadequate feedback, indicators and guidance systems. Chaos theory describes how such initially small errors and deviations driving our techno-economic systems can have been amplified in the large, non-linear chaotic, morphogenetic systems that are human societies. I believe this line of inquiry is fruitful – in fact, it has occupied most of my adult life. Today, our species must make a great leap in knowledge, awareness and wisdom – for our very survival. This leap is possible because we are one of the most adaptable and biologically successful species on the planet. Yet 95 per cent of our human experience has been as members of small nomadic bands of fewer than 25 gatherers and occasional hunters (Tainter 1988). As populations settled and grew, we learned to manage ourselves in rural villages and agrarian societies. Today's requirement – that of reorganizing in sustainable communities our almost six billion-member human family – is well beyond our human experience, as we see clearly in our mega-cities and fracturing nation-states.

Another deep root of today's epistemological dilemma lies at the heart of the Indo-European languages that underlie Western cultures. Such languages reify human behaviour and outcomes and lead to the unrealistic stance of 'objectivity' in scientific research and the operations of its mathematics. Using nouns to catalogue objects and processes in the exterior world has been a vehicle for much genuine human progress. Yet it has also created the epistemological errors of 'confusing the map with the territory', together with Alfred North Whitehead's famous 'fallacy of misplaced concreteness' (cf. Henderson 1996: Ch. 1). These typological errors became encoded in our mathematics, with all those reified nouns viewed as 'objects' and 'quantities' to be manipulated by mathematical operands: adding, subtracting, dividing or multiplying, as mathematician/physician Andrew Hilgartner describes.[1] Hilgartner urges us to cure such epistemological errors and their effects on personal behaviour and policy-making by reclassifying many nouns as verbs – for example, 'language' would be more correctly stated as 'languaging', to remind ourselves that it is a human process. Today's objectified language and epistemology, for example, still confuse money with wealth and well-being, and computers and so-called artificial intelligence with the functions of human cognition as if we were 'Turing machines'. The traditions of Buddhism also caution us against reification, if we are to remain awake. Other wisdom and spiritual traditions in many cultures remind us that we are embedded in that seamless web of complexity – life.

Today we need to re-examine all such cultural programming and how it has 'hard-wired' our responses. Humans must continue to routinize many responses: we cannot pay attention to everything at once. But we have reached a new stage of evolution. It has become a matter of survival to recycle our cultures, reconstruct our academic disciplines and erase old mental models and behavioural programmes in order to be fully awake to our new situation. Only as we awaken from our techno-industrial trance and its now dysfunctional economic programming can we consciously decide what kinds of new 'hard-wiring' may be appropriate. For example, since the end of the Cold War, we have been aware that 'socialism' and 'capitalism' are exhausted categories. We see that capitalism, in fact, has many cultural expressions. We know today that all economies are 'mixed economies' with elements of 'public' and 'private' sectors corresponding to the values, social goals and traditions that make up the 'cultural DNA codes' of different countries. We see the social consequences of 'hard-wired' nineteenth-century economic textbook remedies in Eastern Europe, Russia, China and Latin America, and how their rapid amplification, the result of computerized currency trading in today's $1.3 trillion daily global casino, can disorder some cultures and bypass others, such as many in Africa.

Economics is a malfunctioning strand of our Western cultural DNA code that replicates social, cultural and environmental destruction and now amplifies many of the pathological effects of globalization. How should this incorrect strand of cultural DNA be excised and replaced, splicing in a corrected strand to provide more accurate feedback and a healthier heuristics to attract the evolution of human culture? Today, we are still told by mainstream economists that there is nothing we can do to slow or shape today's economic and financial forces of globalization programmed by their neoclassical formulas. Privatization and ever more global competition driving ever more irrational technological innovation are termed 'natural'. Meanwhile, human real-time efforts at foresight and prevention, so as to politically assess and shape technological change and steer economic growth along more ecologically sustainable paths towards human development and quality of life, are deemed 'intervention in the free market'. This kind of ideology, 'economism', is as deadly as it is faulty. The discipline of economics (even as still taught today) rests on a series of assumptions caricaturing human behaviour and preferences as unchanging, motivated by individual self-interest and insatiable desires to consume material goods and services. These preferences are revealed in the marketplace by prices. The sum of these behaviours of economic actors bargaining in markets with producers is held to lead to a self-regulating macro-economic system in general equilibrium. My fuller critique of economics from ecological and evolutionary perspectives is documented elsewhere (Henderson 1988).

The Love Economy

At least human actors (if not future generations) have always been recognized in economic theories. But the assumptions of their unchanging behaviour and 'human nature', as expressed only in markets and prices, render their collective actions statistically insignificant. This economic model allows for no consumers' role in changing the system's structure or even moving it toward disequilibrium, let alone evolution. Meanwhile, social action is usually volunteered, since few social organizations will pay people to 'rock the boat'. Thus, economics has ignored this kind of unpaid work – along with the unpaid work of women – in what I have termed 'the Love Economy'. Values and technology have been considered parameters, and even producers are assumed to be passive pawns in the market. Ubiquitous evidence of growing oligopolies, corporate trusts and other forms of institutional power and market failures are still taught as 'exceptions' to the model. When such assumptions are criticized, the response from economists is that they know these assumptions are unrealistic, but they continue to employ them so as to make their models work; or they attack the credibility of the critics. While economics has focused on self-interested competition (win–lose), a fuller repertoire of human ways of being and becoming was left to game theorists. They have also described the win–lose games and their outcomes: prisoners' dilemmas and lose–lose vicious circles. Yet game theorists have also studied the 'contrarian' strategies that avoid such herd behaviours and create social innovations, novel win–win games, and virtuous circles based on humanity's age-old cooperation, sharing and altruism, such as the gifts and potlatches of tribal societies (Hyde 1979; Polanyi 1944; Sahlins 1972).

At the Rio de Janeiro UN Earth Summit in 1992, some 20,000 leaders of civic organizations joined in calling for the correction of GNP/GDP so as to include unpaid work and account for environmental costs and the value of natural resources. Fifty per cent of all productive work in industrial societies is unpaid and its counterpart – informal, traditional economies in the developing world, which constitute some 60–70 per cent of all their production – is still invisible to economists. Over 170 countries signed *Agenda 21*, the final document of the Earth Summit, which included the provisions to expand and correct GNP/GDP national accounts so as to include unpaid work, environmental costs and the value of natural resources. Cognitive dissonance grew among policy-makers, professionals, economists and other social and natural scientists whose charge was to implement the provisions under the guidance of the new UN Commission on Sustainable Development.

It remains to be seen whether this kind of social intervention can help reorient the path of industrialism towards healthier, more humane and equitable forms of ecologically sustainable development. In any case, the rapidity with which public awareness has grown worldwide about the deficiencies of steering economies on the GNP/GDP course offers further evidence supporting both the chaos model of human social evolution and the role that determined action-researchers can play in these rapid changes. In 1995, the World Bank released its new Wealth Index, which classifies 60 per cent of the wealth of nations as 'human capital' (education, social organization, etc.), 20 per cent as 'natural capital' (environmental and natural resources), and a mere 20 per cent as 'human-built capital' (factories, buildings, bridges, finance, etc.). This admission that most of the Bank's policies for 50 years have been overly focused on this latter 20 per cent of 'human-built capital' represented a paradigm shift. The fact that, as of 1997, the Bank's actual operations still do not incorporate the shifts required by the criteria of its new Wealth Index, is another example of the stability of social structures and the power of replication (Henderson 1996b: 224–5). Yet on the biological level, this bias in favour of replication over innovation (or mutation) is life-preserving, as in maintaining the stability of DNA.

The system-wide social innovation that would be required to steer technologies and manage their effects to move towards the evolution of human societies and cultures seems to lag behind by decades and sometimes generations (Henderson 1996c). Here Riane Eisler's *The Chalice and the Blade* (1988) provides a key: for some 5,000 years, technology evolved within male-dominated social systems. These correlate with emphases on ecologically incompatible technologies, weapons and social domination rather than partnership with women, other humans and nature. By contrast, social innovation is a subtle, system-wide process, rooted in holistic, transdisciplinary cultural, social, technical, political and economic research and policy analyses. Models of general evolution, disequilibrium, systems, chaos and game theories are necessary – but not sufficient. Social innovations require experimentation by action-researchers, as well as the imaging of alternative futures and scenarios together with ethical motivations beyond self-interest and a time perspective considerably beyond any single human lifespan. Paradoxically, evolutionary action-researchers are motivated to accelerate social innovation and cultural evolution in the short term in attempting to preserve long-term societal options and ecosystems for their descendants.

On a more surface level, the Western scientific/political/economic paradigm reinforces those technological innovations driven by free markets, profit motives and consumer preferences. This may explain technology's focus on weapons and on powerful, ecologically destructive energy and resource utilization, as well as the flood of often trivial consumer product differentiation. Further, the 'free market' economic paradigm masks the role of government subsidies, industrial policies, market power, corporate research and development, as well as advertising and marketing budgets devoted to selling and portraying all such technological innovations as 'progress'. By contrast, social innovation is excoriated in this paradigm as 'social engineering', 'planning', or merely as 'socialism'. Since the end of the Cold War, markets and privatization have accelerated their global penetration and technological development. Economists often equate these globalizations with the spread of democracy, while urging the further downsizing of governments – already in retreat worldwide (Henderson 1993: 322–38).

Action-research on social innovation is an urgent priority. At the same time, all social innovations should be introduced in 'pilot' form as small, reversible, error-friendly experiments to be carefully evaluated for their unanticipated consequences. Today's task is, therefore, to shape our mental, moral and decision-making skills to meet the challenges to our very survival that our misguided technological innovations have created. This requires a flowering of social innovation, rethinking of our paradigms, re-engineering and redesigning of our physical and social architectures. The social and economic restructuring that inevitably follows human invention and technological innovation in the private sector eventually calls forth adaptation in the public sector.

Meanwhile, game theory has codified the equally prevalent human behaviours and motivations toward cooperation, bonding, caring, altruistic concern for the group and the nurturing of children. Clearly, the main body of economic theory also rests on patriarchal assumptions, since all such caring, sharing and altruistic work expected of the world's women, because it is unpaid, remains outside the purview of most economic models. Game theorists also modelled human competition, self-interest and mistrust as 'zero sum' games and 'prisoners' dilemmas', leading to lose–lose 'vicious circles' (such as we see in today's race to the bottom, lowest price common denominator, global economic warfare). The great contribution of game theory has been to go beyond economics' focus on zero-sum games and ensuing 'tragedies of the commons', which systems thinkers have modelled for a generation. Game theorists took insights from psychologists and other social scientists and codified a fuller range of human ways of being and behaving: 'contrarian' strategies (rather than herd behaviour) and all the possible 'win–win' alternatives, many of which create entirely new games, social innovations and 'virtuous circles'. Such terms are creeping into economics papers, with glib claims that economic theory has embraced game theory, as well as anthropology, biology, ecology, and lately, psychology, systems dynamics and chaos theory. Even today, economics does not teach how to recognize systemic changes – such as when all the niches in a market have been filled, and that market transforms into a commons. When this occurs, the win–lose competition appropriate to markets must be changed to win–win rules so as to cooperatively allocate and manage the commons. The penalties for not recognizing such systemic changes are 'lose–lose' vicious circles and multiple 'tragedies of the commons' (Henderson 1995).

We may forget that only 30 years ago, the perennial tug-of-war between the private enterprise market sector and the state was widely believed to be tipping in favour of the state. The sheer scale of technological innovation, already global, seemed to favour large corporations with their broad span of managerial control and ability to capture markets, retain earnings and lobby governments for research and development. Yet all of this corporate power had called forth from governments concomitant national levels of oversight, coordination and the post-Second World War commitments to go from national to macro-policy goals of full employment, economic growth and social welfare. This larger role of the state emerged, driven by experiences of the Great Depression, the military build-ups of the Second World War, the demands of consumers, labour unions and stockholders to correct market failures and abuses, and the actions of the companies themselves. Today, the state is everywhere in retreat. Political hopes and fears are now focused on the ascendance of markets and private corporate power in our globalized economy.

The see-saw struggle between private enterprises and expanding markets versus the state has existed at least since the fifteenth century. European kings chartered private corporations with limited liability for purposes of exploitation of foreign lands and resources. This social innovation has reverberated down the centuries – amplifying today's corporate globalizations. Often early expeditions were bankrolled by monarchs using tax revenues, and involved piracy, subduing indigenous populations, extracting of gold, minerals and local treasure, slave-trading and other opportunities for 'profit', often by outright plunder. In Britain, the Common Law tradition produced legal systems and contracts protecting private property, which fostered private business initiatives. These early charters were narrowly circumscribed social contracts to individuals that suspended some of the rules applied to all other citizens. Today, age-old tug-of-war strategies between private market players versus governments are played out on a global stage. For example, the global financial casino of currency and derivatives trading (90 per cent of which is speculation) resembles the unregulated Wall Street of 1929. International agreements on full disclosure, accounting standards and other measures to police global capital markets are still rudimentary.

Global financial markets not only destroy whole ecosystems and cultures but entail huge risks to investors and the public. Insights from biology and ecology view such tidal waves of financial liquidity as scouring landscapes and ecosystems – sweeping away the 'permeable membranes' of cultures while disrupting community 'cells' and destroying their internal metabolic functions. Governments still rightly fear the unregulated global mobility of today's capital and corporations – all operating on win–lose or lose–lose strategies and rules. Corporations now cooperate in global consortia, often outflanking national governments, yet governments still overlook the game theorists' broad repertoire of win–win strategies for pooling their lost sovereignty in global agreements.[2]

Social policy options for coping with technological abundance prefigured today's recognition of deviation-amplification processes in cybernetic and morphogenetic social systems. Today's globalization of technology, markets, finance, information and mass media are clearly better studied through new lenses beyond those of economics. These are provided by game theory, systems dynamics, chaos theory, sociology, geo-politics, cultural anthropology, psychology and ecology, which all embrace the effects of both positive and negative feedbacks, disequilibrium, expectations, uncertainty and cultural variables.

Today, some economists convert such well-known systems concepts as positive feedback amplification into narrower economic models and terms such as 'increasing returns' (Arthur 1994). The economics fraternity can still confer their Nobel Memorial Prizes on each other for what other disciplines see as back-of-the-envelope trivialities. As the power of economic theories wanes in buttressing corporate prerogatives, lobbyists and politicians allied with corporation special interests look for newer 'scientific' justification for further deregulation and privatization. The stakes are huge – for example, the wholesale privatization promoted by the World Bank of government pension systems, as in the Chilean model, rests on neo-classical economic, but not systemic models (Ralls 1996: 2–6). Advocates of *laissez-faire* policies now cite today's socio-technical complexities and their often counter-intuitive behaviour, along with the uncertainties of dynamic systems in disequilibrium, as new arguments for privatization and non-intervention in markets. Fashionable think-tanks, including the Santa Fe Institute, find their chaos theory models much in demand by corporations, as well as those of the 'economy-as-ecology' school of Michael Rothschild's Institute for Bioeconomics. Both are also very popular with government and political advocates of deregulation (Henderson 1996b: Ch. 8). Yet we humans cannot so easily wash our hands of the responsibility for massive private-sector interventions we have already made – from the evolution of industrial technologies to today's pollution, desertification and ozone depletion. If all this private market activity is simply 'natural' and should, therefore, 'be left to nature' as the new advocates of *laissez-faire* claim, then why is it not just as natural for humans to have developed foresight, community rules, national regulations, insurance liabilities, and become 'green' consumers and investors, social and environmental auditors and consultants, and grassroots globalists, all of which serve as feedbacks to dampen the unwanted, unfair or toxic effects of earlier un-regulated private activity?

Governments often acknowledge the limited options of economics' lose–lose games, in the mantra, 'There is no alternative'. Nations are slow to reorganize today's global economic warfare through cooperation and creation of win–win rules, such as the European Union's EMAS environmental standards. The missing link in both conventional economics and political science involves downplaying the extent to which governments at all levels have allowed themselves to become puppets of corporations and financial special interests (Lydenberg 1981).

Today, a growing moral force challenges corporate power and related government collusion. The astonishing rise of voluntary, grassroots, civic societies is evident in both Northern industrial countries and those in the South. In the USA, for example, 89 million Americans volunteer at least five hours a week in community service.[3] This third sector has taken conventional economics and political science by surprise, since unpaid, cooperative work within the household, the community and traditional societies has been overlooked as 'uneconomic' and, therefore, its some $16 trillion annually is still missing from global GDP (UNDP 1995). This third sector grew around all of these traditional community, family-based, often subsistence activities ignored by conventional analyses, as well as the myriad social, environmental and cultural costs and impacts borne by such ignored populations as a result. This unpaid, informal Love Economy, which underlies much of the civic society and represents at least 50 per cent of all productive work in industrial societies and up to 65 per cent in developing countries, is at last being documented. This has added another coffin-nail to conventional theories of GNP/GDP-measured economic growth and corporate industrialism (Henderson 1996a). The coalescing of the experiences of millions of citizens harmed by such conventional macro-policies of the World Bank, the IMF, GATT, NAFTA and the WTO, as well as the corporations themselves and other institutions of corporation–government détente, is slowly turning these macro-policies on their heads. For example, the Fifty Years is Enough campaign forced reforms at the World Bank, while the Third World Network's crusading analyses documented how conventional policies have exacerbated poverty and ecosystem destruction in the South.

Corporations and Voluntary Standard-setting

We have reviewed the bad news of how corporations consistently violate the rights of citizens. We now turn to examine the slow-motion good news in the bad news. Successful corporations, like species, find niches where they can co-evolve with other species in ecosystems. The social innovations of the 'third force' civic sectors are directly challenging corporations to accept responsibility and accountability formerly demanded of governments. As governments compete to cut budgets, regulations and safety-nets in order to offer corporations 'better business climates', civic groups demand that companies take greater responsibility for social welfare and education functions formerly performed by the state. The power of civic society has yet to reach a critical mass capable of checking global corporations. These global 'corporate citizens', so powerful and financially dominant that their revenues exceed annually the GNPs of all but a few major nations, are what drives the growing feedback of the 'grassroots globalists' of civic society.[4]

The Industrial Revolution, its technologies, enterprises and markets, may be summarized as a set of rapidly evolving complex systems with intertwining political and economic control of various societies (e.g. Lindblom 1977; Tufte 1978). Initially, entrepreneurs served small-scale local markets and captured the local and national standard-setting processes of governments. These enterprises grew through the advantages initially conferred by their charters (in chaos theory models, statistically insignificant variables present in initial conditions grew to improbably dominant effects in human societies, i.e. turbulent or morphogenetic, structurally evolving systems governed by positive feedback loops). After consolidating their local market power, corporations were able to capture national markets via co-opting national regulatory mechanisms. By 1969, for example, many large corporations, such as the big three car manufacturers in the USA, were writing the national clean air standards. They preferred one stricter standard to the different sets of regulations citizens in California and New York had lobbied into state law by 1968. Thus, corporations tend to fight social movements until citizens are powerful enough to enact higher local standards in one or two key jurisdictions. Then corporations tend to 'see the writing on the wall' (that is, recognize a critical mass of demand for reform and acknowledge a win-win game). They cooperate in writing new rules, sometimes opting for the higher standards nationally in order to rationalize their own production, or to reposition themselves in new win–win games (Henderson 1996c). A spate of new management textbooks describes these cooperative strategies, but most do not move societies toward win–win global policies (e.g. Brandenburger and Nalebuff 1996; Moore 1996).

Global corporations continue capturing global markets with foreign direct investment, globalizing production, out-sourcing to weak states and – often overlooked in conventional analyses – by negotiating global standard-setting processes. We are familiar with this standards-capturing process on the downside, as in the efforts of corporations to weaken the Montreal Protocols on ozone depletion and those covering forests and biodiversity agreed to in *Agenda 21*. Similar lowering of global standards has been achieved using the powerful rhetoric of 'free trade', 'national competitiveness' and the 'efficiencies' of market liberalization, deregulation and privatization. Yet we see how corporate standards-capturing also occurs on the upside, where adopting higher global standards in cooperation with government and civic society is seen as a way to jump-start virtuous circles' new ethical markets – a win–win strategy for our global future.

The capturing or escaping of governments' prerogatives during the 1980s included widespread deregulation of banks and capital markets, involving huge losses of tax revenues to states as well. Further consolidation of global corporate and financial power was achieved at the conclusion of the Uruguay Round of GATT and the institution of the WTO in 1995. Regional trade pacts, such as NAFTA, represent competitive capture of selected standards that favoured business and financial interests in the USA, Canada and Mexico. The social, environmental and cultural costs of these trade treaties were ignored, since the consensus now growing for full-cost pricing and overhauling of GNP/GDP national accounting to include human and environmental capital has yet to be implemented. Thus much of today's world trade involves irrational transportation of similar, below-full-cost goods, subsidized by tax-supported transportation and energy infrastructure. As economic and thermodynamic efficiencies are aligned, such entropic world trade will be replaced.

World trade is destructive because it is based on layer upon layer of subsidies: from taxpayers who fund transportation infrastructure, underwriting roads and airports, to the corporate subsidies in most nations' tax codes, which keep energy and resource prices below real costs. Economics textbooks still encourage companies to 'externalize' social and environmental costs from their balance sheets and from the capital asset pricing models (CAPMs) of investors. The exclusion of these costs from national accounts still distorts the GNP, since the costs of cleaning up and repairing economic damage are double-counted as more production. Thus today's world trade is largely irrational. All the agreements, including those of the WTO, serve to subsidize a lowest common denominator economic playing field – a vicious circle sliding into global economic warfare. Today's global economy functions like a global behavioural sink, rewarding corporate and government irresponsibility, levelling rainforests, and homogenizing the world's precious cultural diversity just as it plunders the planet's biodiversity. As prices are slowly corrected to reflect true costs, as taxes are shifted from incomes and payrolls to resource waste, depletion and pollution, and as the world's GNP-based national accounts are overhauled (as agreed to in *Agenda 21*), the wasteful, unnecessary global shipping of similar goods will slowly disappear. This is one key provision of the WTO that, if implemented, would slow down the global 'bidding war' as national politicians 'auction off' their tax bases, workforces, safety-nets and environmental resources to 'lure' corporate relocations. Even *The Economist* frowns on such 'trade-distorting' governmental give-aways and called for WTO enforcement of its own rules. Thus a broad coalition might bring pressure on the WTO.

My vision of a healthy world trade system is one shifting from hardware (goods) to software, services and 'exchanging our cultural DNA'. Most countries are capable of meeting many of their basic production needs and growing their domestic industries, which at full-cost prices will finally be revealed as most efficient. When economic and thermodynamic efficiencies are aligned, British economist John Maynard Keynes will be proved correct: it is better to transport recipes than cakes. But we must also see that we can all win if we also share these recipes, as in the joint implementation strategies promoted by the WBCSD. Countries can make cooperative agreements to share greener and innovative technologies, not hoard them, as in current trade agreements. Information is not scarce and economics is still about scarcity. Information is also cracking the old global money monopolies as high-tech barter and all kinds of direct exchanges are proliferating. Local barter clubs, businesses and governments all engage in counter-trade, now estimated at some 10 to 25 per cent of all world trade. A healthy world trade system will celebrate and reward cultural and biological diversity as we learn to savour each other's music, art, dance, cuisine and biodiversity.

'Good Corporate Citizenship'

Let us examine more closely the role of the creative minority of corporations in fostering good corporate citizenship: the vanguard of some 5 to 10 per cent of corporations that seek 'win–win' niches and cooperative partnerships in the evolving markets of the twenty-first century. These socially responsible, innovative companies see their competitive edge in serving the growing ranks of socially and environmentally conscious consumers, investors and employees (Porter and van der Linde 1995: 120).

Neo-classical economic arguments against social investing still abound, for example that screening portfolios narrows the universe of stocks and increases risks (refuted by many studies).[5] In any case, all mutual funds limit their choice of securities in some way, whether for growth, income or focusing on smaller or high-tech companies. Another hurdle for social investors is the so-called 'prudent man principle' still enshrined in today's statutes defining fiduciary responsibilities of fund managers (based on the age-old charters maximizing the investors' returns). This myopic, short-run approach is based on traditional exclusion of social and environmental costs from company balance-sheets as 'externalities'. In reality, such rear-view mirror investing can end up costing stockholders dearly, as in the bankruptcy due to nuclear power plant cost overruns of Washington state's public power utility, appropriately named WOOPS. Thus the 'prudent man' has been playfully renamed 'the prudent lemming principle', since it also leads to lose–lose, lowest common denominator 'herd' investing behaviour. The movement for socially responsible investing drew much strength from the Reagan administration in the USA and the Thatcher era in Britain. Investors believed that these minimalist governments would fail to protect broader social rights to a clean environment and fail to enforce the regulations that governed employee and human rights – or even roll back those governing the securities exchanges on insider trading, full disclosure, and so on.

While capital markets are 95 per cent driven by the neo-classical economists' win–lose and lose–lose competition, especially speculation in the currency markets, the creative minority performs an active 'enzyme' role, catalyzing much cognitive dissonance and defensiveness. A ground-breaking compendium, Financing Change, shows how to reform capital markets and correct their CAPMs to include social and environmental costs. This can lead to fewer irrational investments, the evolution of risk analyses, and a more creative role for insurance companies, banks, accountants and auditors.[6]

There is new awareness that most jobs in the US economy, as in many OECD countries, are provided by small business – rather than by the downsizing, automating global corporations, still subsidized by most governments, often as quid pro quos for campaign donations. The public furore in the USA over such political corruption has forced both major parties to advocate the repeal of subsidies to large companies while lifting onerous regulations on small companies and encouraging entrepreneurships, start-ups and socially responsible businesses. As media and policy-makers shifted focus to the small business sector, the rise of women-owned businesses was discovered. New research shows that US women-owned businesses employ one in four Americans, more than all of the Fortune 500 companies put together. Further, such business women are rarely profit-maximizers, but are often motivated to make the world a better place and meet new community needs; to avoid the dead-end jobs and 'glass ceilings' in large corporations; and to become economically self-reliant.[7]

Standards and Best Practices

The trend is increasing towards worldwide voluntary corporate standardization of products and services, often in partnership with relevant government bodies, users and civic society groups. The majority of traditional profit-maximizing corporations still seek to capture global standard-setting to prevent higher standards. Yet the vanguard 5 to 10 per cent, already positioned to serve the growing markets for green products and higher social and environmental responsibility, seek to raise these global standards. Only by so doing can they continue their innovative, contrarian efforts to find and expand win–win niches in today's lose–lose global markets. As the global standards are raised through voluntary action and further partnership agreements with governments, employees and civic society, this 'ethical floor' under today's global playing-field can be raised. This will further motivate and help the most responsible 'corporate citizens' to win. Such higher ethical floors under global markets, many ratified under UN protocols and treaties and the WTO, can support the most responsible governments, helping them resist today's pressures to auction their people and resources on the global capital markets to the highest corporate bidder in today's lose–lose game (Henderson 1996b: Ch. 12).

Today, global standard-setting and promotion of best practices have become key arenas for benchmarking corporate performance in twenty-first-century markets. The new battleground is the WTO, where many production processes, such as those re-engineered to be greener or 'eco-labelled', are still considered trade barriers and contested in North–South negotiations. Developing countries rightly accuse industrial giants of unfair trade practices and of influencing the WTO. The WTO's regulations are still based in the nineteenth-century economics of profit maximizing, externalized social and environmental costs, traditional GNP/GDP formulations, and the over-representation of goods over services, which the WTO so far has not well defined. The WTO should be pressured to enforce its rules against governments brokering their tax bases, workforces, safety-nets and environmental resources to 'lure' corporate relocations.

From Stockholders to Stakeholders

Polls in the USA show public outrage at corporate greed escalating, with 69 per cent favouring government action to promote more responsible corporate behaviour and penalize bad corporate citizens. Seventy per cent believe that greed, not competitive pressures, explains corporate downsizing, benefit reductions and moving jobs overseas.[8] A new organization in the USA, the Stakeholder Alliance, a coalition working to reform corporate governance, represents organizations with nearly 5 million members.[9]

Employees, too, are showing greater concern about their companies' policies and products, and those with higher qualifications are exercising selectivity in choosing employers. A national survey by Walker Research, *Corporate Character* in 1995, measured the impact of corporate social responsibility. The study found that next to quality of products, corporate responsibility was the second factor of importance in a company's reputation. While penalties for irresponsibility were higher, the survey showed large rewards in the marketplace for socially responsible companies. Meanwhile, 88 per cent of consumers indicated that they were much, or somewhat, more likely to buy from a socially responsible and good corporate citizen if quality, service and price were equal to those of competitors. Employees rated social responsibility second only in importance to their own treatment. Thus the concepts of intangible corporate assets, such as intellectual capital, address the new situations of many companies: their most valuable assets are human and cannot be owned. This is changing some knowledge-intensive corporate charters into partnerships and increasing employee stock ownership. Twenty-six per cent of traditional investors said that business practices and ethics were extremely important to investment decisions; 60 per cent of current socially responsible investors said that they always or frequently checked on business practices, values and ethics before investing.[10] Clearly the thrust of today's civic society, together with shareholders and employees, is toward a redefinition of corporate mandates to optimize rather than maximize profits – extended beyond stockholders toward the rights of all stakeholders. The stakeholder model is also debated in business schools and boardrooms (e.g. Mintzberg 1983: 23; Hoffman et al. 1990).

So, there is good news and bad news in these great globalizations. They have eroded the sovereignty of every nation and restructured every city and community all over the planet. They have sharpened our concepts of subsidiarity and appropriate levels of policy intervention, the role of monetary regimes and how to integrate social and environmental policy together with an overhauled macro-economics. And no matter what, we cannot go back. Civic society groups and politicians, many of whom oppose globalization, must abandon simple theories of 'restoring equilibrium'. Too much evidence now exists that all life forms, including the human species with our technological tools, have evolved over millions of years on this planet through processes of rapid change and continual disequilibrium. Agrarian rural life, to which many yearn to return, was itself a revolution, which disenfranchised and displaced millions of nomadic peoples. Neither can we romanticize cultural traditions and practices that violate human rights or democratic principles. In reality, how does one 'repeal' the globalization of technology, with satellites, jets, computers and the Internet so intertwined with global corporations? Thus the call for equitable, ecologically sustainable human development that embraces change, however misused, is still a rallying cry. Indeed, these grassroots and democracy trends are effects of the spread of the information technologies that corporations unleashed. The goals of such movements of citizens, employees, stockholders, environmentalists and human rights advocates include democratic control, political transparency and public accountability. Today they need to be aligned and reinforced at the international level.

We must ask ourselves which kinds of globalization, by whom, and in whose interests? Which kinds of globalization are life-threatening, such as nuclear proliferation, the global arms trade, and that of prostitution and child-sex trafficking (now powerful drivers of the AIDS pandemic), destruction of the planet's ozone shield and pollution of our atmosphere and oceans? All of these naturally require global regulation and redirection toward civilian and humane priorities. Which global trends can help evolve human cultures in positive directions? For example, the globalization of information and culture holds much promise. Yet it must be redirected from corporate media conglomerations and 'government by mediocracy' based on spreading wasteful, unsustainable Western-style commercial consumerism and its many addictions. The legal charters of such global corporations cannot be allowed to continue operating under 300-year-old rules that limit their liabilities, making them responsible only to their stockholders rather than to all their stakeholders. We must overrule the mistaken legal interpretation of corporations as 'natural persons' whose financial contributions corrupting our politicians are deemed 'free speech'. We must also support the vanguard of smaller and more socially responsible businesses that are committing to Codes of Conduct, best practices and higher global standards and greener technologies.

We know that micro-enterprises are an essential part of healthy development and that the poorest entrepreneurs pay back their small loans more faithfully than do the rich. We also know that most of the world's livelihoods are still made outside the money economy by careful stewardship and traditional uses of natural resources. Today we know that the Love Economy accounts for 50 per cent of all productive work, even in industrial societies, and up to 65 per cent or more in many developing countries.

By far the most creative response to global corporate and financial power is the recognition by millions of global citizens that pure information-based transactions can now break the global money monopoly. High-tech computerized barter can overcome the necessity for developing countries to earn foreign exchange, just as it allows grassroots communities to barter and use local currencies, and countries to bypass speculators with information transaction-based 'public utilities' for trading commodities, including currencies. All corporate and financial power is based on money systems and their manipulation by governments, banks and financial markets. The very information technologies that today promote corporate consumerism can also be used as alternatives to money – as worried bankers know. As economies 'dematerialize' toward services and the 'attention economies' of time-scarcity continue to grow, money systems must be redesigned to reach all citizens (just as the Grameen Bank in Bangladesh and other micro-credit lenders have proved is possible). If not, all those citizens aware of their new options can simply opt, once again, for pure information-based exchange and barter, building on their existing informal 'Love Economies'.

Let us look at some areas where social innovations are arising and being debated – even if they are not yet amplified in mass media:

1. The rise of civic society and the recognition of the Love Economy all over the world is providing a third force and new voices enriching our options, and creating a new balance of power between business and government, holding both more accountable.
2. Global military budgets have declined some 3 per cent each year since

1987, even though these 'peace dividends' are obscured in budget aggregates.

3. The proposal for shifting strategies of national security from their current focus on military means toward concepts of insurance against risks of aggression. The United Nations Security Insurance Agency (UNSIA) and its companion proposal, The Anticipatory Risk Mitigation Peace-building Contingents (ARM-PC) are similar in structure to the International Tele-communications Satellite Consortium (INTELSAT) and the World Bank. UNSIA would be authorized by the UN General Assembly and report to the Security Council in response to requests from member-nations to provide 'insurance policies' to deter potential aggression. This would allow such countries to shift significant percentages of their military budgets to investments in their civilian sectors and reduce their overall national expenditures. The insurance industry would provide risk-assessment services to such countries to determine their overall insurability: that is, the extent to which they maintain good relations with neighbouring states; eschew nuclear, biological, chemical and other weapons of mass destruction; and do not harbour terrorists or practise or teach violence, 'ethnic cleansing' or other unacceptable policies under international law. Each 'insurance policy' would be individually negotiated and the pool of premiums would constitute a trust fund available to provide the ARM-PC peacekeeping and conflict-resolution contingents (including humanitarian, civic groups already based in the country or invited). Safeguards are structured in to assure openness, transparency, full democratic debate and UN oversight. The UNSIA would negotiate each request and match it with appropriate countries wishing to volunteer peacekeepers and/or humanitarian con-fidence-building groups.

4. A state-of-the art Foreign Exchange for currencies (FXE) would tame today's computerized financial trading systems in our daily $1.3 trillion global casino. The FXE would be operated as a 'public utility' by the largest possible group of central banks in cooperation with the UN. The FXE would offer much-needed competition to the virtual monopoly over global currency exchange by large private banks and currency traders. Since these enormous currency exchange flows are 90 per cent speculative, they have increased volatility. This has sharply diminished the power of central banks to stabilize their nations' currencies as well as reduced domestic sovereignty and macro-economic control over fiscal and monetary policies, interest and employment rates, social 'safety nets' and environ-mental protection. The proposed 'public interest' FXE would provide efficient technology and reporting systems that would allow governments to control and collect fees on currency transactions, and limit speculation, money-laundering and other criminal activities. Central banks could play against private traders on a level playing-field and governments could use the transaction fees collected (many are mandated already in various

countries) to fund multilateral emergency measures. The FXE proposal may yet become a global alternative to regional currency proposals such as those of the EMU and ASEAN.

The Global Commission to Fund the UN and other independent commissions have addressed the urgent need to tame today's global casino, including harmonization of securities and currency-trading regulations, leading to something like a 'Global Securities and Exchange Commission' – now being debated in top financial circles – to create a fairer game for all the players. The FXE infrastructure can be based on the most advanced computer-trading technology, allowing nations and their central banks to add to their trade reporting requirements additional information of great positive value and to curb many of today's abuses. To these reporting systems on each trade a much smaller fee could then be levied than that proposed by Professor James Tobin, since today's volume of transactions now exceeds by orders of magnitude those of the 1970s. Such a very low fee (somewhere below .01 per cent) would be unobjectionable to most traders we have interviewed and yet could still yield large revenues for governments, as well as for relevant UN and other development purposes (Henderson and Kay 1996: 305–24).

Another proposal is to collect user-fees on all commercial uses of the global commons (Cleveland et al. 1996). We all share the global commons and its infrastructures, including the global sea lanes and oceans; airways and atmosphere; the electromagnetic spectrum and the public airwaves that carry our TV, radio and telecommunications; satellite orbits and outer space; Antarctica; and the world's precious store of biodiversity. A further proposal is that nations pursue additional international agreements, not only to collect such user-fees, but also to levy fines and taxes for the abuse of these global resources, including on arms trafficking, cross-border pollution and currency speculation.

The UN is revitalizing itself for the new century. It is capitalizing on its considerable strengths and reshaping itself for the Information Age. The UN continues to be the world's best convenor and broker, networker, standard-setter and fosterer of new norms for our global human family. Some nations have resisted the UN's inclusion of grassroots civic organizations in its activities and conferences. They believe that the UN should remain exclusively an association of national governments. Some nations have used the UN as a 'fig-leaf' and others as a scapegoat – whichever best justifies their national interests and policies.

As systems thinkers, we are beginning to understand that shifting towards more ecologically sustainable, just forms of human development will require policy innovations at seven levels of our societies:

1. Individual: dematerializing and demonetarizing individual and family life-styles toward personal development, earth ethics and sustainable values.

2. Local government: enacting government ordinances to encourage sustainable lifestyles, for example pedestrian and cyclist options; zoning for mixed-use densities; encouragement of local currencies, solar and renewable resource options and recycling; while rejecting the subsidizing through taxes and bond issues of global-scale corporate intrusions.

3. Corporate: enacting redesign of corporate governance toward the stakeholder models and re-engineering manufacturing processes in line with corporate obligations under the 1970 OECD Polluter Pays Principle.

4. National: governments can institute 'green' taxes on resource waste and depletion and pollution, remove taxes on incomes and payrolls, and implement the overhauling of GNP/GDP national accounts toward multidisciplinary, unbundled quality-of-life indicators and broader policy tools beyond macro-economics, while refraining from 'auctioning off' their tax bases and human and environmental capital to corporations, and implementing a 'public utility' FXE.

5. International: redesigning and renegotiating of trade agreements for democratic access for developing countries; democratizing all international financial institutions, central banks and trade negotiations to include representatives of employee unions and voluntary civic society; implementing full-cost pricing, lifecycle costing and application of corrected national accounts and quality-of-life indicators; implementing user-fees for all commercial uses of global commons and taxes and fines for abuses, including UN infrastructure, commercial protocols and peacekeeping operations; moving the World Bank and the IMF towards democracy, transparency and equity, and bringing them back within the United Nations' jurisdiction; reinvigorating ECOSOC, the UN Centre on Transnational Corporations, and other UN agencies; implementing peacekeeping proposals such as UNSIA and ARM-PC.

6. Civic society: strengthening and fostering the growth of civic society and education for global citizenship, including favoured tax status and free public access channels on all global telecommunications media through treaties such as those governing the electromagnetic spectrum and other common heritage resources; implementing electronic democracy, such as COPORA.

7. Biosphere: implementing agreements and the plan of action of the Cairo Conference on Population and Development, the Women's Conference in Beijing in 1995, and the Social Summit in Copenhagen in 1995, as well as *Agenda 21* and previous action plans that can move human societies toward sustainability and protect the planet's biodiversity. Bringing women into full partnership at all decision-making levels can lead to healthier societies, stable populations and sustainable, truly human development.

Some of these social innovations are being promoted through the Global Commission to Fund the United Nations and other coalitions of support. To some extent their merits are being debated by leaders and the public.

Some are more easily understood and may be adopted more quickly, while others are unlikely to make much headway in the USA without a social crisis. Some of the innovations may find more fertile ground in other countries. Two rubrics: 'the power of prevention' and 'the cooperative advantage' codify many of the lessons learned from these and earlier historical experience. Such win–win and 'contrarian' strategies can complement economics' 'win–lose', competitive view of globalization, now leading to vicious circles and today's many 'races-to-the-bottom'. By contrast, game theory maps a broader, overlooked repertoire of human behaviour, altruism, cooperation, nurturing and contrarian rather than 'herd' behaviours – verified by generations of cultural anthropologists and psychologists. These complementary human behaviours in such new movements as those of socially responsible investors, global codes of conduct, standards and treaties can lead to 'virtuous circles'. This can eventually raise the ethical floor under today's lowest common denominator global economic playing-field so that the most ethical corporations and countries can win. Today's human challenges can channel and employ all the energies and talents of every man and woman on earth. At the same time, this great effort to steer our technical genius can build more peaceful, prosperous and conscious paths to sustainable human development and further evolution of all life on this planet. If humans fail to evolve culturally and morally, the planet, of course, will survive without us.

Notes

1. C. A. Hilgartner, 'The method in the madness of Western man' (unpublished ms).

2. See e.g. the catastrophe mathematics of René Thom (Thom 1975), which captures organic, non-linear processes, bifurcation modes and the role of positive feedback and attractors in rapid structural change.

3. The Independent Sector, 1828 L Street, NW, Washington, DC 20036.

4. See e.g. *Citizens: Strengthening Global Civil Society*, CIVICUS, World Alliance for Citizen Participation.

5. See e.g. The Council on Economic Priorities, New York, and Guerard 1966, which found no significant difference.

6. Schmidheiny et al. 1996. Progress on global standards for 'good corporate citizenship' has continued since the pioneering ILO 'Tripartite Declaration on Principles Concerning Multi-National Corporations'; the United Nations 'Mutually Agreed Equitable Principles and Rules for the Control of Restrictive Business Practices'; and UNCTAD's 'Transfer of Technology Code'. More recently, voluntary codes of conduct include the Caux Principles, promoted by a group of Japanese, European, and North American corporations; the CERES Principles on Environmentally Responsible Economies, which include mandatory progress reports, with over 50 large signatories, including Sun Oil and General Motors; the Minnesota Principles on Corporate Responsibility and the standards for social responsibility under development by the UK-based SustainAbility Ltd and by Green Audit of New York, and other consulting firms and member companies of the Social Venture Network in the USA and Europe (Social Venture Network, San Francisco; and Interfaith Center on Corporate Responsibility, special issue of *The Corporate Examiner* 1995).

7. National Association of Women Business Owners, Silver Springs, MD, 1996.

8. Poll conducted by Preamble Center for Public Policy, Washington, DC, September 1996.

9. The Stakeholder Alliance, Center for Advancement of Public Policy, Washington, DC.

10. Walker Research (1995) *Corporate Character*, Indianapolis, IN: The Walker Group.

References

Arthur, W. B. (1994) *Increasing Returns: Path Dependence in the Economy*, University of Michigan Press, Ann Arbor.

Brandenburger, A. and B. Nalebuff (1996) *Co-opetition*, Currency/Doubleday, New York.

Cleveland, H., H. Henderson and I. Kaul (eds) (1996) *The United Nations: Financing Alternatives*, Global Commission to Fund the United Nations, Washington, DC.

The Corporate Examiner (1995) 'Principles for global corporate responsibility: benchmarks for measuring business performance', 1 September.

Eisler, R. (1988) *The Chalice and the Blade*, Harper and Row, New York.

Guerard, Jr, J. B. (1996) 'Is there a cost to being socially responsible in investing?', Vantage Global Advisors, New York.

Henderson, H. (1988) *Politics of the Solar Age*, Knowledge Systems, Indianapolis.

— (1993) 'Social innovation and citizen movements', *Futures*, 25 (3): 322–38.

— (1995) *Paradigms in Progress* (reprint), Berrett-Koehler, San Francisco.

— (1996a) 'What's next in the great debate about measuring wealth and progress?' *Challenge*, November–December.

— (1996b) *Building a Win–Win World*, Berrett-Koehler, San Francisco.

— (1996c) *Creating Alternative Futures* (reprint), Kumarian Press, Hartford, CT.

Henderson, H. and A. F. Kay (1996) 'Introducing competition to the global currency markets', *Futures*, 28 (4): 305–24.

Hoffman, W. M., R. Frederick and E. S. Petry, Jr (eds) (1990) *The Corporation: Ethics and the Environment*, Quorum Books, London.

Hyde, L. (1979) *The Gift*, Vintage, New York.

Lindblom, C. E. (1977) *Politics and Markets*, Basic Books, New York.

Lydenberg, S. D. (1981) *Bankrolling Ballots, Update 1980: the Role of Business in Financing Ballot Question Campaigns*, Council on Economic Priorities, New York.

Mintzberg, H. (1983) *Power in and around Organizations*, Prentice Hall, Englewood Cliffs, NJ.

Moore, J. F. (1996) *The Death of Competition*, Harper Business, New York.

Polanyi, K. (1944) *The Great Transformation*, Beacon, Boston, MA.

Porter, M. and C. van der Linde (1995) 'Green and competitive', *Harvard Business Review*, September–October.

Ralls, J. (1996) 'Pensions systems: defining the holy grail', *International Fund Strategies*, September: 2–6.

Sahlins, M. (1972) *Stone Age Economics*, Aldine de Gruyter, Hawthorne, NY.

Schmidheiny, S. and F. J. L. Zorraquin, with the World Business Council for Sustainable Development (1996) *Financing Change*, MIT Press, Cambridge, MA.

Tainter, J. (1988) *The Collapse of Complex Societies*, Cambridge University Press, New York.

Thom, R. (1975) *Structural Stability and Morphogenesis*, WA Benjamin, Reading, MA.

Tufte, E. R. (1978) *Political Control of the Economy*, Princeton University Press, Princeton, NJ.

UNDP (1995) *Human Development Report*, Oxford University Press, New York.

6

The Mosaic of Global Taxes

HOWARD M. WACHTEL

As globalization weakens national borders, governments in both developed and developing countries are discovering that their tax bases are being eroded, especially their ability to tax the proceeds and profits from corporate investment and finance.

From the developed world, financial and tangible forms of capital roam the globe, rendering it difficult either to define profits for tax purposes or to decide in which country the taxable profit is earned. Less developed countries (LDCs) find themselves under such pressure to grant tax holidays, tax abatements and generous land give-aways that they cede their tax base in an obsessive competition for foreign investment. Corporations have then used these concessions from LDCs to press for tax reductions in their home countries in what is by now a well-tuned orchestration of political pressure. 'Tax degradation' is the phrase used by the IMF's director of its Fiscal Affairs Department to characterize this general phenomenon, 'whereby some countries change their tax systems to raid the world tax base and export their tax burden' (Tanzi 1996).

The erosion of the tax base from capital has increased the burden of taxation on labour. In the countries of the European Union, taxes on capital have been drifting downward since 1980, those on labour upward. From around a 50 per cent share of total tax receipts in 1980, the tax take on capital and self-employment fell to 35 per cent by 1994, and the tax share from labour rose from around 35 per cent to over 40 per cent.[1] The wide gap between higher tax proportions from capital in 1980 and those from labour were steadily eroded, as the former fell and the latter rose, until 1991 when they became equal; they subsequently reversed course with the tax proportions from labour exceeding capital. The gap now goes the other way, with tax shares from labour exceeding those on capital, opening a new steadily growing gap between them.

In the United States the corporate profit tax share of federal government tax receipts fell from 27 per cent in 1965 to 17 per cent in the mid-1990s.[2]

Taxes on labour translate into higher employment costs, and higher employment costs translate into higher unemployment. Setting aside the debate over the causes of unemployment in Europe from other sources, this tax distortion contributes to the problem. Any increase in employment costs will increase unemployment.

A labour tax at the point of employment is comparable to a higher wage in that both increase labour costs; the difference is the beneficiary. A labour tax increases unemployment; a higher wage benefits the employee and may or may not contribute to unemployment, depending on whether the higher wage is offset by higher productivity. A higher wage can be mitigated by higher productivity; labour costs need not rise at all, or could fall. A substantial body of research, called efficiency wage theory, finds empirical support for the proposition that higher wages can in fact induce higher productivity under certain conditions.[3] If labour is taxed at the point of employment, however, the impact on labour costs is unambiguous. The cost of employing labour will be higher, without any incentive on the part of labour to increase productivity, and fewer people will be employed than would otherwise be the case if employment taxes were lower.

The tilt of the tax system toward reliance on employment taxes and away from taxes on capital has two origins: one is the increasing burden of social security payments on the modern state and the other is associated with the enhanced mobility of capital, which allows it to escape the higher tax rates and broader tax base in developed countries.[4] To put this in context, taxes on labour and capital are taxes on factors of production. The third factor of production that is typically taxed is land. Historically, tax systems were developed along with the creation of the nation-state; indeed one of the motivations for state creation and defined geographical jurisdiction was the desire of authorities to capture the tax base, which was originally land. Modern tax theory has pursued a balanced set of taxes on all three factors of production and offered the three 'E's' as controlling criteria in the tax mix: efficiency, equity and effectiveness, by which is meant cost of compliance and simplicity of administration.

A government's ability to tax depends on its ability to maintain its tax jurisdiction. Factor mobility erodes this. Of the three factors of production, capital is most mobile and land is least mobile. Labour is somewhere in between but definitely at the immobile end of the spectrum, except for some very high-profile, extremely wealthy individuals. Globalization, therefore, has forced governments to take into account a fourth criterion: *taxing the factor of production that is less mobile*.

Taxation and Factor Mobility

'The heart of the problem', according to *The Economist*, derives from the fact that 'modern tax systems were developed after the Second World War when cross-border movements in goods, capital and labour were relatively small. Now, firms and people are more mobile – and can exploit tax differences between countries.'[5] In economists' language, governments can more effectively tax factors of production if there is a high degree of inelasticity. The taxed factor cannot escape by fleeing the tax jurisdiction if there is immobility and inelasticity. One moment's reflection is sufficient to understand why the proportion of tax revenues emanating from capital has been declining while that from labour has increased. The mobile factor of production – capital – can more readily jettison an unfavourable tax jurisdiction and seek refuge in a Third World tax haven. A government can raise the tax *rate* on capital but discover that its tax receipts have declined because the *base* on which the tax is calculated drops proportionally more than the rate has risen. Capital flees the high tax jurisdiction; the tax on capital is more elastic.

This is more easily accomplished by owners of financial capital but increasingly can also be attained with physical capital, while inelastic labour remains confined to the tax jurisdiction in which it resides. Profits are a moving target; labour is stationary and more readily targeted for taxation. Even if labour wanted to move to another tax entity, it could not do so easily. Immigration laws restrict labour mobility but not capital movements. There are also other reasons why picking up and relocating half-way around the world is not as easy for humans as it is for stateless and rootless capital. The difference in opportunities for movement of capital as opposed to labour, therefore, accounts for the shifting of taxes onto labour and away from capital, with consequences for unemployment, equity and efficiency.

A vast corporate 'underground economy' avoids taxes but absorbs benefits from others' tax payments. The OECD surrenders to this reality when it comments that 'with growing international mobility of both fixed investment and financial investment there may be a need to reduce taxes on income from capital. Thus, most of the tax burden will have to fall on labour as this is the less mobile factor' (OECD 1997: 9).[6] If the underground capital-taxed economy is not sufficiently complicated for contemporary governments, globalization threatens to attack another source of tax revenue: consumption taxes. Here the Internet and the worldwide web assert themselves. The technological revolution that has brought us the computer and information systems now introduces cyberspace, a jurisdiction belonging to no government and therefore outside any taxing capacity. Though just beginning and now a small problem of tax control, commercial transactions over the web are quickly becoming large and untaxable.

When a Dutch consumer buys software from a shop in The Hague, VAT is collected. But what if he or she simply purchases the same software over the Internet and downloads it? First of all, which tax rate applies: the rate where the item was purchased or where it originated? And second, how can governments track these transactions, because as *The Economist* points out, 'the Internet eliminates not just national borders but also the identity of firms and individuals doing business' (31 May 1997: 22). The most rapidly growing bookseller in the United States is not one of the mega-stores that are popping up in every large city in the country, but a web site out of Seattle called Amazon. With few overheads and a 'stock' of millions of titles it can price its product and offer a convenient 'service' – browsing at home at any time of the day or night – that a fixed-site store cannot. The insertion of quotation marks here is not an affectation but deliberately done to call attention to how conventional usage of the language has different meanings in the cyberspace of today and tomorrow, as against the physical space that has governed tax transactions between government and citizen. The next item to be marketed easily over the net is CDs, as new-generation computer technologies will allow the downloading of CDs as readily as the downloading of software is today, to be followed by a basket of goods and services that encompasses the spectrum of consumption. Today the total of consumer purchases over the net is only a tiny 0.1 per cent of total purchases in the United States, but this is estimated to climb to some 25 per cent in the next 35 years (*The Economist*, 31 May 1997: 22).

Reform constituencies with an interest in global taxes are not necessarily in accord with each others' objectives. Fault lines exist between the interests of Third World and industrial countries, eco-tax advocates and labour constituencies, redistributionists from rich to poor countries and defenders of lower-income recipients in developed countries.[7] These divisions among groups that might otherwise coalesce weaken them as a whole in challenging transnational corporations and financial interests that have a unified position against any global taxation whatsoever. This group has on its side a general aversion to tax increases of any kind in the current ideological epoch in which the debate would have to take place.

Notwithstanding these obstacles, there may be space for a global tax proposal that has other purposes aside from raising revenue or redistributing income. If along the way redistribution is also obtained it will be all the better, but my political antennae report back that a direct statement of purpose that puts revenue-raising and redistribution front and centre would fail. Revenue-raising and redistribution can occur but in the form of a flea hitching a ride on a dog.

The Tobin Tax

With new forms of taxation on capital that speak to globalization, a distinction must be made between financial transactions and tangible investment in such items as buildings and equipment. The most prominent global tax proposal treats the issue of financial capital as opposed to tangible investment in plant and equipment. It is associated with the Nobel Prize economist James Tobin, who in 1978 launched a proposal for a turnover tax on the sale of financial assets (Tobin 1982).[8] He was writing at a particular historical moment and his scheme was designed to address the problems in financial markets of the late 1970s: currency instability following on the collapse of the Bretton Woods system, the OPEC oil price shock, a collapsing dollar and intense speculation in other currencies and gold, and difficult early days for the system of flexible exchange rates.[9] Speculation in financial markets further destabilized what was already a fragile balance in financial markets. Tobin's proposal was, therefore, initially designed to promote financial stability by adding a cost to speculation. If along the way it raised revenues, that was a secondary benefit. At the time his proposal was launched, the use of new tax receipts was not a primary consideration. He did say in passing that the 'tax proceeds could appropriately be paid into the IMF or World Bank', but only later did the use of the Tobin tax receipts become a principal part of the discourse on global taxation (Tobin 1982: 494).

Tobin's ideas build on those of one of the great twentieth-century designers of the modern state, John Maynard Keynes, who wrote with prescience a half century before the personal computer, information techno-logy and satellite telecommunications: 'as the organization of investment markets improves, the risk of the predominance of speculation does, however, increase. ... Speculators may do no harm as bubbles on a steady stream of enterprise. But the position is serious when enterprise becomes the bubble on a whirlpool of speculation' (Keynes 1935: 158–9). In what has now become an equally famous metaphor from Tobin, he talks about throwing 'some sand in the well-greased wheels' of financial speculation to restrain financial markets from deviating too much from fundamental values (Tobin 1982: 493).

Tobin's original formulation was an international uniform tax on all spot foreign currency conversions.[10] The tax would have to be introduced simul-taneously in all countries and it would have to be identical, otherwise financial houses would move their foreign exchange transactions 'offshore' and escape the turnover tax (cf. Eichengreen, Tobin and Wyplosz 1995: 165). Such a tax would restore a degree of control over monetary policy for central banks that today have lost some monetary autonomy and have become passive responders to private financial markets (Wachtel 1990). Tobin's 1978 proposal consisted of a 1 per cent tax rate, and that has remained the benchmark in subsequent discussions.

Many governments currently place a tax on the sale of securities – bonds or stocks – as a way to dampen speculation in these financial markets.[11] None, however, taxes foreign exchange turnover. The evidence from securities taxes is that transactions do not move offshore, but there are reasons for this that may not apply to foreign exchange markets. Securities still rely heavily on a fixed site. There are information requirements, face-to-face meetings that sustain the comparative advantage of a fixed site, and complex clearing mechanisms that must be precise, rapid and error-free. These attributes of securities markets apply less in foreign exchange dealings where the computer terminal and sophisticated information technologies replace the hands-on conditions of securities markets.[12]

Tobin could not have foreseen the explosive growth in daily foreign exchange transactions during the 20 or so years after he launched his proposal in 1978. From around $150 billion[13] per day during 1985, foreign exchange transactions have mushroomed to one trillion dollars per day in the 1990s. Not all of this involves spot transactions – some are in futures contracts and not addressed by the Tobin proposal, others involve duplication through resale piled upon resale. Any turnover tax today, therefore, would have to decide how to treat resales and futures contracts as opposed to spot trading to arrive at a net turnover base for purposes of imposing the Tobin tax.[14]

Calculations have been done on the proceeds of a Tobin tax by the United Nations Conference on Trade and Development (UNCTAD), which has been at the centre of Third World efforts to collect data on global capital flows, provide estimates of the size of potential tax receipts, and offer ideas for how these tax revenues could be used as a resource for redistribution. Based on the one trillion dollar per day marker and using a 1 per cent tax rate, UNCTAD comes up with $720 billion per year in new tax revenues – a staggering sum considering the small tax rate.[15] For the sake of argument, UNCTAD simply splits the proceeds, $360 billion for the collecting governments and $360 billion for a fund for redistribution from rich to poor countries. There is no other global tax scheme that would raise as much revenue.[16] This one has the added advantage of a small tax rate with minimal impact on capital markets, low distortion effects and ease of administration.

In political terms the tax would have to be sold to a public that is averse to any new or old taxes primarily on the basis of curbing speculation, not on raising revenue or redistribution. A political constituency may be found in the G-5 countries for restraining speculation and potential financial instability by playing on populist scepticism about making profits from unrestrained speculation that require mop-up operations from tax-payers when modest speculation escalates into frenzy and subsequent crisis.[17]

Criteria for the Success of Global Taxes

With the Tobin tax as a prototype, it is now possible to ponder the criteria for judging the success or failure of a global tax. It should, first, have the advantage of simplicity and ease of administration, including minimal costs of tax compliance. Second, a global tax should have primary objectives that are necessary for sound and sensible economic policy, are defensible, and can be sold to a sceptical public with an aversion to all taxes. Any global tax that contends for acceptance must, third, raise sufficient revenue to make the political battle over its introduction worth the effort. Scarce reformist political capital should not be squandered on quixotic schemes that have limited payoff. Fourth, and finally, the global tax should involve at least several groupings of countries in the world – the core, semi-periphery and periphery in Wallerstein's classification scheme or the more popular usage of North/South, with the south broken down into three categories of newly industrializing states, middle–income LDCs and the poorest countries.

On these criteria, the Tobin tax does quite well. It satisfies the first three easily. It has an elegance of simplicity, is easy to administer, raises large sums of revenues, and can be defended on its own terms as a brake on potentially damaging financial speculation. It fails on the fourth criteria in that it is a tax policy aimed exclusively at the G-5 at best and at a G-3 in particular: the United States, Japan and the United Kingdom, where essentially all of the foreign exchange trading takes place on a 24-hour clock in a global market.

The Third World in all its segments falls outside of the foreign exchange markets in any meaningful sense as a proportion of the trillion-dollar-a-day trading system.[18] It is a claimant for redistribution and UNCTAD has taken this up in its campaign. We have seen these schemes before. The Brandt Commission of the 1970s proposed a global armaments tax with redistribution from North to South, and this became part of the Third World's and UNCTAD's proposal for a New International Economic Order. The Brundt-land Commission took up this idea and added a global environmental tax to the redistribution platform. Whatever one thinks about such plans for global redistribution, they must be advocated as moral or ethical demands for economic justice and do not fit into a scheme for economic redistribution via a tax proposal that has redistribution organically built into it.

The Tobin tax and its inclusion in UNCTAD's advocacy for global resource redistribution fall into the category of ethical claims. The tax itself does not incorporate a redistribution logic because it is purely a tax on the very wealthiest countries and their foreign exchange speculators, who have limited economic relations with the poorer countries of the world. Nevertheless, the Tobin tax definitely belongs in the mix of new global taxes, because it meets so clearly three of the four tax criteria offered here.

Taxes on Fixed Capital

The Tobin tax is designed to mitigate the speculative dimension of foreign exchange markets. A second aspect of taxes on capital pertains to foreign direct investment (FDI) – corporate investments in buildings, the equipment that goes into them, and the technology that powers the equipment. The two are connected. If wealth is absorbed by paper financial transactions and direct investment is neglected then countries face the risk Keynes identified in the 1930s. He said the 'job is likely to be ill-done ... [w]hen the capital development of a country becomes a by-product of the activities of a casino' (Keynes 1935: 159). Restoring economic vigour to the industrial economies requires, therefore, attention to both financial and tangible capital accumulation. The tax structure can assist this process, ignore it, or operate against it. The Tobin tax on one form of financial speculation is a piece of the tax puzzle; the other involves taxes on fixed capital and its most injurious contemporary aspect, foreign direct investment.

Taxes on corporations have conventionally focused on profits as the base. This was an effective tax for several decades after the Second World War, and corporate taxes on profits produced a fair share of revenues for governments. The problem is that globalization has rendered profit taxes increasingly difficult for governments to impose because of the mobility of capital and its ability to escape high tax jurisdictions.

From the early 1970s, corporations have perfected their ability to avoid taxes through several devices. The most important is transfer pricing, which started initially in manufacturing and has now spread to the delivery of services (cf. Tanzi 1995). A corporation making a complex product in several countries engages in internal transactions within the company that are off the market. It produces parts in different countries, provides services at various locations, combines the parts into a finished product somewhere, conducts its research and development, sells in many countries, and manages production and sales at one or several headquarters sites. This is real political space in which governments, workers and civil society reside with and contest each other, not the politically neutered cyberspace celebrated by some futurologists. With transfer pricing, the corporation assigns a 'price' to these activities within its own internal market in such a way as to show high costs, and therefore low profits, in high tax jurisdictions and low costs (high profits) in low tax jurisdictions. The company, rather than the market, establishes these transfer prices in order to minimize taxes by manipulating the location of its profits. Since taxation on profits as it currently works is based on the revenues and costs in the taxing jurisdiction, the company has an incentive to present high costs in high tax places, and transfer pricing allows it to do this.

Take, for example, the production of Nike shoes. The company assigns a high price to its cost activities – research and development, marketing and management – in the USA, where it wants to show low profits for tax purposes. It shows low costs in Indonesia. Profits evaporate in the United States and appear in low-taxed Indonesia. There would be an inclination in this direction without transfer pricing, but this intra-company device allows it to frame an overall global tax strategy. It is difficult, if not impossible, for governments to audit the company's manipulation of internal prices to its tax advantage. If they tried, the costs of such tax audits would barely justify the tax recovery.

The problem is that profit is an elusive concept and a slippery accounting category for tax purposes. It involves both revenues and costs, and the costs can be shown to originate in the corporation's country of choice. A tax on capital as a factor of production in the globalized economy must, therefore, find some other accounting strategy, another element of corporate activity that is not as susceptible to tax avoidance.

Tax on Foreign Direct Investment

There are two tax systems that would fulfil the objective of capturing the base lost through capital mobility: one is a direct levy on foreign investment, the other identifies more precisely the profits earned in each country of operation and addresses the transfer pricing conundrum. With respect to foreign investment, one potential objection must be cleared up at the outset. The FDI tax is *not* meant to prohibit foreign investment. Because FDI carries with it political and policy consequences for both the recipient country and for the country of origin, however, tax policy that sorts out these consequences has merit. For the recipient country, FDI promotes low wages, the absence of core labour standards, environmental neglect and tax give-aways.[19] The same country typically has all of these policy characteristics. Some of the largest recipients of FDI have the poorest record on labour and environmental policy and offer the largest tax holidays. On a scale from good to bad, China, for example, would fall on the bad side of all of them and is the world's largest vessel for FDI.

Foreign direct investment has increased five-fold in ten years, from an annual flow of around $60 billion in 1985 to $315 billion by 1995. A share of this flow is more than ever directed toward Third World countries, around 40 per cent during the second half of the 1990s. From 1990 to 1995 alone the share went from 20 per cent to 35 per cent. This amounts to about $130 billion of FDI from OECD industrial countries to Third World countries. Nearly one-third of this goes to China, over $40 billion per year (WTO 1996).

The problem with taxation on capital as concerns FDI intersects with another global policy issue, namely the integration into the global economy of low-wage countries that do not adhere to internationally sanctioned core labour standards concerning the right of employees to form a trade union and the use of child labour, prison labour and bonded labour.[20] The modern manufacturing and service corporation has discovered how to produce in the poorest countries in the world with the least educated workforce, reversing conventional wisdom that only low-tech products and services fabricated and delivered by uneducated workers could survive in low endowments of human capital. Up the learning curve companies have climbed, and they are now able to move the most sophisticated high-wage, and what were formerly thought to be human capital-intensive activities, to low-wage, low human capital and low-taxed enclaves in the Third World.

Trade unions and their members in DCs view this a threat – to their wages, working conditions and job security, notwithstanding the body of research that does not find major job displacement resulting from low-wage international competition (Slaughter and Swagel 1997). Companies, however, and their academic and governmental supporters, must know otherwise. Low-wage international competitive pressures are invariably mentioned during collective bargaining, or when governments justify a call for more flexible labour markets, or a company threatens to close a factory. Corporate executives, the media and academic economists cannot have it both ways. They cannot claim that factories and offices have to shut down because of global competition from low-wage countries, and at the same time stand behind the academic research that purports to show that this has no bearing on locational decisions.[21] The OECD cannot assert the necessity for what it euphemistically calls labour market flexibility in the face of global competition from low-wage countries – lowering wages, cutting social security benefits and reducing job protection – and then say in the same document that such competitive forces have no impact on locational decisions. Either one or the other of these assertions is right; both cannot be.

A tax on FDI should be designed to address the twin problems of tax-avoiding capital mobility and the erosion of core labour rights in recipient countries. It is not meant to quarantine LDCs from FDI, dictate decisions as to where companies can invest, or distort international labour markets. Rather, such a tax would correct distortions in international labour markets caused by the suppression of core labour rights, reward those LDCs that are trying to promote progressive social policies by levelling the playing field with their LDC competitors, and promote economic development through labour policies that enhance incentives for investment in people.

Here is how such a tax would work. A foreign direct investment tax would be introduced on corporations and would apply wherever there was FDI, in an LDC or DC. The tax would vary, however, depending on the rating a country received from the ILO about its adherence to core labour standards. Included in the rating should be a judgement about how rapidly and effectively countries are moving towards the adoption and implementation of core labour standards. The standards can be modified to account for differing levels of development. Nothing is implied about the wages paid in an LDC in this rating scheme. Only the core labour standards concerning trade union rights, child labour, bonded labour and prison labour are in dispute. A country that adheres to the ILO standards should, other things being equal, have higher wages because of the powerful indirect effect from free labour markets and from the adherence to core labour standards. To keep wages below free market levels is precisely why governments suppress these rights, putting those countries that score higher on labour rights at a competitive disadvantage. The result is a lower wage outcome than an unrestricted labour market would produce. For those who argue that this will intrude on free trade, precisely the opposite is the case. When labour rights are denied, a critical market, the labour market, is not free. Free trade requires free markets throughout and an 'unfree' labour market is, in fact, incompatible with the free trade argument.

To see how a foreign investment tax would work, graded by adherence to core labour standards and level of development, start with a tax rate of, say,

20 per cent on all FDI, whatever the recipient country. This tax would apply to those countries at the lowest end of the spectrum of core labour rights. The tax would be adjusted downward to a minimum tax of 10 per cent on the FDI base if a country had a better record on core labour standards or was making progress toward their implementation. Such a tax makes a policy statement: it says companies can invest wherever they wish, but must pay a higher tax if they choose to invest in those countries with the worst labour standards. It says countries are not required to do anything about their core labour standards if they do not want to. It does say that such countries with poor labour standards would have to attract FDI from companies that are taxed more heavily than they would be in some competitor LDC. The justification for any FDI tax in the first instance is that governments of FDI origin have to pay some of the costs associated with capital mobility – for unemployment and community impacts – out of the taxes levied on the affected populations, the immobile factors.

This tax would have several salutary benefits. For LDCs it would promote equitable economic development and encourage economic and social policies that invest more in human capital. It would reward those countries with strong core labour standards, allowing them to resist pressures to dismantle their social policies. Evidence from economic history is unambiguous that the route to economic development and social progress is through exactly such a strategy of growing, not declining, wages and aggressive investment in human capital. The present regime of low-wage competition to attract FDI, through the suppression of labour rights, dooms poorer LDCs to remaining poor. Such a competitive race to the bottom makes a country more attractive for FDI by lowering wages, prohibiting trade unions, encouraging the use of or turning one's back on the employment of child labour, bonded labour and prison labour. These 'low road' policies of development, however, are not conducive to sustainable economic development. They are short-sighted and trap poor countries in a cul de sac. There is never a way out. If a country tries to introduce progressive labour and social policies, it is trumped by some competitor who offers Western companies the low wages and restriction on labour rights they want. This graduated FDI tax encourages the sort of economic development that is sustainable, socially progressive and consistent with the historical route to economic development.

For DCs the tax also has benefits. It makes a clear statement that companies can invest offshore but will have to decide where to do this, based on adherence to core labour standards. The ability to leverage low wages and poor working conditions elsewhere back into DCs can be partially broken by the graduated FDI tax. It offers some defence against a globalization that has contributed to wage and work problems in DCs, without being strictly prohibitive on the ability of companies to invest wherever they wish. A healthy debate about globalization would occur once the linkage between FDI and core labour standards was exposed.

The tax receipts would not be as high as they are for the Tobin tax, but their policy effects would be more extensive and would nudge them in a positive direction in both DCs and LDCs. A maximum tax of 20 per cent on FDI would produce annual revenues of anywhere from around $65 billion, based on the mid-1990s rates of FDI, to half that, $32.5 billion, with the actual sum found somewhere in between.[22] This tax's primary advantage, however, is found in its joint policy improvements, which in the long run may have more important consequences for both DCs and LDCs than a Tobin tax, whose benefits for LDCs would only accrue after a very difficult redistribution battle and would not address the internal structural problems that promote low-wage and inadequate human capital policies. The FDI tax encourages a breakout from a competition in LDCs to see who can be poorest and attract the most FDI. It mitigates pressures for lower wages and labour market flexibility in DCs. A combination of the two taxes suggests itself if the Tobin tax redistribution could also be linked to core labour standards and internal policy reforms in LDCs that promote a higher wage and human capital strategy of development.

The FDI tax meets enough of the criteria to remain in the global tax mosaic being constructed here. It does not raise large sums of revenue, but has more currency in its policy effects and in its promotion of economic and social policies that are of consequence for both DCs and LDCs. It has sufficient simplicity and administrative elegance to satisfy the criteria presented earlier. Most importantly it engages every country in the world and, therefore, scores well on this criterion. It has a potential political constituency that can be mobilized around issues of fairness, buttressed by the economic argument that a critical market – the labour market – is not free in many parts of the world and should be reformed to bring it into line with other markets.

Unitary Profits Tax

The second task for a reconstituted tax structure on capital has to address the transfer pricing problem discussed previously: the device corporations use to evade high-tax governments and leverage weaker countries into tax give-aways. Profits have to be accounted for differently. A way has to be found to identify more effectively where profits are earned for tax purposes. A modified version of what in the United States is called a 'unitary' tax can accomplish this. It starts with accounting categories that are known and cannot so easily be fudged: aggregate worldwide profits, total global revenues received, and revenues earned in a particular tax jurisdiction. To discover the profit base for tax purposes, a calculation would be made as follows: divide revenues earned in the tax jurisdiction by total worldwide revenues. To identify profits earned in the tax jurisdiction, apply this percentage to global profits. This becomes the profits base on which a tax is levied.

For example, assume Nike makes worldwide profits of $1 billion. It receives 40 per cent of its worldwide revenues from sales in the United States. The profit earned in the USA is then $400 million and the corporate profits tax rate is applied to that base. The advantage of this unitary tax is that the problem of transfer pricing disappears. The three statistics – worldwide profits, sales revenue and sales revenues in the tax jurisdiction – are known or can readily be obtained by tax authorities. Opportunities for evasion are few.

With reference to the criteria for a successful tax reform plan, this one has multiple merit.[23] It is easy to administer and clear in its purposes. A political constituency could be mobilized on the grounds of tax fairness, especially after examples of transfer pricing fiddles were publicly exposed. It collects large sums of money, which today escape taxation by any government, either of FDI origin or FDI recipient. It does not involve any new tax, only a new way to identify and administer an old tax. It engages the North and the South and reduces the pressures on Third World countries to offer tax havens, because there are no longer ways to avoid profit taxes.

Summary

Globalization has rendered nation-state-based tax systems ineffective. Mobile factors of production, such as capital, can evade taxation, leaving labour and consumers bearing ever higher burdens of taxation. Conservative political interests, supported by the very corporations that have evaded taxes, then lead tax revolts on behalf of the immobile citizenry and against weaker and poorer labour and consumer constituencies in both developed and less developed countries. This takes the form of opposition to social security systems in DCs and to foreign assistance and redistribution from rich to poor countries. One way out of this paradox is to develop systems of corporate taxation that address this aspect of globalization.

Three have been offered: the Tobin tax on foreign exchange turnover, a foreign direct investment tax to support labour and social reforms throughout the world, and a unitary corporate profits tax that undermines transfer pricing. This is a tax mosaic that is supportable on the criteria of ease of administration and simplicity, with minimal costs of compliance; is based on sound and sensible economic policy; raises sufficient revenue so that the benefits derived are worth the political costs of advocacy; and engages the North and the South in a discourse over redistribution. The taxes also have a political bite to them. Issues of fairness are explicitly introduced, as well as an equitable sharing of tax burdens, reconstituting a corporate tax base, and modernizing the tax system so that it is compatible with contemporary globalization.

This last point may be one of the most important. As political and opinion elites use modernization and globalization to attack social security systems, the poor in DCs, and the poorer countries among the LDCs, opposition forces can make use of the modern and the global on behalf of those constituencies that threaten to be triaged by globalization and modernization.

Notes

1. Data taken from a chart 'Taxing matters', *The Economist*, 5 April 1997, p. 50.

2. To arrive at these proportions, I deducted social security taxes from total federal tax receipts. What remains, therefore, is the percentage of tax receipts, net of social security taxes, which corporations contribute. See Council of Economic Advisers 1995: 367.

3. This literature is reviewed in Wachtel 1992; Ch. 5.

4. Tax receipts depend on both the tax rate and the tax base. The rate is some percentage applied to a taxable source, the tax base. Tax competition among governments in LDCs to attract investment from DCs involves both.

5. *The Economist* 1997: 21.

6. The OECD reviewed the empirical research on capital mobility and conducted its own econometric study of capital mobility. It concluded that 'capital mobility is substantially higher than suggested (by other researchers) and ... has increased over time' (OECD 1997: 22).

7. In this chapter I am deliberately avoiding an analysis of eco-taxes in order to preserve the conceptual unity around the issue of corporate taxation and taxation on other factors of production. The literature on eco-taxes is also far more extensive and does not warrant as full a treatment as the one posed here on the discordance of factor taxation that has developed as a consequence of globalization.

8. Tobin points out that he first offered this proposal in 1972, but the 'idea fell like a stone in a deep well' (1982: 490).

9. The Tobin tax has had a revival in the wake of the 1997 Asian financial disruption, which was perceived superficially as caused by speculative 'hot money' fleeing Asian economies.

10. By limiting the tax to spot transactions, Tobin implicitly exempts speculation in foreign exchange futures contracts.

11. Most EU countries have such taxes, as does Japan. In the United States the taxes are not national but confined to state and local jurisdictions (Summers and Summers 1989: 177). By the end of the 1980s, seven EU countries, Switzerland, Japan and three other Pacific Rim countries had such taxes (Felix 1995: 204).

12. For a discussion of how a turnover tax on securities would affect different types of traders see Stiglitz 1989: 101–15.

13. All currency figures are in terms of US dollars.

14. There are adequate reasons for including futures contracts in the Tobin tax since they are part of the speculative universe. Resales, however, raise the issue of double taxation. The literature does not carefully address these issues.

15. UNCTAD uses a gross turnover base and does not deal with the issue of resales or futures contracts. For the revenue calculation, see Felix 1995: 205.

16. The other new global tax idea, eco-taxes, would collect less, have higher rates, and produce potentially larger distorting effects.

17. The G-5 includes the United States, France, Germany, Japan and the United Kingdom.

18. The 1997 Asian financial crisis was not about foreign exchange speculation but caused by short-term capital flight from tangible investment projects with roots in the corrupt and undemocratic regimes that permeate Asian economies.

19. Core labour standards concern trade union rights, child labour, bonded labour and prison labour. They are classifications used by the ILO in Geneva, which promotes their improvement and monitors them among its member countries.

20. Much the same analysis would pertain to environmental standards and FDI.

21. For a rare dissenting point of view among academic economists that is consistent with the analysis presented here, see Rodrik 1997.

22. This calculation is derived from a mid-1990s base of around $325 billion in FDI per year. Tax receipts would grow along with the growth in FDI. Revenue raised depends on the average labour standards rating and the resulting effective tax rate. A maximum 20 per cent tax rate yields $65 billion; a minimum 10 per cent rate yields $32.5 billion.

23. Tax proceeds require a complex calculation that is beyond this exploratory excursion into global taxes. They would be large, falling somewhere between the Tobin tax and the FDI tax.

References

Council of Economic Advisers (1995) *Economic Report of the President*, Government Printing Office, Washington, DC.

The Economist, 'Disappearing taxes', *The Economist*, 31 May 1997.

Eichengreen, B., J. Tobin and C. Wyplosz (1995) 'Two cases for sand in the wheels of international finance', *Economic Journal*, 105.

Felix, D. (1995) 'The Tobin tax proposal', *Futures*, 27 (2).

Keynes, J. M. (1935) *The General Theory of Employment, Interest and Money*, Harcourt, Brace and Co., New York.

OECD, 'Taxation and economic performance', 3 March 1997

Rodrik, D. (1997) 'Has globalization gone too far?', Institute for International Economics, March.

Slaughter, M. and P. Swagel (1997) 'The effect of globalization on wages in the advanced economies', IMF Working Paper, April.

Stiglitz, J. E. (1989) 'Using tax policy to curb speculative short-term trading', *Journal of Financial Services Research*, 3: 101–15.

Summers, L. H. and V. P. Summers (1989) 'When financial markets work too well: a cautious case for a securities transactions tax', *Journal of Financial Services Research*, 3.

Tanzi, V. (1995) *Taxation in an Integrating World*, Brookings Institution, Washington, DC.

— (1996) 'Globalization, tax competition and the future of tax systems', IMF Working Paper, December.

Tobin, J. (1982) 'A proposal for international monetary reform', *Essays in Economics: Theory and Policy*, MIT Press, Cambridge, MA, pp. 488–94.

Wachtel, H. M. (1990) *The Money Mandarins*, rev. edn, ME Sharpe Publishers, Armonk, NY.

— (1992) *Labour and the Economy*, 3rd edn, Harcourt Brace Jovanovich, New York.

WTO (1996) 'Trade and foreign direct investment', 9 October.

7

An Alternative to Global Marketization[1]

SAKAMOTO YOSHIKAZU*

Paradoxes of the End of the Cold War

There was scarcely an international relations scholar who predicted the end of the Cold War. Why was this? Realists, whose conception of international relations is based on power politics played out between nation-states, conceived of the Cold War as a fixed structure or 'system' that constrained the choices of actors; a structure that was considered to be ahistorically perpetual. As possible choices within those structural boundaries, realists concentrated on devising various diplomatic and military 'strategies'. Thus they almost entirely failed to predict changes in the very structure of the international system; changes that resulted in the end of the Cold War. It may well be that the end of the Second World War can, at least in part, be interpreted in power political terms because the Allied victory was achieved through the military devastation and occupation of Germany and Japan. The end of the Cold War, however, did not occur with the Western countries militarily defeating and occupying the East.

What, then, led to the end of the Cold War? Of course many factors were involved, but the most decisive one was the progressive weakening of the Eastern states through an erosion of regime legitimacy. This was not a result of the military weakness of the Eastern states such as the Soviet Union, as illustrated by the fact that Russia is still a nuclear superpower. The loss of legitimacy was propelled by two factors in particular. First, the oppressive rule and political stagnation characteristic of authoritarian regimes. Suppression of human rights bred a deep distrust of and opposition to the ruling political regimes. Second, the stagnation of the command economies. Low productivity and inefficiency gave rise to discontent and distrust of the economic system. Although this kind of distrust and scepticism toward the

* Reprinted from *Alternatives: Social Transformation and Humane Governance*, vol. 24, no. 2. Copyright © 1999 by Lynne Rienner Publishers, Inc. Reprinted with permission of the publisher.

governing regime emerged within certain sections of the elite, the main actors who challenged the legitimacy of the system were, above all, the dissenting citizens. This challenge erupted as a 'civil revolution'. While most of those of the elite who felt apprehensive about the inefficiency of the economy aimed to preserve the existing political system of one-party rule through partial economic reform, the citizens were rejecting outright the very political system that lay at the base of the economy's inefficiency. Thus, in this way, what was initially a double challenge to the legitimacy of both the political and economic systems became primarily a challenge to transform the political system. This challenge reflected the reality that the command economy was in essence integrated into the political system through state control. In this sense, the transformation that took place had as its driving force above all a 'civil revolution' that signified the formation of a *political* civil society.

What we see here are the dynamics of political change. Once the apparently inconsequential dissenting opinions and actions of citizens reach a critical mass, they suddenly crystallize and generate huge amounts of energy. Furthermore, this is not a Leninist type of revolution where people are mobilized and organized according to the grand design of a charismatic, avant-garde leader. It is a 'civil revolution' with the following characteristics: first, a crystallization of power resulting from the *autonomous* decisions and actions of a countless number of seemingly powerless citizens; second, *unpredictability* in that no one, not even the citizens themselves, can predict when and in what way the critical point will be reached; and third, once the avalanche of change begins, a new civil leadership secures a 'transformational hegemony' through non-violence in areas where dissident groups had already formed under the former regime the *core of a nascent civil society*. This kind of revolution is neither a rebellion of the mob, nor a plotted insurrection, but is rather a form of transformational power manifested through the autonomous actions of 'the powerless'. This kind of civil power first extended beyond the boundaries of individual countries in Eastern Europe and then played a decisive role in ending the Cold War as a system prepared for global war. That this 'civil revolution' transcended national boundaries and linked people together to bring about such fundamental global change is a historically unprecedented development.

What can be seen here is a power that only the powerless can exert, namely, 'the power of the powerless'. This is the first paradox that manifested itself with the end of the Cold War. Present Czech President Václav Havel wrote in an underground article in 1979, when the Communist Party was still in power, that the source of 'the power of the powerless' lies in 'living within the truth' through a rejection of official lies and hypocrisy of the state (Havel 1985). These words bring to mind Gandhi's 'power of truth' (*satyagraha*). Both Havel and Gandhi speak of the negation of the legitimacy of the system. It is small wonder that a transformation brought about by 'the power of the powerless' was not predictable by conventional realism with its tendency to conceive of state military power as the prototype of all power. My reason, however, for emphasizing the 'power of the powerless' is not just that it brought about a massive transformation in international politics, namely the end of the Cold War, but that at a more fundamental level, 'the power of the powerless' constitutes the basic principle of democracy that those who are ruled are in fact the rulers and sovereign.

The fact that international politics, which has tended to be defined as power politics, can now be increasingly defined in terms of 'the power of the powerless' was shown dramatically with the end of the Cold War. The end of the Cold War by 'the power of the powerless' points to a global-wide progression of the formation and establishment of civil society independent of state power, whether it be at the level of international order or domestic regime. Thus it is no accident that, in parallel with the collapse of the international Cold War system, from the late 1980s to the early 1990s citizens' democratization movements were able to change old regimes in countries such as South Korea, the Philippines, the Republic of South Africa and many Latin American countries. From this perspective, it may even be argued that the creation of a democratic world order in the twenty-first century is unattainable unless it is based on 'the power of the powerless', a fact that calls for the reconceptualization of 'power'.

Thus far I have discussed the paradox regarding the crucial factor that accounted for the end of the Cold War. Next I would like to move on to the paradox seen in the result of the war. As I have said, although the end of the Cold War appears at first glance to have been a victory for the Western states, what in fact prevailed over the East was the Western system, with its pillars of a capitalist market economy and political democracy founded on civil society. A common characteristic of the market and civil society is that both seek to be autonomous. It is ironic that at the very time Western states were proclaiming victory over the East and an end to the Cold War, markets and civil societies in the West were strengthening their independence from the state and thus weakening the power of the state in the West. In other words, the Western states' demonstration of superiority toward the East coincided in the West with an erosion of state power *vis-à-vis* the market and civil society. This is the second paradox of the end of the Cold War.

In the final phase of the Cold War, American President Ronald Reagan and British Prime Minister Margaret Thatcher promoted two policies from a neo-conservative platform. The first was the forging of a large-scale military build-up aimed at establishing superiority over the East with programmes such as the massive Strategic Defence Initiative, the feasibility of which is highly problematic. The second was the enforcement of economic liberalization, deregulation and privatization policies aimed at reducing the size of government. While the first of these policies aimed at a strong state and the second at a weak government, the large-scale military build-up of the former was rendered irrelevant when the arch enemy disappeared at the end of the Cold War. Thus what remained was the pursuit of a weak state, that is a small government, in relation to the market.

The issue here is the relation between the market and civil society, which form the two pillars of the Western system. As stated above, the common characteristic of both the market and civil society is their tendency to seek autonomy. In fact, the phrase 'civil society' began to be used in the latter half of the eighteenth century in an age when the market was seeking to establish independence from the mercantilist state. This development signified the emergence of what Marxists later termed 'bourgeois (civil) society' as a new bearer of liberation at the time. But that was as far as the commonalties between the principles of market and civil society went. The fundamental contradiction between the two became unmistakably clear in the latter half of the nineteenth century, when the division of capitalist society in terms of class conflict and the division of the world into imperialist powers and colonized societies came to the fore. This uncivil, often violent, conflict at home and abroad contributed to the demise of the concept of 'civil society' in the mainstream of Western social and political thought.

With the present-day situation in mind, rather than engaging in historical discourse I would summarize the contradiction as follows: whereas the market is characterized by the *commodification* of social relations, civil society is oriented to the *humanization* of social relations. Furthermore, while the market is a system of exchange based on the pursuit of self-interest and is centred on such instrumental values as productivity and efficiency (the 'system of wants' in the words of Hegel), civil society refers to social relations that form a public space in which human dignity and equality of rights are mutually recognized and continually redefined by citizens as end values in the context of changing historical processes. In the market humans are treated as means, but civil society conceives of humans as ends in themselves (Sakamoto 1997), and it is from this perspective that the inequity and alienation that emerge from the market are critically viewed.

Further, not only is there a fundamental tension and contradiction between the market and civil society, but the market with its overriding penetrating power is prevailing over civil society, which is falling behind in its resistance to the market. As such it is unavoidable that to the extent that market liberalization and deregulation proceed, issues such as widening social disparities, increasing inequality and rising unemployment and poverty, all of which are in contradiction to the idea of human beings as ends in themselves, will become prominent even in the developed countries in the North, let alone in the relatively late-developing countries. In the latter, the gap between the rapid penetration of the market and the lag in the formation of civil society is even starker. In fact, this is precisely the defining feature of late-developing countries.

For example, in post-war Japan the penetration of the market affected not only politics but also society and culture, giving rise to categories such as 'economic animal' and 'corporate man', which are incompatible with civil society. In South Korea also it is said that the potent penetration of the market has led to a decay of social and human relations. Furthermore, in the sense that the Korean Peninsula now remains the only arena of the Cold War in the world, the formation of civil society in a unified country is far from complete.

In South Korea, however, as the recent statements of President Kim Dae Jung show, the development and strengthening of democracy as a political culture to counter the dominance of market culture is being emphasized. When Kim Dae Jung was elected, he proclaimed two cardinal tasks for his country – the 'development of the market economy' and the 'development of democracy'. In contrast, almost no Japanese politician calls for the 'development of democracy'. In no way is this because democracy has been sufficiently realized in Japan. As has been exposed by prosecutors over the last few years, the extent of the relationship of structured collusion between conservative politicians, bureaucracy and big business in Japan is beyond description. This is not just a problem of ethics. It unquestionably implies a crisis of democracy where vital decisions about the allocation of resources that affect the lives of citizens are made in places far from their scrutiny. We see, however, virtually no Japanese politicians warning the people of a crisis of democracy.

No doubt anti-democratic practices exist in both Japan and South Korea. The question is whether or not a *sense* of crisis that calls for the 'development of democracy' exists. In this respect there seems to be a huge difference between Kim Dae Jung and Japanese politicians. This has to do with the fact that compared to South Korea, where the people had to achieve democracy through waging their own struggle, the Japanese experience of post-Second World War democratization was much different. Thus even if the political contexts of Japan and South Korea differ, the commonality of confronting the conflict between the market economy and democracy based on civil society exists. Indeed, this is not an issue confined to Japan and South Korea, as we shall now examine.

The Penetration of Market Logic

As history shows, the simultaneous and interlinked progression of the formation and development of a capitalist market economy and democratic civil society was limited to a small number of countries that had industrialized and developed early, such as Britain, later followed by France and the United States. In that sense Britain was the exception rather than the classic model for capitalist development. In other countries, including those that had been colonized, the prevalence of a capitalist market economy with overwhelming penetrating power advanced more quickly than the formation of democracy based on civil society. Although the degree may differ, many of these countries opted for state-protected industrialization and a state-led export orientation in attempting to catch up with the already developed Western nations. These countries also gave priority to statism as opposed to democracy, and to 'ethno-national' community as opposed to civil society. Although important differences exist, such as the fact that Japan and Germany became imperial powers while the newly industrializing economies (NIEs) such as South Korea experienced colonization, there are many similarities between these countries in terms of development models.

In post-Second World War Japan and Germany the formation of civil society began with externally imposed democratization through defeat, while in the NIEs, such as South Korea, it emerged through an internal democratic struggle. However, in the cases of both Japan and South Korea, the state-led market economy, which we may call 'state capitalism' and which defined the political economic structure previous to democratization, exhibited a deeply rooted dominating power that continued to prevail over civil society even after democratization. The state, which did not undergo a civil society-rooted, thorough democratization, inherited a traditional power structure and political culture. It is from here that we see the persistence of a 'crony capitalism' characterized by favouritism, the dominance of former *zaibatsu* and *choebol*, financial irregularities and corruption in the form of the privatization and commodification of power. In post-war Japan, the iron triangle of politicians, bureaucrats and big business, the peculiar form of holding company organization, and the surprisingly widespread structural corruption that has been gradually exposed over recent years all remain strongly rooted as a system, and form what we may call the 'corporate state'. This system, which may be summed up as 'structured collusion', was not just domestic. It also spawned an international complex of corrupt elite linkages between Japan and South Korea, before its democratization.

State institutions and traditional practices performed the function of maintaining the opaqueness of the market and breeding a lack of accountability in both state and market. With that being the case, promotion of market deregulation and liberalization aimed at achieving market independence from the state is bound to promote a broad 'economic rationalization'. In this sense, the IMF intervention presently taking place in Northeast and Southeast Asia should contribute to the 'rationalization' of both state and market.

But will the 'rationalization' of the state and market mean their 'democratization'? In other words, if the state, in a reaction to the globalization of the market economy, becomes a 'market state' giving priority to the logic of the market, will that lead to a democratization of the market and state? It seems likely that making corporate management more transparent will contribute to its rationalization, particularly from the perspective of investors. Unless, however, the state acts in the favour of citizens as a control mechanism against markets and corporations, the result of the rationalization of markets and corporations is likely to reinforce further the logic of the globalization of the market. In fact, previous IMF structural adjustment programmes implemented in mainly Latin America and Africa have paid no more than rhetorical attention to political democratization while giving overwhelming priority to the rationalization of the market economy. There is therefore a necessity to examine the implications of the rapid globalization of the market economy for democracy and civil society.

Contradictions of the Global Market Economy

In the post-Cold War world, the point has been reached where the global market economy holds a dominant position in relation to the state and civil society. This dominance is demonstrated clearly by the recent power of the IMF, the international agent of the logic of globalization, over Asian states. This power has compelled severe sacrifices on the part of the citizens and workers of these countries. Within this primacy and penetration of the global market economy, at present we can delineate three global trends.

The first is the rapid growth of global capital, that is, capital that exhibits a high degree of autonomy from the state, treats the world as a single market, and exercises significant influence on the global market. At the global level, massive amounts of capital are being accumulated at an alarming rate with an increase in multinational corporate mergers and acquisitions, restructuring, alliances and groupings. The top 50 corporations in the world, listed as the 'Global 50' in the magazine *Fortune*, are examples of such globally active corporations earning huge profits. Over 60 per cent of these multinational corporations are US-based. Although they may be referred to as 'global capital', their 'home base' is in the United States where their R&D, essential for competitiveness, are almost exclusively conducted. The fact that these corporations are experiencing high growth is undoubtedly related to the steady growth of the US economy in the last seven years.

The 'Global 50' is made up of, among others, the manufacturing industry (automobiles, etc.), the information and communications industry, the oil industry, and the banking and insurance business. Related to this category are short-term bank loans and portfolio investment (e.g. hedge funds) geared to speculative high profit-making, which have a tremendous impact on the international economy, as was shown by the recent Asian financial crisis. Again related to this speculative global capital is the third type of global capital, which produces huge profits through the speculation and commodification of money itself, namely, foreign exchange. It is said that on an average day more than US$1 trillion, 500 billion are traded in this market. This is a massive amount, equivalent to the GDP of France or Great Britain in 1996.

In the case of the first type of global capital, that is, non-currency 'industrial' multinationals, we can observe large amounts of untaxed earnings due to 'transfer pricing' in which imports and exports are treated as in-house dealings on corporate accounts, utilizing 'tax havens'. In a similar way, the second and third types of cyberspace-based speculation are also hard to capture within the tax system of the modern state, which is in essence based on the idea of territory. In this way, global capital contains a system for tax evasion, increasing the ability to achieve high profits.

Second, the reverse side of the growth of global capital has been destitution at the national level, what we may call 'national impoverishment'. In most countries, we are witnessing state and local government fiscal deficits; deficits in medical, pension and unemployment welfare programmes; and particularly in developing countries household financial deficits, which amount to an absolute decline in income levels. Even in the advanced countries of the North, unemployment gives rise to an increase in households experiencing absolute deprivation. Restructuring and downsizing has led to a large-scale transfer from full-time to part-time work. An increase in the number of 'migrant' people moving from one short-term, part-time job to another is also becoming more apparent.

In short, while it is possible for those who benefit from the high growth of global capital to increase their incomes and to accumulate large amounts of wealth, the citizens who are excluded from these benefits experience relative or absolute deprivation. Public finance is either left to fall into deficit or attempts are made to reduce the deficit through privatization, leaving the destitution of the people to take its own course. At the same time, citizens residing within the territory of the state must faithfully pay taxes.

The increase in this kind of disparity, which accompanies globalization of the market, is prominent even in the United States, which is currently enjoying the highest rates of growth. For example, if we divide the United States' working population into five income brackets and compare 1996 real average income with that of 1990, we see that the top 20 per cent is experiencing by far the highest rate of increase, followed by the next 20 per cent. The average income for the bottom 40 per cent has actually declined. We see here a clear tendency for wealth to concentrate in the higher-income brackets.[2]

'Neoliberalism', which is at the foundation of present-day globalization of the market, is similar to the ideology originally put forward by the most advanced capitalist country of the first half of the nineteenth century, Great Britain. This ideology purports that 'a small government and free competitive market will enrich the nation'. Just as by the 1870s it had become obvious that this logic was leading to a deepening of domestic class conflict and disparity, it seems certain that in today's world this logic will give rise to an increase in the disparity of global wealth.

The third global trend is the universalization of democracy. As mentioned above, this occurred even more in the process of the ending of the Cold War. The fact that the idea of civil society, that is, the idea of the rejection of inequality and injustice and the pursuit of human equality and human rights, has acquired legitimacy on such a broad scale around the world is historically unprecedented. This third trend is in contradiction to and incompatible with the first trend of the high growth of global capital and the second trend of the increased poverty of the state and nation, which are also in contradiction to each other. As long as these fundamental contradictions exist, it is unavoidable that deep-seated tensions and conflicts will emerge.

The ideology of liberal capitalism, which glorified free competition and was centred in Britain in the nineteenth century, now has as its standard-bearer the United States. This ideology is stamped by the traditional American ideal of individualist liberal democracy, as opposed to that of social democracy widely held in Europe, which draws from the history of class conflict and growing disparity since the nineteenth century. It is clear that arguments in favour of the 'global standard' generally mean globalization of the 'American standard'. The real problem, though, is that such arguments only assert 'deregulation' and 'privatization', and neglect the idea that 'global social regulation' is necessary in relation to global capital. What can be seen here is an ideology of market supremacy, what may be called 'market fundamentalism'.

From the various contradictions and conflicts that emerge here, two may be pointed out as particularly important.

The first is the increase in alienated, marginalized people who have failed to be 'winners' in the competitive global market. These include domestically discriminated-against ethnic and racial minorities, women, migrant workers, the low-skilled and low-educated unemployed overtaken by technological innovation, the low-income elderly, the ill, the physically disabled and the homeless. These people are concentrated at the bottom of the social pyramid in large cities around the world in both the North and South. If the globalization of the market and the accompanying increase in disparities continue to spread in an unregulated way, what kind of situation can we expect to arise in the twenty-first century?

It would not be surprising to me if the 'powerless citizens', economically trampled on and concentrated in large cities around the world, indignant over increasing injustice and inequality and driven by a deep despair about the future, were to one day erupt into riot, and that the riot of one city were to spread rapidly in the age of the Internet and CNN to other cities around the world, leading to widespread disturbances. Given that future events cannot be predicted with any degree of certainty, one cannot say that an uprising will definitely occur, but if the present globalization of the market continues in an unregulated fashion, it should come as no surprise if such an uprising actually occurs, since the necessary structural conditions do indeed exist. This kind of uprising would not be limited to a democratic rebellion calling for equality of human rights. Violent exclusionist actions aimed at other races and ethnic groups, together with fascist or fundamentalist direct actions and terrorism, are also possible. In any case, there is no doubt that an extremely destabilized political and social situation would arise.

Neither would this situation of uprisings be particularly new. It has a long history dating back to the nineteenth century — the workers' protest movements, the rebellion of indigenous peoples against colonial rule, the nationalization of foreign assets by developing countries, and more recently the 'nuclear revolt' of the likes of India under the pretext of protesting against the inequality of the Non-Proliferation Treaty regime. The more the logic of global capital is realized, the less the chances of interstate war. However, a global urban uprising might just be the 'world war' of the twenty-first century. This revolt may be even more serious if the growth of global capital were to stop and a worldwide depression were to set in. In order to avoid the danger of such 'war', an idea that transcends the logic of competition is essential.

The second problem that emerges is that the logic of a global *laissez-faire* market can only worsen the degradation of the global environment without having in any way power to prevent ecological crisis. Leading up to the Kyoto conference on the prevention of global warming in 1997, American big business campaigned vigorously against major cuts in greenhouse gas emissions, with the American government also maintaining a negative attitude throughout negotiations. This demonstrates quite clearly that as long as corporations and states, the main two competitive actors in the global market, do not act in a way that transcends the logic of competition, the conservation of the global environment is extremely problematic.

A large number of individuals, and not just corporations and states, also have their own interests legitimated by the logic of competition. For example, in the United States the low price of gasoline is made possible by the strong competitive power of American multinational oil companies. Provided that the American people continue to consider consuming cheap gasoline and driving their automobiles as if it were a 'natural right' to do so, it is difficult for the US government to levy an environmental tax on gasoline. But this is everyone's, and not just the American people's, problem. Somewhere in our consciousness lies the idea that strong competitive power and the possession of material wealth give rise to rights and entitlements, while the 'have-nots' have no rights. As long as this idea, which has been called 'possessive individualism', remains deeply rooted, it will be difficult to solve global environmental issues (Macpherson 1962).

What is vital in coping with the global environmental crisis is the idea of 'cooperation and solidarity' as against 'competition'. At the most fundamental level, what is badly needed is a way of thinking that conceives of human beings and nature from the perspective of end, and not instrumental, values. This perspective is no longer simply an idealistic notion, but has become a physical imperative with the survival of future generations at stake. Looking into the twenty-first century, environmental degradation and the depletion of the earth's natural resources harbour the potential to trigger new forms of conflict and war.

Global Regulation of the Global Market

Despite this, the wave of market liberalization covering trade, finance and currency markets continues to sweep across Asian countries. With the realization of the principles of 'competition' and 'self-help', workers, farmers and small and medium-sized businesses will be immediately exposed to severe international competition, causing large numbers of 'losers', dropouts and unemployed. For neoliberals, this is the result of 'fair competition'. But a good possibility exists that the people who experience head-on the inhumanity of the logic of the global market economy and the resulting breakdown in social linkages could be swept back to the traditional 'imagined communities' of the ethno-national group and state. Yet it is inconceivable that this regressive tendency will generate an effective alternative to the logic of the global market.

In this regard, it must be noted that the global market and global capital are able to exert such profound influence because they possess the means for the rationalization of the exploration and utilization of the world's resources, in other words, the ability to create wealth with a high degree of efficiency. Therefore it would be a mistake to reject this entirely and fall back into 'state capitalism', 'state socialism' and the 'economic bloc' of the 1930s that was centred on a regional hegemonic state. The issue here then is not the outright rejection of the globalization of the market and global capital, but how to regulate them to minimize their negative effects from the perspective of civil society-based public values. And since such regulation solely at the national level is not very effective, the issue of how to establish international public regulation needs to be considered.

Of course, one may expect the regulation of global capital to be carried out by an international organization at the global level. In the 1970s the New International Economic Order was launched in response to the demands of developing countries opposing the gap between the North and the South. In response to this, an information and research centre on multinational corporations was set up at the United Nations, but it had absolutely no powers of regulation. In fact, if one looks at the United Nations system at large, it has been the Bretton Woods institutions of the IMF, World Bank and GATT/WTO that have exercised considerable influence on the world economy. These institutions have, generally speaking, aggressively promoted the logic of market globalization. In the debate about reforming the United Nations, it has been proposed that an 'Economic Security Council' with powers comparable to that of the Security Council be set up to guarantee global equity and welfare in the world economy (Commission on Global Governance 1995). The developed countries in the North, however, have been negative toward the proposal and there seems little possibility of its realization in the near future.

Nevertheless, ignoring the fact that the globalization of the market is turning the world into an economic battlefield of the survival of the fittest is not only unacceptable from the point of view of civil society, but is also dangerous for capital itself. We do find some serious discussion under way on the social regulation of this increased competition. The bare minimum of restrictions that have been suggested so far include: an appropriate global capital tax to check the growth in global disparity; a tax on massive currency speculation (the so-called 'Tobin tax'); a tax levy and legal restrictions to halt and reverse environmental degradation; and international restrictions aimed at abolishing child labour and other forms of excessively low wage labour (see Martin and Schumann 1997 and Group of Lisbon 1995). In order to make the corporate activities of global capital compatible with the requirements of global equity, the objective should be to, on the one hand, regulate its corporate activities, while on the other hand, redistribute tax revenues at the national and global levels. What is necessary is further technical analysis in a variety of areas regarding specific regulatory policies.

In implementing capital regulation, what becomes immediately apparent is that cooperation, and not competition, between states is imperative because past experience has shown that regulating capital in one country leads to its flight to another country. There is no urgent need, however, for all the countries in the world to cooperate in this regulation of capital. It is not profitable for capital to move or flee to another country unless there is a comparable degree of technology and infrastructure in the receiving country. In reality, therefore, it would take only the cooperation of the OECD countries and the NIEs at large to achieve a highly effective global regime of capital regulation.

There is no doubt that Japan and South Korea are continually faced with the problem of how to respond to the globalization of the market and protect their national interests. However, if individual states separately pursue their own interests, the protection of those very individual state interests becomes more problematic. This is one of the severe realities of the globalization of the market.

Of course it would not be easy for an agreement to be reached between the main countries of the OECD and the NIEs. Even if the European Union were to agree, gaining the same acceptance from the United States would not be easy. In contrast to the European Union, where the idea of the 'social economy' – that is, of a certain degree of social regulation of the market – is commonly accepted, the neoliberal United States stands to gain much from the globalization of the market economy. Taking this situation into consideration, Japan and South Korea must face the reality that there is a limit to the resolution of domestic problems, however imminent they may appear, without the implementation of global regulation. To achieve equity and welfare for them, Japan and South Korea should cooperate and internationally call for the promotion of global regulation, without which there is no way to counteract the globalization of the market and the logic of global capital.

Regional Regulation of the Global Market

Such global regulation may not be immediately feasible, but it will sooner or later be unavoidable in some form or other so as to prevent the collapse of world order through the kind of 'world war' mentioned earlier. This should be kept in mind as an issue for the twenty-first century. In the meantime, cooperation for regional regulation by Japan and the Asian NIEs should be initiated so as to take even a small step towards global regulation.

However, as touched on above, in East Asia (for convenience defined as including Northeast and Southeast Asia) the penetration of the logic of the global market performs a double-edged function in the following two respects. First, there is the historical dimension. While the penetration of the logic of the market can be beneficial in sweeping away cronyism and corruption rooted in the traditional regime and culture, it has led to the breakdown of social linkages and fragmentation of the emerging civil society. It seems, therefore, that a critical reconstruction of the traditional culture of the people is also necessary in various social contexts as a way of addressing the problem of how to strengthen a public sphere of citizens' cooperation and solidarity. In a larger context it could be said that later-developed countries have to deal simultaneously with both 'the requirements of modernization' and 'the problematic of modernity'; that is, they must deal with both the 'pre-modern' and the 'postmodern' as inseparable issues.

The second issue concerns the international dimension of the East Asian countries. While they have to a considerable degree succeeded in building national economies, they have been incorporated in the post-Second World War period into the world capitalist economy without experiencing an intermediary regional integration similar to the EC/EU. They have been incorporated into the process of globalization through the almost exclusive mediation of the United States as their largest export market, and a foreign exchange system linked solely with the US dollar as the key currency. In short, it has been asymmetric bilateralism with the United States, not horizontal regional multilateralism. For this reason, the later-developed countries of East Asia have to fulfil simultaneously the tasks of retaining the limited autonomy of their national economies, of building a new regional framework of multilateral cooperation, and of coping with the impact of global market-ization in order to regulate global capital, all for the purpose of protecting and enhancing the democratic rights and legitimate interests of citizens.

In response to the Asian monetary and financial crisis of 1998, Japan, which relies heavily on East Asian markets, has to a certain degree extended external financial assistance, but has been strikingly devoid of ideas for shouldering its responsibility as a country of Asia by increasing domestic demand. Leading Japanese government officials initially resisted US and Asian requests for Japan to increase domestic demand, claiming interference in internal affairs. Even when Japan's position changed to reluctant acceptance, the predominant reason was a concern for relations with the United States, the demands of Asian countries being only a secondary factor. This illustrates clearly just how fragile the sense of a regional identity is despite the existence of an East Asian regional economic network closely linking the domestic with the international.

Thus the East Asian countries are confronting a common historical challenge. They must define their present position while dealing simultaneously with the two dimensions of 'past and present' and 'state, region and world'. If countries find themselves facing common historical issues, it is desirable that common agents be created to deal with those issues. And the presence of common historical tasks suggests the existence of shared conditions for a common response. If the world, moving into the twenty-first century, can be characterized by the primacy of the globalization of the market and the dangerous contradictions inherent in that process, then a fundamental issue will be how to establish agents that are in resistance to the market in order to realize the basic values of civil society such as equity, equality and public welfare. Of course this is a complex issue requiring a diverse approach. Here I would like to suggest two tasks to be undertaken by the countries of East Asia.

Creating a Transnational Public

The first task concerns the issue of how to create agents for regional co-operation in East Asia. The recent currency and financial crisis in Asia has brought to the surface the reality that the region already is, despite the diversity of the conditions of respective countries, in a state of economic interdependence, and, in a sense, has already in practice created an 'economic community' with a common destiny. On the other hand, the fact that the current situation was something that no one had predicted ruthlessly exposed the reality that a conscious, proactive, political framework for regional co-operation has been decisively lacking. So, how might we begin looking for an agent to promote a regime for East Asian regional cooperation that would impose public regulation on the unrestrained globalization of the market?

As I have stated in my book referred to above (Sakamoto 1997), there is a strong possibility that the United States and China as superpowers will define a regional bipolarity in East Asia in the twenty-first century. The existence of Japan and Russia will also be important, but the basic pattern of the United States and China forming a bipolarity will be dominant. Here, despite the many differences in historical conditions between Europe and East Asia, Japan and South Korea must take the initiative for regional cooperation in Northeast Asia within the Sino-US bipolarity, just as Europe, between the poles of the United States and the USSR, took autonomous initiative for regional integration during the Cold War. This is by no means intended to exclude the United States, China and Russia, but only to emphasize that the necessity for Japan and South Korea to take autonomous initiative for regional cooperation is self-evident. If Japan and South Korea become a driving force for regional cooperation in Northeast Asia, and if there is also a deepening of cooperation with ASEAN, there is no doubt that this will lead to an increase in East Asia's regional autonomy *vis-à-vis* the United States and China.

I have argued (Sakamoto 1997) in favour of regional cooperation in terms of the creation and institutionalization of a multilateral East Asian security framework, and there is no doubt that the necessity for this will increase in the future. With the recent regional financial and currency crisis, however, we find the emergence of a pattern where countries hit by the crisis are caught between the United States and the IMF on the one hand and China, which has so far refrained from devaluing its currency, on the other. This pattern suggests a regional international structure for the twenty-first century that has the United States and China forming two economic, as well as security, poles. Such a conception urges Japan and Korea to act promptly as the driving force for regional cooperation.

Given the present-day permeation of the global market force, it is obvious that any regional regulatory response will have certain limits. However, as has been proposed by various sources in the latest financial and currency crisis, a number of measures are possible. Although such measures would require further technical refining, the following could be considered:

1. the establishment of a regional Asian monetary fund for responding promptly to a monetary crisis and preventing a currency speculation spillover to other countries in the region;
2. the employment of a currency basket in line with the conditions of respective countries that would include not only US dollars but also the yen and other currencies in the region, and from next year the Euro;
3. the monitoring and regulation of short-term speculative foreign capital;
4. regional cooperation in the reduction of corporate taxes to prevent countries from falling victim to competition against each other in a bid to attract foreign investment; and
5. mutual humanitarian aid, particularly aid from Japan, for the protection of marginalized people who suffer from a lack of food and medical supplies, economic hardship due to structural unemployment, and so forth.

It must be stated here, however, that the greatest barrier to the building of a firm base for realizing regional cooperation in East Asia lies with Japan, especially with regard to Japan–South Korea relations. The postwar regional integration of Europe would not have been possible had West Germany not reflected deeply on its responsibility for the war, taken positive steps to compensate victims of the Nazis, and reconciled with France, its 'natural enemy' for over two hundred years, and other concerned countries. In contrast, Japan, while making some state-to-state reparations or similar payments, has continued to be ambiguous regarding its responsibility for warfare and colonial rule, and to this day continues to refuse to pay any state compensation to victims. Under these conditions how can reconciliation between Japan and South Korea be possible? And without reconciliation, how can an autonomous initiative for cooperation between the two nations become possible? The gravity of the situation is daunting. Many Japanese citizens are troubled by this problem. For example, many are not convinced by the government's insincere response to the so-called 'comfort women' issue and are left feeling guilty.

At root here is the gap between the state and concerned citizens, but this gap is not just limited to the recognition of historical responsibility. It also relates to the problem of whose cooperation is referred to when we talk about 'the promotion of Japan–South Korea-led regional cooperation'. In fact, in the past under the name of 'cooperation' there were numerous cases of anti-democratic collusion between the Japanese and South Korean governments that were antithetical to the principle of civil society, as illustrated by the ambiguous 'political settlement' of the abduction of Kim Dae Jung in 1973.

The second task is to create not interstate cooperative relations as such, but cooperative relations based on democratic accountability to civil society. Otherwise, regulation of the globalization of the market runs the danger of preserving the vested interests of the privileged within the state. The Suharto regime of Indonesia is a case in point. In contrast, Kim Dae Jung has emphasized the importance of linking the global market-driven rationalization of the economic system with the development of political democracy in South Korea. Kim Dae Jung's idea of a 'democratic market economy' has the potential to become a design for restricting market-driven globalization through the growing transnational linkages of civil society and democracy. It is only this kind of restriction that we can justly call 'public' regulation.

To sum up, cooperative relations should be based on the recognition of the following conditions that characterize the contemporary world. Regulation of global capital cannot be achieved by any single 'sovereign state', and inter-state cooperation is indispensable. Inter-state cooperation will not ensure the protection and promotion of the rights and interests of citizens unless states are under the democratic control of civil society, which is sufficiently powerful to counteract the impact of the globalized market and the corresponding tendency of the state to turn into a subservient 'market state'. The power to be exerted by civil society in the tense relations *vis-à-vis* the state and market will be a critical factor. For civil society to counteract the power of the globalized market, civil society has to, and in fact does, transnationalize itself, providing the state with a transnational foundation for democratic inter-state cooperation. Civil society, including transnational civil society, however legitimate the stand it takes may be, has no formal institutional mechanism of its own to exercise effective, at times coercive, control over the global market. It must, therefore, exert democratic influence through the instrumentality of the state machinery that ensures the enforcement of international rule for the regulation of global capital. It is therefore only on the basis of an association of states which I call 'civic states' that *public* values such as equity, justice, social welfare and human rights can be put into effect to counteract the global market force.

The 'Civic State' in Perspective

The term 'civic state' was coined by myself. 'Civic state' is an abbreviation for 'civil society state', but it is entirely different in meaning from a city-state such as ancient Athens, where 'civic' and 'state' were merged into one notion. In modern terminology, 'civic' and 'state' are separate and even antithetical. Thus the idea of a 'civic state' itself contains contradictions in two respects. First, while it is in the nature of the state to rule based on unequal relations, civil society comprises equal social relations founded on the mutual recognition of human dignity and equal rights. Second, while the state has boundaries and clearly distinguishes between the internal and external, ins and outs, nationals and aliens, civil society, which has generally coincided in modern history with the nation-state, is today in the process of rapidly growing into a set of transnational social relations cutting across national borders, as is shown by countless NGOs and Internet and media networks. One of the reasons I use the term 'civic state' as distinct from 'democratic state' is that, in contrast to a democracy as a political institution that tends to be incorporated into a state framework, contemporary civil society is rapidly developing beyond state boundaries.

In these two respects, the idea of the civic state contains contradictions within itself. In my view, however, these very contradictions inherent in the civic state have positive implications and dynamic potential for the future of world order. States not based on transnational civil society, and contemporary 'nation-states' and civil societies that have clung to the institutional and conceptual framework of exclusionist national sovereignty, will not be viable in the twenty-first century.

An association of civic states, that is, a system of international cooperation formed by civil society-based states, might at first appear to be a Utopian idea, but this is not the case. To a considerable extent it is already becoming a reality with the formation of the European Union. While conflicts of national interests and various private interests are obviously still present in the EU, we can also point to the following four basic characteristics that have sustained the viability and strengthening of the European Union as an organization of regional cooperation and integration despite passing through many deadlocks and crises over the years:

1. Member governments have based their actions on the principle of democratic accountability toward their citizens. A prerequisite for this has been the democratization of political regimes. The European Union would not have been possible if Germany were still under Nazi rule.

2. Based on the first, efforts have been made to achieve regional integration through rational inter-state coordination and compromise, minimizing the risk of the recurrence of the irrational confrontations and warfare that characterized Europe for centuries.[3]

3. A political culture has been consolidated where the state acts in cooperation and consultation with NGOs. A cooperative division of labour is becoming increasingly common for governments and NGOs, for instance in the running of domestic welfare programmes, the implementation of foreign aid, and international conferences on the environment, human rights and disarmament.

4. The civil society of each country acts on the basis of the transnational development of a similar political culture in neighbouring nations. In other words, while preserving cultural diversity, a general convergence of *political* culture is under way, with transnational linkages between civil societies and NGOs becoming an everyday practice.

In short, there has been a parallel development of international cooperation at the state level and transnational linkages at the civil society level. These two layers interact in a tense relationship of civic checks on the government on the one hand, and a cooperative division of labour between civil society and the state on the other, with democratic accountability acting as the linking and mediating principle. Only with this kind of regional cooperation based on 'civic states' has the possibility emerged for Europe to pursue a 'social market economy' model that values the public good and social welfare, which includes regulation over the American, neoliberal type of globalization of the market. Of course, for similar conditions to be fulfilled in East Asia, numerous changes and reforms are necessary. However, the fact that this is already occurring in Europe, where the sovereign state system first came into being, provides significant new ideas for envisioning the future of East Asia with the twenty-first century on the horizon.

A transnational civil society that counteracts the dynamics of a transnational economy, while expanding in parallel with it, lies at the base of the transformation of the sovereign state and the emergence of a new regional cooperation. This process is leading to the creation of region-wide democratic public spaces based on the 'power of the powerless'. Achieving global regulation of the globalized market, based on cooperation between these region-wide democratic public spaces, may not be easy. However, just as we saw when the seemingly impossible end of the Cold War was realized, we would be advised to take heed that one of the salient features of the contemporary world is 'the power of the powerless' and its potential to act as the driving force of great transformation.

Notes

1. Revised version of keynote address, Hallym University Symposium, Seoul, Korea, 29 May 1998. Translation assisted by Gregory C. Ellis.

2. *Yomiuri Shimbun*, 15 December 1997; *Asahi Shimbun*, 18 June 1998.

3. These first two characteristics of the civic state can also be seen in reactions by certain states to the issues of nuclear armaments and proliferation. Argentina and Brazil were long considered as two major powers poised to engage in a nuclear arms race in South America. With the fall of military regimes in both countries through the process of democratization, we have witnessed an abandoning of the nuclear option, and a move toward the creation of a common market and a 'zone of peace'. In South Africa also nuclear weapons were renounced in the process of the democratic transformation of the apartheid system.

References

Commission on Global Governance (1995) *Our Global Neighbourhood*, Oxford University Press, New York.

Group of Lisbon (1995) *The Limits to Competition*, MIT Press, Cambridge, MA.

Havel, V. (1985) 'The power of the powerless', in J. Keane (ed.), *The Power of the Powerless: Citizens against the State in Central-Eastern Europe*, Hutchinson, London.

Macpherson, C. B. (1962) *The Political Theory of Possessive Individualism*, Oxford University Press, New York.

Martin, H. P. and H. Schumann (1997) *The Global Trap*, Zed Books, London.

Sakamoto Yoshikazu (1997) *Sotaika no Jidai* (The Age of Relativization), Iwanami Shinsho, Tokyo.

II

Collective Action and Development

8

The Local Dimensions of
Global Reform

FANTU CHERU

Globalization, a phenomenon brought about by technological revolutions, is an increasingly important dimension of international economic relations in terms of its implications for trade, productive investment and finance. In both the mainstream media and corporate boardrooms, globalization is presented as the only avenue that will bring unprecedented world prosperity and freedom in the post-Cold War era (Barnet and Cavanagh 1994). Others, however, characterize globalization as the greatest threat to potential human development. They point out that as the remote forces of globalization hobble governments and disintegrate the bonds of social solidarity, anger is growing among those whose existence is being threatened (Barber 1996; Mittelman 1996). Despite these divergent points of view, the long-term implications of globalization remain unclear. Furthermore, whether it is possible to build a strong transnational civil society movement to curtail the growth of the structural power of capital remains to be seen.

Although it is tempting to indulge in an academic exercise of constructing scenarios or proposing the creation of special UN agencies for specific global reforms, the best contribution I can make as an African is to highlight the constraints to be overcome, and the opportunities that remain to be exploited, in African societies for constructing a just and sustainable social order at local and national levels, and how these local efforts can be used as stepping-stones towards global reform. For progressive movements in the North, an understanding of the African reality on the 'ground' is the first step towards developing joint programmes on issues of common concern that affect the future of humanity. *Effective social formations of resistance, redistribution or trans-formation cannot be theoretically prescribed or academically engineered. Instead of focusing on a unifying conception of society and transformation, we must look for a workable sense of cohesion to emerge out of the seemingly irreconcilable modes of resistance waged from below.*

This chapter attempts to map the contours of the 'pro-globalization' versus 'resistance to globalization' debate and to present some concrete suggestions on how both Northern and Southern social movements, through joint actions, can carve out a middle ground aimed at harnessing the opportunities offered by globalization while pre-empting its negative consequences. Specifically, the experiences of African governments in reconstituting hegemonic accords in the neoliberal restructuring of their economies are examined, as well as the latent resistance from the citizenry to these policies. Finally, the chapter presents the appropriate parameters of state–society–market relations required to build a just, egalitarian and democratic global community.

Globalization and Neoliberalism

Globalization and liberalization are depicted as the fast lane to higher levels of development. With the collapse of communism, the neoclassical liberal economic model has emerged as the dominant model of the new global economic order. The proponents of neoliberalism argue that the debt-ridden countries in Africa and the newly emerging countries of Eastern Europe can pull themselves out of poverty and underdevelopment by shifting their development paradigm from development planning, with an active and commanding role for the state, to devaluation, deregulation, liberalization and privatization – in short, installing market fundamentals under the iron discipline of the trinity of the IMF, World Bank and WTO. And in the process, these countries are expected to replicate the successful experiences of the newly industrializing countries of East Asia.

Since the early 1980s, a large and growing number of developing countries have embarked (some reluctantly, under pressure from the multilateral development banks) on the liberalization of their trade and foreign investment regimes, as well as the adaptation of their domestic economic structures and strengthening of their export capacity. Between 1980 and 1986 alone, 36 sub-Saharan African countries initiated 241 adjustment programmes. Most have had multiple programmes, with 11 implementing 10 or more. One decade later, the role of the state in Africa has been significantly curtailed, the dominance of market forces is now in place, and economies have been opened wide to external penetration. In short, globalization and structural adjustment are mutually reinforcing.

The initial expectations that structural adjustment programmes could bring rapid economic recovery were unrealistic. Substantial economic turnaround has not occurred in any of the countries that introduced them, living standards for the majority have declined, and investment in the productive and social sectors of the economy has dwindled. The retreat of the state in key areas of social services has left enormous gaps that have at times been filled by local survival initiatives. Reform has become necessary to satisfy external creditors, and not adequately internalized as a domestic requirement for growth (Gibbon and Olukoshi 1996). This has given way to popular resistance from below.

Although developing countries can learn a lot from the experience of NICs, the recipe they followed was entirely different from that being prescribed by the apologists of liberalization and deregulation (Smith 1991). First, the Asian countries developed as an extension of an American economic and military strategy in the context of the Cold War. Large amounts of capital were provided to these bastion outposts of the East–West confrontation, and their access to markets in the United States was relatively free (Broad and Cavanagh 1988; Frank 1991).

Furthermore, the Asian 'Tigers' never entrusted to the market or to foreign investors the task of deciding which industries should prosper and which ones should fail. Instead, the respective governments devised different incentives to encourage their infant industries until they carved out a competitive niche in the world market. In the case of industries that were not competitive, programmes were developed to help them diversify or phase out, and their workers were retrained. Land reform, the upgrading of infrastructure, the development of indigenous technological capacity and the strengthening of domestic demand, consumption and investment followed this (Bello and Rosenfeld 1990; Fishlow et al. 1994). Only once this had been achieved, did they reorient their investments to the export market. Therefore, they managed to achieve market-driven economic restructuring without incurring high economic and social costs.

The experience of Africa, in the context of economic globalization and onerous debt accompanied by disciplinary neoliberalism, has been quite the opposite. Notwithstanding the adoption of misguided national policies and mismanagement by local elites, economic adjustment and liberalization have been forced down the throats of African people against the background of depressed commodity prices, declining foreign assistance, withdrawal of private lending, increased Northern protectionism and unsustainable levels of debt (Cheru 1989; Barrat Brown and Tiffen 1992; Mihevc 1995). Therefore, few African countries have achieved creditably in terms of any of the indicators that measure real, sustainable development. Instead, most have slid backwards into growing inequality, ecological degradation, de-industrialization and poverty. Adjustment has been achieved by curtailing investment in social services and by incurring more debt.

As the NICs' case demonstrates, it is important to recognize that the state has an important role to play in national development, and that the state is not necessarily or inevitably parasitic or corrupt. Indeed, the G-7-supported reform process in Africa and the former East European countries actually requires a strengthening of key aspects of the state apparatus, although the rhetoric of structural adjustment and 'systemic transformation' suggests otherwise. In its latest *World Development Report* (1998), which focuses on the state, the World Bank now acknowledges the central role of the state in national development. This, however, does little to undo the damage already done in the Third World over the last decade, all in the name of efficiency and global integration.

Limits of Globalization 'from Above'

Despite increasing global linkages, however, the process of globalization is by no means complete, and developing countries should not pin their hopes on liberalization to pull them out of the current economic and political crisis. While most developing countries will gain economically from the globalization process, some will benefit more than others. A number of countries with initial conditions that make them less suited to take advantage of globalization will lose out and become more marginalized in relation to other countries.

For example, East Asia has gained the most to date from globalization, and the situation of much of Latin America, though still fragile, appears promising. Sub-Saharan Africa, on the other hand, shows little sign of being able to benefit at this time despite more than a decade and a half of liberalization efforts under the watchful eye of the IMF. These reforms have been necessary to satisfy external creditors, and have not been adequately internalized as domestic requirements for growth and transformation. The basic institutional, infrastructural and human resources required for initiating meaningful transformation are in short supply.

The most crucial impact of globalization and liberalization has been on the role of the state in national development. As Cox (1987) suggests, the state no longer primarily acts as a buffer against the world economy, but plays an integral role in facilitating globalization. This situation is not entirely limited to Third World governments. Surrounded by impersonal forces beyond their control, leaders have a diminished scope. In many European countries, such as France and other social democracies, there has always been the conviction that political planning should prevail over the whims of the market. Yet, with growing unemployment and profound malaise, there is little governments can do to help alleviate the problems of high unemployment and declining living standards. These governments are bound by strict spending curbs mandated by European economic integration, partly a response to the competitive demands of the global marketplace.

The resentment and rebelliousness they provoke among the governed further compound the problems facing leaders. Many people have a sense of uncertainty, a feeling of futility and a worry that uncontrollable forces are now at large. The losers in global restructuring try to reassert themselves through organized resistance (Cheru 1989; Beckman 1992). In some countries, the immediate public response is withdrawal from the political process; in others, there is outrage and criticism. As antagonisms increase, energies and efforts are dissipated and leadership is at risk of losing credibility. The real challenge now is how to channel this discontent towards a more constructive and transformative project aimed at establishing a post-hegemonic and post-globalizing world order.

Marginalization: a First Step towards Transformation

Many countries in Africa and elsewhere have tried to respond to the challenge posed by globalization in two ways. The first has been to *embrace globalization* as a development strategy. 'If you can't fight globalization, you may as well join it' is the slogan most used by aspiring countries such as Mexico. The state becomes a conduit for capital as opposed to an arbiter and enforcer of social equity. However, this strategy will do nothing to reduce dependence and marginalization. As the recent Mexican crisis demonstrated, such a strategy is not sustainable politically and economically in the long run.

The second response has been to *resist globalization* and liberalization. A handful of Third World countries have openly tried to defy the policies of the institutions of the world system, particularly the policies of structural adjustment and repressive reintegration. The World Bank and Western donors successfully countered these feeble efforts, and the agitators were brought back in line one by one, without defaulting a cent on the debts they owed to creditor nations.

The failure of both 'accommodationist' and 'resistance' strategies in the past forces us to examine a particular African discourse on transformation that suggests that large-scale marginalization should not necessarily be viewed negatively. It could instead provide a compelling occasion to redefine African priorities away from global integration and toward self-reliance and new regionalism, to recognize informal economies, and to encourage informal politics, particularly civil society at a regional level (Shaw 1994). As the late Claude Ake succinctly put it:

> Perhaps marginalization, so often decried, is what Africa needs right now. For one thing, it will help the evolution of an endogenous development agenda, an agenda that expresses the aspirations of the people and can therefore elicit their support. Because of exogeneity, and its contradictions, Africa does not even at this late stage have a development agenda. (Ake 1996)

In sum, Ake concludes that ordinary Africans cannot escape from under-development until public policy becomes an expression of their democratic will and connects again with social needs. This does not imply de-linking. Rather, it suggests that Africa will have to force its way into the new global arrangement on its own terms rather than be pulled into it. In order to do this, Africans must continue to expand the self-scrutiny and 'decolonization of imagination' that have been under way for some time now. To be specific, development can be related to and driven by social will only in the context of democracy.

Northerners might find Ake's analysis troubling, since it does not fit their world view and the appropriate route for global transformation. Unfortunately, processing politics through categories more appropriate to the political reality of Western societies often misses the logic of politics in the Third World. To reject alternative intentions as a legitimate expression is to deny others unlike oneself the capacity to structure life along different notions of social development. These issues are central to the discourse on globalization.

Globalization 'from Below' and Transformative Resistance

Both state and market have more often than not proved unable by themselves to offer solutions to the numerous problems that humanity faces. They are part more of the problem than of the solution. Citizens and their associations, together forming what Nerfin (1987) calls 'the third system', may be better able to ensure the continuation of life on this planet. The 1990s began with extraordinary public protest against systems that left little room for citizens' participation on matters that affect their lives. The flag-bearers of this new renaissance are based in the church, the informal sector, human rights movements, grassroots ecology movements and development NGOs that have sprung up all across Africa in the last decade to articulate alternative visions of survival and democratic governance (McCormick 1989; Scott 1990; Cheru 1996). They employ both overt and hidden forms of resistance, thus pressing demands on the state through the 'politics of claims', non-payment of taxes and open insurrections. These new social movements advance the idea that development is a human right, and that its achievement requires popular participation and control.[1]

Even in the United States, a country that has benefited a great deal from globalization, internal contradictions and the call for reform are growing louder. Wypijewski describes the extensive organizing sweeping across the United States, largely promoted by the stirring of labour, the dismemberment of welfare as we knew it, the boldness with which big money controls the law-making machinery of the country: organizing is in the air again:

> Privatization, globalization, a corporate system that rewards the average CEO at a rate 173 times the wage of the average employee (in real terms, executive pay is up about 300 percent since 1980, workers' wages down 12 percent); the explosion in temporary work, part-time work, low-wage work; the ascendance of workfare, of prison labor; the assaults on immigrants and poor people, of unions, currently losing 150,000 souls each year. (Wypijewski 1997: 17–25)

The fundamental issue around which people are organizing principally deals with the distribution of wealth and power, and the subordination of human rights to corporate rights. In the process, such groups have become politically conscious and are educating themselves in organizational dynamics and self-government at the local level.[2]

Local-level resistance in isolation from potential allies in other countries and regions will have limited impact. And indeed many social movements have discovered that their possibilities were limited within the framework of existing domestic political institutions. Consequently, many have made the jump directly from local activity into the international arena (Korten 1990). A worldwide network of NGOs devoted to specific issues (ecology, human rights, indigenous peoples' movements, etc.) has served as a conduit for leaders of social movements from many countries to bring their concerns to international attention (for example in Rio, Beijing, Copenhagen and Istanbul) often putting their governments on the defensive. In the North American context, for example, hundreds of citizen groups (with both left and right orientations) from Mexico, Canada and the USA mobilized to challenge elite perspectives in the NAFTA debate (Rupert 1997). This strategy is necessary because problems that affect the poor and the marginalized cut across national borders. The North–South popular alliance becomes even more crucial when viewed in the context of the considerable power held by elites and firms that underpin the globalization process.

Cautious Pragmatism

Despite tremendous strides made in the past decade in building global movements around specific issues of mutual concern, the eventual destination of new social movements in many parts of the world and their prospects for reaching critical mass are far from clear; they are not nearly as clear as the supporters of the NGO movement claim (e.g. Mathews 1997). In the specific case of Africa, the vibrancy of these new institutions of civil society contrasts with the paucity of their strategic power and resources. Organizing around daily subsistence increasingly consumes much of people's energy and meagre resources, thus making the task of developing a counter-project exceptionally difficult and slow.

It is particularly unrealistic to expect overburdened African social movements to divide their limited energy and resources between pressing local 'livelihood' issues and global reform. The more the representatives of African social movements spend their time on worthy international campaigns that are little understood by their own constituencies, and devote less time to critical local 'bread-and-butter and rights' issues, the more they risk losing legitimacy and fostering an ethic of isolationism. The most visible civic movements, including NGOs, could not function effectively or even survive without external financial support. The groups subsist on life-support systems provided by the North. This dependency limits independent initiatives and influences their priorities and agendas, unless by some coincidence the external agencies and the local groups have identical plans, aspirations and goals. Therefore, in our effort to link local resistance to global reform, we must find answers to the following question: how can the negative effects of external funding – on agenda-setting, prioritization of issues, accountability to foreign interests, external ideological direction and the ability to survive over the long-term – be addressed?

The biggest challenge in the coming decades is therefore three-fold: how to strengthen those internal forces that are best placed to defend the democratic project in their respective communities; how to enable them to develop a long-range strategic and sustainable economic agenda; and how to mobilize the necessary resources to fulfil these objectives. When people overcome the local/national obstacles to their development, they are prepared to make the jump to global struggles. In other words, in our effort to mount global reform, we should not neglect the most pressing issues at the local level. As Mary Hollnsteiner (1979) observed in the Philippines, it takes a long time for poor people living on the margin to move from simple, concrete and short-term personal issues to more complex, abstract, long-term and systemic issues. Until the tasks of local capacity-building and awareness-creation are completed, we should not waste people's time and limited resources on a hopeless intellectual exercise.

The idea of resistance is simply not enough. We have to come up with innovative proposals at local, sub-regional and regional levels aimed at the rehabilitation of both states and market, the democratization of civil society, capacity-building and institutionalization, and the continued coordination of activities and exchange of information and best practices with other social movements at all levels. Central to this undertaking is the recognition and respect of 'people's knowledge and reality' that may be expressed in non-Western discourse. There is no single formula for how individuals and communities go about 'decoding' the ideology of developmentalism or globalization. Even in areas where there is consensus across continents, the steps communities take will differ, depending on local conditions and a realistic assessment of risks and gains.

Now the most common form of transnational organizing for global reform is the practice of lobbying governments through the vehicle of specialized UN conferences. Important though the declarations are that have come out of the numerous UN conferences in recent years, the various global agreements have been ignored. The key problem has been the emphasis on the global institutional fix, such as the creation of specialized UN agencies and the signing of global agreements whose enforcement is questionable. For example, the most recent review by the United Nations on progress in the implementation of the Rio agreements concluded that finger-pointing and foot-dragging on the part of governments has led to self-destruction and little progress in implementing what had been agreed upon in Rio. This is partly attributed to the inability of local/national groups dealing with environmental issues in each country to make their own governments accountable. Therefore, the lesson from Rio is that civil society groups must always be vigilant if they are to succeed in realizing the objectives they have set out.

What is to be Done?

Despite increasing contact among people across the globe, it is premature to declare and celebrate the emergence of a cohesive global civil society movement. We must avoid making broad generalizations from the few transnational social mobilizations for global reform on specific issues that have been successful. Even in the highly publicized case of global ecology movements, implementation of the Rio Treaty, which they helped negotiate, has fallen far short of expectations. While NGO access to global institutions has improved, the door remains firmly shut to certain key institutions that have tremendous power to affect our lives (Krut 1997). Social movements in the South, with limited resources and weak organizational bases, have in particular not been able to monitor compliance by national governments, let alone gain access to key powerful global institutions. Because these local social movements are engaged in many other issues besides the environment, their meagre human and financial resources are stretched too far. It would be irresponsible to ignore this African reality in our discussions of future world orders.

While we should strive to build a global civil society movement to counter the growing structural power of capital, we should also acknowledge that a significant portion of that work has yet to begin. The first observation is that, with respect to many Third World institutions and social movements, the basic institutional pillars and the means required to strengthen them are not yet in place. While some NGOs in the popular sector have become more effective, many have not. We should not lump all NGOs and organizations together. There exist different forms of hierarchy in the popular sector, in terms of resources, strategic vision and analytic and lobbying skills. In addition, many factors such as culture, race, class and gender divide the popular sector more than the issues are able to unite it. These problems are prevalent at the local, national and regional levels.

Concerning resistance against globalization and marginalization in parts of the Third World and Eastern Europe, the evidence is rather mixed now. Some forms of 'democratization' may not necessarily involve the development of progressive forces. The proliferation of new social movements can splinter civil society and fragment political life. For example, in the East European countries, we have witnessed a rise in right-wing populism and a resurgence of fascist political movements. In the Third World, resistance to the process of commodification and rationalization of social life has given rise to religious fundamentalism, some of which has a socially repressive character (Gill and Cheru 1997). It is therefore important to identify potential agents of transformation in diverse contexts and to build a durable transnational civil society movement to check the excesses of the forces of globalization.

The third observation deals with the dilemma of the agenda mix for social movements in their relations with the state. Should civil society always be in confrontation with the state, or should civil society be viewed as one stage in the development of community on the way to becoming a state? Or should it be viewed in terms of the relationship of the state to people – as an interface between people and the state? A comprehensive development alternative cannot go far enough without a basic change in power structures. Until this happens the popular sector can only pressure government for some policy changes and accumulate little victories here and there. This implies that the popular sector has to come up with a state agenda of its own and suggests entering the terrain of the nation-state: national politics.

Here lies precisely the dilemma of people's organizations. By their nature, their main concern is social politics – in other words, self-governance whose success is measured mainly in terms of the circles or poles of popular power that they create at the base. In this context, state politics is of a different world. And yet, civil society has to grapple with the unavoidable agenda mix. In an attempt to navigate through this dilemma, they face other problems that tend to confuse their identity and undermine their core values, such as autonomy, pluralism, diversity, volunteerism and closeness to the grassroots, bottom-up perspective. Therefore, they will have to find the appropriate combination of strategies to handle effectively the contradictory trajectories of state politics, which is integrative or centralizing, and social politics, which is horizontal or centrifugal.

Stages in between Local Resistance and Global Reform

In the final analysis, resistance against the forces of globalization and against the social coalitions that continue to perpetuate poverty and oppression in Africa will take many forms, and the outcome will depend on the capacity of the forces of civil society to gain sufficient influence to qualify as a genuine counter-project rather than merely as a societal tendency confined to the margins of policy. This implies that the popular sector must have another political agenda over and above its main business of disempowering central-ized structures. In other words, it has to come up with a state agenda of its own. This will depend on progress in the following areas:

CONSOLIDATING THE STRUGGLE FOR DEMOCRACY Some of Africa's problems can be addressed by extending the process of political reform and governmental restructuring downwards. Democratizing democracy is the only real option for reducing corruption, making political systems more responsive and bettering the lot of the poor. Decentralization and the strengthening of local governments are essential for opening up new avenues for people's participation in public life. The consolidation of democracy could make an important contribution towards framing policies conducive to economic recovery, equity and accountability at the local level, and could facilitate efforts for regional and global reforms.

Since 1989, Africa has witnessed a democratic revolution, which has shaken the foundations of authoritarianism and autocracy across the region. That revolution, driven by popular demands from below, is unfinished and under a twin threat: from unrepresentative regimes bent on retaining power at any price, and from the social tensions generated by poverty. The conditioning of aid on the implementation of free elections and free markets further compounds the problem. Almost all the donor-driven democratization initiatives are designed to secure peaceful political order and not necessarily political freedom.

STRENGTHENING CIVIL SOCIETY MOVEMENTS One cannot hope to build a vibrant global civil society movement when its constituent parts – the local social movements – are weak and fragmented. People's capacity for participation in the creation of sustainable communities must be strengthened through efforts to expand rapidly people's organization and awareness. Only by enlarging visions and raising consciousness can people undermine the vicious circle of mass exclusion and marginalization. Democracy cannot work without a high level of information and knowledge. This is a crucial area too often neglected when we talk about mobilizing people and involving grassroots organizations. Capacity-building entails leadership training for both men and women. Building locally based research capacity, developing networking/ negotiation and lobbying skills, and dissemination of information are all necessary. Institution-building would also involve improving communication flow between communities and different sets of institutions, both urban and rural, thus helping peasants become a catalyst for change.

BUILDING INCLUSIVE ALLIANCES Alliances must be built across classes and sectors. It is important to recognize and work with natural allies within existing institutions, including government and the international donor and financial institutions, who share the vision or can be enlisted to its cause. Those who are working for international reform can benefit from the pressure of citizen action. Care must be taken, however, to avoid co-optation, recognizing that the objective requires the transformation, not simply the fine-tuning, of inappropriate institutions. Many of Africa's problems may demand interventions at the local, national and/or regional level. The interventions at each level could include input drawn from local, national or global partners. Therefore, to the extent that North–South solidarity is deemed necessary, the ultimate responsibility for defining African priorities must rest with Africans themselves.

PROMOTING COLLECTIVE SELF-RELIANCE/SOUTH–SOUTH COOPERATION The greatest assurance of Africa's security would be for the continent to seek economic relations that emphasize the imperatives of our own self-reliance more than charity does. South–South cooperation, in the context of globalization and liberalization, need not aim at some kind of autarchy or self-contained growth, whether on a sub-regional or even inter-regional basis. It should seek rather to profit from such opportunities that globalization and liberalization might provide as well as the limitations of the process (Cheru 1992). The strategy should aim at speeding up and supplementing South–South linkages that are likely to emerge spontaneously as the economies of developing countries expand.

South–South cooperation faces its greatest obstacle in the failure to elaborate effective mechanisms to facilitate South–South transfers; in other words, to establish the modalities that would permit active, meaningful and regular exchanges among the countries concerned. This would, for example, involve the establishment of sub-regional and regional networks connecting different professions (i.e. chambers of commerce, research institutions, consultancy firms, professional associations, labour confederations, etc.) whose services and expertise could be accessed by policy-makers, community groups and the private sector.

INCREASING PEOPLE'S ACCESS TO INFORMATION The future of humanity depends on a basic transformation in thought and action, leading people to rediscover their essential humanity and to recreate their relationships with one another and between themselves and their environment. This requires expanding people's access to relevant information so that social and environmental impact can be assessed, and they can take necessary actions to protect their interests.

A good example is UNDP's Sustainable Development Network (SDN) programme. A direct result of the 1992 Rio Earth Summit, SDN has already linked together government organizations, the private sector, universities, NGOs and individuals in 24 developing countries through electronic and other networking vehicles for the express purpose of exchanging critical information on sustainable development (Rawkins et al. 1997). Accessibility to information for all levels of civil society is particularly important in developing countries that are undergoing difficult transitions to democracy.

North–South solidarity must be built on the basis of equal partnership and on the recognition that poor people's knowledge about their own reality (and how they might go about solving their problems) counts most, even when that local perspective appears on the surface to be inconsistent with (or less relevant than) the analysis and wishes coming from the North. After all, the local is part of the global, and one should not treat it differently. The vast majority of people in the developing world have living memories of development failures, and of domination and manipulation from outside. Previous experiments concerning North–South solidarity that were not based on the principle of partnership have done nothing but cast doubt and confusion. Unless mutual confidence is developed between Northern and Southern social movements and a real partnership is established, new and externally developed cooperative initiatives will continue to be seen as a threat to local initiatives and self-reliance.

The key to building durable social solidarity will depend on the degree to which Westerners are willing to accept and learn from Third World political expression that explores religious or historical themes using non-Western or indigenous means. Instead of insisting that the people of the Third World join in the debate on global transformation using terms and political discourse appropriate to the reality of Western societies, we must make the effort to build true partnership with Third World people by recognizing the validity of their analysis, and by trying at least to understand those cultural, historical and religious forms of political expression.

Notes

1. UN Economic Commission for Africa, 1990, *African Charter for Popular Participation in Development and Transformation*, Addis Ababa; Asian NGO Coalition and the Environmental Liaison Center International, 1990, 'The Manila Declaration on People's Participation and Sustainable Development', *IFDA Dossier*, no. 75/76, pp. 45–50.

2. For a sympathetic account of such undertakings, see Pradervand 1989 and Ekins 1992.

References

Ake, C. (1996) *Democracy and Development in Africa*, Brookings Institution, Washington, DC.

Barber, B. (1996) *Jihad vs. McWorld*, Ballantine Books, New York.

Barnet, R. and J. Cavanagh (1994) *Global Dreams: Imperial Corporations and the New World Order*, Simon and Schuster, New York.

Barrat Brown, M. and P. Tiffen (1992) *Shortchanged: Africa and World Trade*, Pluto Press/ TNI, London.

Beckman, B. (1992) 'Empowerment or repression? The World Bank and the politics of African adjustment', in P. Gibbon, Y. Bangura and A. Ofstad (eds), *Authoritarianism, Democracy and Adjustment*, Scandinavian Institute of African Studies, Uppsala, pp. 83–105.

Bello, W. and S. Rosenfeld (1990) *Dragons in Distress: Asia's Miracle Economies in Crisis*, Institute for Food and Development, San Francisco.

Broad, R. and J. Cavanagh (1988) 'No more NICs', *Foreign Policy*, 72: 81–103.

Cheru, F. (1989) *The Silent Revolution in Africa: Debt, Development and Democracy*, Zed Books, London.

— (1992) *The Not So Brave New World! Problems and Prospects for Regional Integration in Post-Apartheid Southern Africa*, Bradlow Occasional Series no. 6, South African Institute of International Affairs, Johannesburg.

— (1996) 'New social movements: democratic struggles and human rights in Africa, in J. Mittelman (ed.), *Globalization: Critical Reflections*, Lynne Rienner, Boulder, CO.

Cox, R. (1987) *Production, Power, and World Order: Social Forces in the Making of History*, Columbia University Press, New York.

Ekins, P. (1992) *A New World Order: Grassroots Movements for Global Change*, Routledge, London.

Fishlow, A. et al. (1994) *Miracle or Design? Lessons from the East Asian Experience*, Policy Essay no. 11, Overseas Development Council, Washington, DC.

Frank, A. G. (1991) 'No escape from the laws of world economics', *Review of African Political Economy*, 50: 20–31.

Gibbon, P. and A. O. Olukoshi (1996) 'Structural adjustment and socio-economic change in sub-Saharan Africa', Research Report no. 102, Scandinavian Institute of African Studies, Uppsala.

Gill, S. and F. Cheru (1997) 'Democratization and globalization: the G-7 "nexus" and the limits of structural adjustment in Africa, Eastern Europe and Russia', in S. Gill (ed.), *Globalization, Market Civilization, and Disciplinary Neoliberalism*, Macmillan, London.

Hollnsteiner, M. (1979) 'Mobilizing the rural poor through community organization', *Philippine Studies*, 27 (3): 387–411.

Korten, D. (1990) *Getting to the 21st Century*, Kumarian Press, Hartford, CT.

Krut, R. (1997) *Globalization and Civil Society: NGO Influence in International Decision-Making*, UNSRID Discussion Paper no. 83, Geneva.

McCormick, J. (1989) *Reclaiming Paradise: The Global Environmental Movement*, Indiana University Press, Bloomington.

Mathews, J. (1997) 'Power shift', *Foreign Affairs*, January/February: 50–66.

Mihevc, J. (1995) *The Market Tells Them So: The World Bank and Economic Fundamentalism in Africa*, Third World Network, Accra.

Mittelman, J. (ed.) (1996) *Globalization: Critical Reflections*, Lynne Rienner, Boulder, CO.

Nerfin, M. (1987) 'Neither prince nor merchant: citizen, an introduction to the third system', *Development Dialogue*, 1: 170–95.

Pradervand, P. (1989) *Listening to Africa: Developing Africa from the Grassroots*, Praeger, New York.

Rawkins, P., F. Cheru, E. de Silva, M. Gonzales and M. Kesseba (1997) *Global, Inter-Regional and Regional Programmes: An Evaluation of Impact*, UNDP, New York.

Rupert, M. (1997) 'Globalization and contested common sense in the United States', in S. Gill and J. Mittelman (eds), *Innovation and Transformation in International Studies*, Cambridge University Press, Cambridge, pp. 138–52.

Scott, A. (1990) *Ideology and the New Social Movements*, Unwin Hyman, London.

Shaw, T. (1994) 'The South in the new world (dis)order: towards a political economy of Third World foreign policy in the 1990s', *Third World Quarterly*, 15 (1): 17–30.

Smith, S. C. (1991) *Industrial Policy in Developing Countries*, Economic Policy Institute, Washington, DC.

World Bank (1998) *World Development Report 1998*, Washington, DC.

Wypijewski, J. (1997) 'A stirring in the land', *The Nation*, 15 August: 17–25.

Poverty and the Politics of Alternatives at the End of the Millennium

MICHAEL WATTS

The 19th century is not yet over. (Richard Sennett)

[Modernity] is a mode of vital experience ... that is shared by men and women all over the world today. To be modern is to find ourselves in an environment that promises us adventure, power, joy, growth, transformation of ourselves and the world – and at the same time that threatens to destroy everything we have, everything we know, everything we are. (Marshall Berman, *All that is Solid Melts into Air*)

It is perhaps a sign of our times that any discussion of reimagining development or development alternatives in the 1990s begins with the word, with language and with discourse. And from there it is a very short step to the 'idea' of poverty, to the 'invention' and social construction of development, and, within a cybercultural moment, to the virtuality of everything (to Baudrillard's Nietzschean cry: 'down with all hypotheses that have allowed a belief in the true world' (1983: 15)). Alternatives, like everything else, can be imagined at will; it's construction all the way down. Alternatives must be built *with,* not on, the ruins of capitalist modernization – a conundrum that Richard Falk (1996) calls 'rooted Utopianism'.

The intellectual field that constitutes the new critiques of development – one thinks of the work of Arturo Escobar, Gustavo Esteva, Wolfgang Sachs and the new *Post-Development Reader* (Rahnema 1997) as its compendium – is complex and differentiated, replete with the language of crisis, failure, apocalypse and renewal, and most especially of subaltern insurgencies that are purportedly the markers of new histories, social structures and political subjectivities (Nederveen Pieterse 1996). The Delhi Centre for the Study of Developing Societies – to invoke one such important and visible cluster of erstwhile anti-development Jacobins, latterly referred to by Fred Dallmayr (1996) as a Third World Frankfurt School – includes among its pantheon the likes of Ashis Nandy, Rajni Kothari and Shiv Visvanathan, who in their own way represent a veritable heteroglossia of alternative voices from the South, encompassing a massive swath of intellectual and political territory on which there is often precious little agreement. I have chosen, however, to provide a perhaps questionable unity to these critiques – drawn variously from post-Marxism, ecofeminism, narrative analysis, poststructuralism, postcolonial theory and postmodernism[1] – by emphasizing their confluences around development as a flawed, in some quarters a catastrophically failed, modernist project.[2] Much (but by no means all) of this critique draws sustenance from the idea of the third leg of modernity – the dark side of modernity and the Enlightenment produced the disciplines and normalized subjects – as much as by the Marxian leg of capitalist exploitation and the Weberian (and Habermasian) leg of colonization of the life world by monetization, rationalization, calculation and bureaucratization. This tale of disenchantment carries much of the tenor, tone and timbre of earlier critiques of development – most vividly of the 1960s, but also of the 1890s and earlier, as Michael Cowen and Robert Shenton have admirably demonstrated (1996) – readily apportioning blame to the multinational behemoths of global capitalism. However, as David Lehmann (1997) has noted, it seems to reserve its most virulent prose for the development establishment itself. Much of this work rightly takes on the professions of development, proposing ethnographies of those development institutions that in the name of building freedoms (from hunger, from oppression, from arbitrary rule) create forms of classification, exclusion, individuation, normalization and discipline: in short, the conversion of 'a dream into a nightmare' (Escobar 1994: 4). Globalization – the dialectic of indigenization and cosmopolitanism – now projects Foucault's birth of the clinic onto an unsuspecting global society. In the name of development we confront the world sanatorium in which First (and occasionally Third) World Nurse Ratchets preside over billions of docile, sedated Southern normalized subjects. In a world in which discourse seems to carry implausibly robust, powerful and hegemonic efficacy, post-development and alternatives reside in the hybrid (Escobar), in critical traditionalism (Nandy), in strategic essentialism – in the 'discursive insurrection' of the Third World (this is Escobar citing Valentin Mudimbe).

Is this new – by which I mean the broad sweep of poststructural, post-colonial and post-Marxist analysis – deconstruction and reimagining of development really a distinctively new vision? What sort of vantage point does it provide for a post-development imaginary? To employ Escobar's own language in representing 1950s development economics, what sort of 'world as a picture' is contained within the scopic regime of alternatives to development? On the one hand, there is a certain sense of 1960s *déjà vu*. A number of accounts of globalized political economy in this work – in spite of its aversion to metanarratives and totalizing history – rests clumsily on a blunt, undifferentiated account of world capitalism, in which institutions like the

World Bank have untrammelled hegemonic power, and the Third World appears as a monolithic, caricatured and often essentialized realm of at worst normalized subjects and at best hybridized, subaltern emancipatory potential. Has Ernest Gellner's (1979) Big Ditch simply been replaced by the Big Panopticon?

There is a historical repetition of another sort of course, which resides in the contradictory experience of capitalist modernity itself. The creative destruction of capitalist development has, as Marshall Berman (1974) notes, typically produced the experience of, and the reactions to, the solid melting into air. Modernity *contains* the tragedy of underdevelopment: development and its alternatives – the millenarian populists, the romantics – are dialectically organized oppositions within the history of modernity. This is not simply to fold the current antipathy to development into the grand master narrative of modernity, but to observe that there is a danger of not learning from history, of losing touch with the roots of our own modernity, of not recognizing that modernity in any case cannot be unproblematically located in the West, and of not seeing development and its alternatives as 'oppositions that contain the other' (Harvey 1993: 15).

What *is* different from the 1960s crisis of development is the degree to which the state as a necessary and appropriate vehicle for national aspirations, and the universalistic (and anti-imperialistic) claims for liberation, are no longer axiomatic and taken for granted. Locality, culture, authenticity are the forms of identification that stand in opposition to states, and the very fictions of the nation-state and nationalism are supplanted by what Lehmann (1997) calls 'multi-national populist subcultures' in search of cultural difference ('cultural difference is at the root of postdevelopment' as Escobar [1994: 225] puts it).[3] One might say that the practical and strategic content of this vision is rooted firmly in the soil of civil society rather than in the state or market. But it is civil society of a particular sort: of grassroots movements, of subaltern knowledge, of cultural economics (in which to return again to Escobar, the economy is 'not principally a material entity' [1994: 59]), of hybrid autopoetic politics, of the defence of the local, of cybercultural post-humanism. Much less is said about the civil society that Alexander (1995: 101) refers to as countervailing processes of decivilization, polarization and violence – which are typically modern themselves.

The factors I find striking about much of the more recent critiques of development are the following (if I may be permitted a brief shopping-list):

- the curious, and perhaps appropriately ironic, extent to which a postmodern or poststructural sensibility (replete with its own essentialisms, its own magisterial claims, and its own antipathy to forms of universalistic liberal rights upon which its own position is typically predicated) is attached to claims and critiques of extraordinary totalizing power, certainty and rectitude – development, as Escobar has it, is 'a historically *singular* experience' (1994: 10, my emphasis);

- the extent to which the unalloyed celebration of popular energies of grassroots movements is not subject to the sort of hypercritical discourse analysis that might permit an understanding of their achievements, their political strategies, and the limits of their horizons and vision;
- how there is a curious confluence between elements of the neoliberal counter-revolution (the World Bank's account, for example, of Africa's postcolonial modernization failure, its anti-statism and the need to harness the energies of 'the people') and the uncritical celebrations (and often naïve acceptance) of postdevelopment's new social movements and of civil society itself;
- how the important critique of economic reduction and class determinism (the Marxian master-narrative) – and, it should be added, the deconstruction of the free market myopia (the Smithian master narrative) – have produced, to quote Stuart Hall (1995: 258), not alternative ways of thinking about economic questions, but instead 'a massive, gigantic and eloquent disavowal'.

In making these abbreviated assessments of a complex and diverse field, I am simply attempting to position myself in relation to other discussions of imagining, or what I prefer to call *reworking* development (Pred and Watts 1992). Such an imaginative effort must come, in my view, from within the complex and contradictory experiences of modernity, and implicit in this judgement is a belief, if I may quote Perry Anderson (1994), that the Enlightenment, in all of its complexity and depth, must be defended and developed.

Poverty

Not all people exist in the same Now. They do so externally, through the fact that they can be seen today. But they are thereby not yet living at the same time with others ... They rather carry an earlier element with them; this interferes ... [the old] contradicts the Now; very strangely, crookedly, from behind. The power of this untimely course has appeared, it promised precisely new life, however much it merely hauls up what is old. (Bloch 1932)

Impoverishment and well-being have always been central to the language and practice of development. Poverty constitutes, as the famous ILO declaration put it in 1944, 'a danger to prosperity everywhere'. However, since the end of the Second World War this danger has not receded: poverty eradication around the globe in the age of development has been, at best, disappointing. Of course, it is not all a narrative of failure: the proportion of the world's population that enjoyed per capita income growth rates of over 5 per cent tripled between 1965 and 1980. Some newly industrialized states in East Asia have experienced historically unprecedented rates of 'industrial compression':

Taiwan and South Korea were, after all, war-torn, impoverished and arche-typically postcolonial 'underdeveloped' exporters of sugar and rice in the 1950s. But on balance the record is mixed, and nowhere more so than with respect to the plight and privation – the structured inequality – of women. Of the 1.3 billion people in poverty, 70 per cent are women. Between 1965 and 1988 the number of rural women living below the poverty line increased by 47 per cent; the corresponding figure for men was less than 30 per cent (UNDP 1996).

Mass poverty has been stubbornly resistant to the changing fads and fashions of development policy. If the incidence of poverty declined as a proportion of the world's population in the postwar period (itself perhaps contestable), the total number falling below the absolute poverty line has unequivocally increased. In the period since 1980, economic growth in 15 countries has brought rapidly rising incomes to 1.5 billion people, yet one person in three still lives in poverty and basic social services are unavailable to more than one billion people.

Locating poverty on the larger canvas of postwar development allows us to see two important historical forces at work. First, some key constituencies did not participate in the growth and productivity achievements of the 1945–80 period (women and rural landless, for example): that is to say, growth was accompanied by *exclusion*. And second, the record of the poor in participating in the market successes of the post-1980 period was constricted in the absence of redistribution: market-driven growth was marked by *marginalization*. One hundred countries totalling 1.6 billion people actually experienced economic decline; in almost half of them average incomes are lower now than in 1970. The gravity of these figures is only deepened by recognition of the growing polarities within the global economy as a whole. According to the UNDP, between 1960 and 1991 the share of the richest 20 per cent rose from 70 per cent to 85 per cent of global income, while that of the poorest fell from 2.3 per cent to 1.4 per cent. Between states, the ratio of the shares of the richest to the poorest increased from 30:1 to 61:1. The problem is polar-ization: the proportion of the globe experiencing low income growth rates per head has grown, and since the 1980s has grown substantially.

The eradication of poverty, and by extension the universal achievement of full states of well-being, are central to the very idea of development. But why should poverty be taken seriously? Why should it be an object of specific state policy that demands immediate action and eradication? Should we not take seriously Christ's words: 'The poor always ye have with you' (St John ch. 12 v. 8)? Is not the existence of poverty in the midst of plenty simply 'all for the best in the best of all possible words' as Voltaire's Candide believed? Two centuries ago poverty – what was in late eighteenth- and early nineteenth-century Europe referred to as 'pauperism' – and its relation to political economy were part and parcel of what Karl Polanyi (1944) called 'the discovery of society'. The debate over pauperism in Britain was not simply a discussion about who were the nation's poor – those that cannot, or will not find work – but was part of the very invention of liberal government and of new modes of governance and social regulation. Thomas Malthus, in his essays on population and the poor, spoke to the question of the rights to subsistence at a time of political radicalism and nascent civil rights in the wake of the events of 1789 on the one hand, and of debates within classical political economy over growth and capitalist stability on the other. Society was in this sense discovered as a part of moral, social, political and economic struggles, conducted over almost a half-century, on how the existence of poverty amidst plenty raised the most profound questions of civil, political and economic liberties. In the *Communist Manifesto* Marx composed a narrative of revelation, to depict what had hitherto been hidden with the specific intention of providing a basis for political organization (Thomas 1998). Indeed, as utterly improbable as it might have seemed from the vantage-point of Malthus and the victory of liberal governance in the repeal of the Poor Laws, the European capitalist states were to be transformed by the rise of organized political movements (Hobsbawm 1998: 20). What distinguished Marx from the anarchists was politics, what had to be done. Marx provided a political enterprise – which of course drew upon the popular radicalism of an earlier era – to rethink the figure of the pauper and the role of civil society. Global inequalities in the late-twentieth century have posed these questions anew with a compelling urgency.

Poverty Eradication

World history ... is a house which has more staircases than rooms. (Bloch, 1932)

To break through barriers of stagnation in a backward country, to ignite the imaginations of men ... a stronger medicine is needed than the promise of better allocation of resources or even the lower price of bread ... What is needed ... is faith – faith in the words of Saint-Simon that the golden age lies not behind but ahead ... [this] requires a New Deal of the emotions. (Alexander Gerschenkron)

Most cultures have sought to explain poverty and typically to devise moral and economic approaches to it. But in the history of ideas about the poor, this 'first transition' in Europe was quite fundamental because the questions and dilemmas it generated are still relevant to development thinking and the world of *realpolitik*. The question of the pauperism in rural England during the 1790s has, in other words, its counterpart in the Cairo slum-dweller or the Bolivian peasant in the 1990s. The ethical and economic thinkers at the dawn of European industrialization were tackling many of the issues of poverty and policy that are central to development economics today. In Europe the struggles for civil liberty were opposed by those fearful of tyranny in the same way that the fight for political participation drew fire from those who saw enslavement for the masses. These battles over the dimensions of what we might now call human development were not easily won, and the fight is far from over. There are always, as Hirschman (1991) noted, reactionary setbacks and counter-thrusts. The extent to which free-market capitalism could eradicate poverty was controversial in 1820, and it remains so in the 1990s.

In this sense Marx and Malthus's engagement with the discourse of the poor, of rights, of popular radicalism, of consultation with the power, and the wretched power of the state, enables us to make connections with the work of Amartya Sen (1992) and his notions of capability and different forms of life. The life a person leads can be seen as a combination of various 'doings' and 'beings' (what he calls 'functionings'). These functionings vary from such elementary matters as being well nourished to more complex doings or beings such as having self-respect or participating in civic life. The capability of a person is therefore the various combinations of such functionings that are available; that is, the freedom a person has to lead one kind of life. Focusing on capability implies less an emphasis on goods *per se* than what they enable a person to do; it also means downplaying the utility associated with doing it. Poverty is not about low income or low utility (or the failure to meet basic needs of specified commodities) but about a capability failure. To have an inadequate income is not a matter of falling below some specified poverty line but to have an income below what is adequate for generating, via functionings, the appropriate capabilities for the person in question (Drèze and Sen 1990). Poverty eradication must address the root causes of the problem: namely, capabilities. At its core is the creation of an enabling environment, that is to say a people-centred development capable of meeting citizenship rights. Poverty eradication is, in this sense, about the acquisition of a full sense of human security, what we refer to as citizenship (Dasgupta 1994).

By emphasizing the question of politics and rights there is a way in which poverty and capability can be drawn into a more embracing theory of human needs – a theory of development, in my view – based on the work of Doyal and Gough in their book *A Theory of Human Need* (1991). In this model all persons seek to avoid serious harm that prevents them from pursuing their vision of the good life, whatever it may be. To pursue preferred forms of social life – what Sen calls freedom or well-being – presumes that persons can participate in the forms of life in which they find themselves (Cohen 1994). Basic human needs are, then, those universal preconditions for a successful and critical participation in a form of social life – what Sen calls a capability set. In Sen's language, the freedom to lead different types of life is reflected in the person's capability set, which contains a number of functionings representing the various alternative combinations of beings and doings, any one combination of which a person can choose. Capability is a space of functionings that defines a person's state of being. However these ideas are expressed, the fundamental prerequisites can be considered to be physical health and critical autonomy (i.e. the capacity to make informed choices about what should be done and how to go about doing it). These basic needs can be met in a variety of ways – through satisfiers or functionings. Universal satisfier characteristics (intermediate needs) are those properties of goods, services, activities and relationships that enhance physical health and human autonomy in all cultures. Functionings represent parts of a state of a person – in particular the various things he or she manages to do or be in leading a life. The different functionings of a person will be the constituent elements of the person's being seen from the perspective of his/her welfare. Universal satisfier characteristics – which can be regarded as goals for which specific satisfiers can act as the means – contribute, in other words, to improved physical health and critical autonomy. The characteristics of these need satisfiers or functionings are:

- adequate nutrition and water;
- adequate housing;
- non-hazardous work and living environments;
- security in childhood;
- adequate health care;
- significant primary relationships/self-respect and dignity;
- economic and physical security;
- safe birth control and childbearing; and
- appropriate basic and cross-cultural education.

These needs, if they are to be met, and hence if poverty is to be eradicated, demand intermediate needs or functionings – that is, procedural and material preconditions for enhancing needs satisfaction. The former relate to the ability of the poor to identify and appropriate needs satisfiers in a rational way, and to the necessity of the means for political participation and claims-making whereby people express their felt needs and dissatisfactions – which itself implies forms of democratic resolution. The latter refer to the capacity of economic systems to produce and deliver necessary and appropriate needs satisfiers and to transform them into final needs satisfaction. There is a strong moral case for codifying these intermediate needs into state guaranteed rights (Ghai and Alcántara 1995).

Development stands at the centre of a theory of needs. On the one hand, poverty is the result of capability failure – the failure to secure the universal prerequisites for critical and successful participation in one's social form of life. On the other, poverty as a failure of human needs provision identifies the failure of universal procedural and material preconditions for enhancing needs satisfaction. Capability and the theory of basic human needs has identified the societal preconditions necessary for optimizing needs satisfaction (negative and positive political rights) and for securing the material preconditions for basic needs provision (Gore 1995).

Development is always about much more than income and consumption. And poverty alleviation is necessarily about much more than a wage-packet and a better food supply. But the likelihood of the poor being such beneficiaries necessarily takes us well beyond labour and food markets, and into the sphere of the social contract and associative development to a wider sense of well-being, and most critically to an unleashing of the productive energies and capacities of the poor. At its core is a strong sense of society: of a vibrant civil society in which community action is encouraged, grassroots mobilization is facilitated, and the popular energies and creativities of the poor are unleashed; and necessarily of what Gerschenkron calls faith. It is also a vision of society in which development typically occurs through dialogue, negotiation and the notion of irreducible rights. But the danger of conceiving development as dialogue and negotiation – even if the powers of rights-driven social movements are upheld and enforced – is that development's primary reality remains struggle, strife and conflict. Work and security cannot be provided without infringing on massive corporate or state power, any more than gender equity can be realized without confronting the vast economic costs of maternity. Here, as Perry Anderson (1994: 43) has noted, the model of dialogue, and even social movement, may be a lure, a siren call up the dark side of modernity. What sorts of faith – what sort of New Deal of the emotions – might be capable of encapsulating the realities of strife and of constituting a model of dialogue? I would return again to the emancipatory potential of rights and the challenges to governance which they might liberate.

It is often suggested that this sort of discussion of development and need suffers from a surfeit of universalism and, as Aronson (1995) puts it, an abstract conception of needs that suggests an abstract and timeless quality (needs are constructed, discursive and historical). My own position, however, is similar to that of Nussbaum, who argues that social science, if it is to be critical of oppression, must be essentialist to invoke common extra-discursive capacities for human suffering; and because these inescapable and basic needs 'allow in its design for multiple specification' (1992: 224). In this regard, my model of needs is not incompatible with Nancy Fraser's (1989) account of 'needs talk' (that is to say, the politics of needs interpretation through discourse). Needs will always need to be politically validated, they will be interpreted and struggles over meaning and definition will ensue, and there will be conflicts over provision (that is to say, satisfaction). Like Fraser, I take it as axiomatic that these needs – always marked by difference, relativity and variation in the discursive realm of needs talk – as justified claims must be translated into social rights[4] (van Parijs 1992).

Capitalism and Struggle

The practical application of the principles will depend, as the Manifesto itself states everywhere and all times, on the historical conditions for the time being existing. (Marx and Engels 1872/1998: Preface)

What then are the prospects for a popular radicalism of rights and for the collective organization of the poor? What, in sum, are the 'historical conditions for the time being existing'? First, the liberation from capital is, as Miliband (1994: 188) puts it, nowhere on the agenda of politics. The new world (dis)order is and will be for some time dominated by corporate capital and states for whom some version of neoliberalism is the touchstone. In conditions marked by new forms of complexity and uncertainty, reforming capitalism is – to employ Habermas's (1990) language – marked by a 'fallibilist consciousness'.

Capitalist development is none the less an open process; this openness resides in its contradictory and dependent character. Openness precludes the possibility of a telos (capitalism has no purpose except, as Joan Robinson noted long ago, to keep the show going), but capitalism can and does reveal developmental tendencies. At a moment of capitalist expansion and deepening, the theory that nothing risks killing off capitalism more effectively than an excess of capitalism has special salience. As Schumpeter (1942) noted long ago, the capitalist's rational frame of mind that destroyed so much of pre-modern life turns against its own, by attacking private property and the whole scheme of bourgeois values. These 'built-in defects are not like tonsils', said Schumpeter, but are 'the essence of the organism that displays them'. Capitalism is neither self-contained nor self-reproducing.[5]

Imagining development as an exercise in *realpolitik* must reside in the structural constraints and the conjunctural opportunities of the multiple trajectories of national and regional capitalisms. Capitalism depends on an unstable balance between its value and non-value forms, which, as Jessop says (1997: 562), 'rules out the commodification of everything'. Instead we find 'uneven waves of commodification, decommodification and recommodification as the struggle to extend the value moments of the capital relation encounter real structural limits as well as increasing resistance, and then it seeks to overcome these again in new ways' (ibid.: 562).

In providing the contours of what is new there is a danger of invoking a neomodernization theory replete with the universalisms, linear histories, and pragmatisms of old. Modernity in the 1990s is less about universalism than about the issues of universalization (rather than well-defined universal categories) and norms of complementary reciprocity (what Arato and Cohen (1990) call the 'ability to identify with the non-identical').

The dimensions of a modern development alternative must, in my view, embrace four themes (Anderson 1994): work (equity and distribution of);

social security/welfare (addressing the eviscerated forms of social solidarity through open and enabling forms of security); democracy/citizenship (the deepening democratic self-determination capable of generating new, broad forms of voluntary action; Fox 1995); and peace (the diminution of violence). At the heart of these concerns is the broad question of *exclusion* (from work, from land, from markets, from security, from protection, from human and political rights) and its relation to something called globalization.

I wish to emphasize the prospects of such need achievements in relation to the fact that capitalisms are not self-contained but are (to use Jessop's term) structurally coupled to their environment – which implies (i) trajectories that are open but path-dependent/non-arbitrary and (ii) recurrent interfaces between the developmental tendencies of capital on the one hand and 'the instrumental and communicative rationalities and its environing institutional orders and lifeworld together with their distinctive forms of struggle and resistance' (Jessop 1997: 577) on the other. Development alternatives can be explored, to put it differently, within the circumference of the following two processes: the incompleteness of capitalist societalization, and the social and institutional embeddedness of capitalist development.

The globalization of capitalism, triumphalist neoliberal claims of a world market and the collapse of actually existing socialisms perhaps suggest that we are in the midst of a second 'great transformation' (the refiguring of Atlantic Fordism, the replacement of Keynesian welfare with Schumpeterian workfare, the decomposition of civil society around exclusion and the erosion of citizenship rights). In the same way that Polanyi (1944) talks of the 'discovery of society' in the debates over the late eighteenth- and nineteenth-century working poor, might there not be a rediscovery of society (development) in the belly of this second Great Transformation?[6] Here development alternatives can grow from the soil of the disembedded nature of the market (in its global forms) and the resistances to the universalization of capitalism (the struggle to establish accumulation as a dominant principle of societalization that embraces class and non-class struggles) (Jessop 1997).

Development, in this account, is about the re-embedding of economy and society (i.e. relations between people, between organizations and institutional orders) and defence of non-capitalist societalization (the building of a hegemonic bloc, i.e. a historical unity of durable social forces around the colonization of the lifeworld). At the heart of this strategy is an egalitarian economic and social contract that embraces effective demand- *and* supply-side practices: egalitarian productivism and a social infrastructure of collective goods (Rogers and Streeck 1994; Dahrendorf 1996). Key to this social contract is necessarily an organizational capacity on the part of the poor and a robust conception of popular rights.

Reworking development is, then, unreconstructedly modernist. It succumbs neither to the pop high-technology Utopias of an Alvin Toffler nor to the anti-modernist austerity of Ivan Illich. My antipathy to the project of modernity is matched by the possibilities for re-enchantment, what Gellner (1979) called *contra* Max Weber the 'Rubber Cage' of modernity. The normative content of this vision is derived from the so-called sins of modernist theorizing (that some forms of universalism, essentialism, reductionism and functionalism are desirable and inevitable in analysis, and by implication that theory must be interpretive and causal (McLennan 1996; Sayer 1997)) and from a radical humanism that grapples with the ironic fact that one of the strongest cases against capitalism (at the global level) is seemingly where socialism is weakest.

Coda

> The concept of progress is to be grounded in the Idea of catastrophe. That things 'just go on' is the catastrophe. (Walter Benjamin)

Things 'just going on' indeed result in catastrophe: polarization, exclusion, social disintegration, civil strife. But Benjamin goes on to say that the blithe optimism of the Left is as much about just going on as is the market triumphalism of the Right. Alternatives, in Benjamin's view, spring from the remembrance of history (rather than the imaginaries of emancipated futures) and from that moment when the human species 'traveling in this train [of history], reaches for the emergency brake'. I am not sure what such a gesture might mean in the late twentieth century, any more than I can uncritically endorse histories flashing up at a moment of danger (as Benjamin puts it). In so far as his is a revolutionary stance I am not at all sure from where this sentiment might emerge in the context of our age – and hence of a revolutionary imaginary. The prospect of an alternative socialist imaginary that grows from the realities of the moment – globalization, particular patterns of inequitable asset distribution, market-driven political regimes and neoliberal development trajectories – turn on what Perry Anderson (1992) calls the possibilities for transvaluation, mutation and redemption of the socialist tradition. Short of invoking some sort of faith in hope and humanity – a Utopia does not need an eschatological horizon, as Bloch put it; its power does not reside in its coming to being – my own emphasis would be on the emancipatory aspects of modernity, which draw from the still selective ways in which modernization has been carried out. As Arato and Cohen (1990) emphasize, this leaves space for social movements to continue the differentiation begun by modernity leading to new forms of rights, forms of self-determination and mutual identification, respect and reciprocity. In the context of growing global polarities these movements may increasingly and effectively operate at the level of a transnational civil society. For many countries occupying the broad space of global poverty, modernity surely must have emancipatory potential within its circumference. Perhaps, indeed, the nineteenth century has barely begun.

Notes

1. Much of this literature is drawn together in Rahnema (1997) and Sachs (1990). The work of the so-called Delhi School (Ashish Nandy, Shiv Visvanathan, Rajni Kothari) is also key, as is Schuurman (1994) and Booth (1994). I have written on this literature in Watts (1995).

2. This disenchantment is not, of course, the prerogative or monopoly of the subalterns and their organic intellectuals. In the celebration of the fiftieth anniversary of Indian Independence, Prime Minister Gujral's address struck a note of total pessimism in his reference to the hopes and idealism of the past having been 'squandered' (*Guardian*, 24 August 1997, p. 5).

3. There is strong continuity here between Escobar and the cultural emphasis in the work of Kothari (1988), and his stress on alternative modes of thought, and Nandy (1987), on 'cultural frames' and critical traditionalism.

4. It is unclear to me how a strong social constructivist sense of needs drawn from poststructuralism can address the fact that a radical humanism *requires* a form of essentialism and universalism, and does not dispense with it in the name of cultural authenticity.

5. Jürgen Habermas made the point that capitalists themselves cannot reproduce on their own the conditions that make capitalism possible (Sassoon 1996: 766).

6. I fully recognize of course that the Great Transformation of which Polanyi spoke is far from complete in the Third World, where an industrial working class is still in formation. The great arch of Polanyi's transformation is thus not complete. The second transformation refers in this sense to a deepening of market relations in the wake of a Keynesian revolution, and new frontiers of market disembeddedness in a diverse Third World characterized by a long, but not complete, transformation of the Polanyi sort.

References

Alexander, J. (1995) 'Modern, anti, post, neo', *New Left Review*, 321: 63–104.

Anderson, P. (1994) 'Comment', in D. Miliband (ed.), *Reinventing the Left*, Polity Press, Cambridge, pp. 39–44.

— (1992) *A Zone of Engagement*, Verso, London.

Arato, A. and J. Cohen (1990) *Civil Society and Political Theory*, MIT Press, Boston, MA.

Aronson, R. (1995) *After Marxism*, Guilford, New York.

Baudrillard, J. (1983) *Simulations*, Verso, London.

Berman, M. (1974) *All that is Solid Melts into Air*, Harper, New York.

Bloch, E. (1932) *Heritage of Our Times*, University of California Press, Berkeley, CA.

Booth, D. (ed.) (1994) *Rethinking Social Development*, Longman, Harlow.

Cohen, G. (1994) 'Amartya Sen's unequal world', *New Left Review*, 203: 117–29.

Cowen, M. P. and R. W. Shenton (1996) *Doctrines of Development*, Routledge, London.

Dahrendorf, R. (1996) 'Economic opportunity, civil society and political liberty', *Development and Change*, 27 (2): 229–50.

Dallmayr, F. (1996) 'Global development?', *Alternatives*, 21: 259–82.

Dasgupta, Partha (1994) *An Inquiry into Wellbeing and Destitution*, Clarendon Press, Oxford.

Doyal, L. and I. Gough (1991) *A Theory of Human Need*, Guilford, New York.

Drèze, J. and A. Sen. (1990) *Hunger and Public Action*, Clarendon Press, Oxford.

Escobar, A. (1994) *Encountering Development*, Princeton University Press, Princeton, NJ.

Falk, R. (1996) 'An inquiry into the political economy of world order', *New Political Economy*, 1 (1): 13–26.

Fox, J. (1995) 'Governance and rural development in Mexico', *Journal of Development Studies*, 31 (5): 621–44.

Fraser, N. (1989) *Unruly Practices*, University of Minnesota Press, Minneapolis.

Gellner, E. (1979) *Spectacles and Predicaments*, Thames, London.

Ghai, D. and C. de Alcántara (1995) *Globalization and Social Integration*, UNRISD, Geneva.

Gore, C. (1995) Introduction, in G. Rodgers, C. Gore and J. Figueirredo (eds), *Social Exclusion: Rhetoric, Reality, Response*. ILO, Geneva.

Habermas, J. (1990) 'What does socialism mean today?', *New Left Review*. 3–21.

Hall, S. (1995) 'When was the postcolonial?', in I. Chambers and L. Curti (eds), *The Post Colonial Question*, Routledge, London.

Harvey, D. (1993) 'From space to place and back again: reflections on the condition of postmodernity', in J. Bird et al. (eds), *Mapping Futures: Local Culture, Global Change*, Routledge, London

Hirschman, A. O. (1991) *The Rhetoric of Reaction*, Harvard University Press, Cambridge, MA.

Hobsbawm, E. (1998) Introduction, in K. Marx and F. Engels, *The Communist Manifesto*, Verso, London.

Jessop, B. (1997) 'Capitalism and its future', *Review of International Political Economy*, 4 (3): 561–81.

Kothari, R. (1988) *Rethinking Development*, Ajanta, Delhi.

Lehmann, D. (1997) 'An opportunity lost', *Journal of Development Studies*, 33 (4): 568–78

Malthus, T. (1798) *An Essay on the Principle of Population*, Johnson, London.

Marx, K. and F. Engels (1872/1998) *The Communist Manifesto*, Verso, London.

McLennan, G. (1996) 'Postmodernism and the four sins of modernist theorising', *New Left Review*, 218: 53–74.

Miliband, R. (1994) *Socialism for a Sceptical Age*, Polity, Cambridge.

Nandy, A. (1987) *Traditions, Tyranny and Utopias*, Oxford University Press, Delhi.

Nederveen Pieterse, J. (1996) 'My paradigm or yours?', Working Paper no. 229, Institute of Social Studies, The Hague.

Nussbaum, M. (1992) 'Human functionings as social justice', *Political Theory*, 20 (2): 202–46.

Parijs, P. van (ed.) (1992) *Arguing for Basic Income*, Verso, London.

Pred, A. and M. Watts (1992) *Reworking Modernity*, Rutgers University Press, New Brunswick.

Polanyi, K. (1944) *The Great Transformation*, Beacon Press, Boston, MA.

Rahnema, M. (ed.) (1997) *The Post-Development Reader*, Zed Books, London.

Rogers, J. and W. Streeck (1994) 'Productive solidarities', in D. Miliband (ed.), *Reinventing the Left*, Polity, London.

Sachs, W. (ed.) (1990) *The Development Dictionary*, Zed Books, London.

Sassoon, D. (1996) *One Hundred Years of Socialism*, New Press, London.

Sayer, A. (1997) 'Essentialism, social constructionism and beyond', *The Sociological Review*, 45 (3): 453–87.

Schumpeter, J. (1942) *Can Capitalism Survive?* Harper, New York.

Schuurman, F. (ed.) (1994) *Beyond the Development Impasse*, Zed Books, London.

Sen, A. (1992) *Inequality Re-examined,* Harvard University Press, Cambridge, MA.

Thomas, P. (1998) 'Seeing is believing', in L. Panitch and C. Leys (eds), *The Socialist Register,* Merlin Press, New York, pp. 205–17.

UNDP (1996) *Human Development Report 1996,* Oxford University Press, New York.

Watts, M. (1995) 'A new deal for the emotions', in J. Crush (ed.), *Power of Development,* Routledge, London

10

Environmental Justice as a Force for Sustainability

JOAN MARTINEZ-ALIER

Rather than providing a blueprint for a future society, or a map to show how to reach it, this chapter identifies new issues (ecological distribution conflicts) and new social forces (the environmental justice movement and environmentalism of the poor) at the end of the twentieth century.

There are several varieties of environmentalism, with correspondingly different environmental politics and policies. Environmentalism is sometimes seen as a 'postmaterialist' single-issue movement, but it cannot be single issue because the human economy and society are embedded in ecosystems. In this chapter the trend called ecological modernization (decreased use of energy and materials through technical change and through the application of economic instruments such as eco-taxes) is not seen as the only trend that counts. On the contrary, several manifestations of the growing environmental justice movement, considered a major force in the next decades for achieving an ecologically sustainable society, are analysed here. Thus this chapter first considers briefly whether economic growth improves or harms the environment, and whether it is plausible to rely on technical change and on the 'internalization of externalities' in the pricing system to achieve a sustainable economy. Examples are given of different types of local and international externalities. Externalities must be understood as ecological distribution conflicts, which sometimes give rise to environmental movements. Here some environmental movements of the poor are considered from the angles of both their local forms and their global implications. For instance, resistance to oil exploration in the tropics because of local negative externalities is at the same time resistance to the global greenhouse effect.

In the chapter's futurist conclusion, a trend towards an eco-feminist society and economy is foreseen, which encompasses environmentalism of the poor and the environmental justice movement. However, eco-feminists need to consider the balance between the human population and natural resources, and therefore the final section also discusses the Malthusian question that remains central to all forms of environmentalism.

Pervasive Externalities

The conflict between economic growth and the environment is nowadays often perceived as necessitating wide-ranging social changes. In this section I shall discuss indicators of environmental impact, externalities and the failed attempts to calculate the money values of the externalities.

The larger the world's economies become (because of population growth and increased consumption of energy and materials), the more they use natural resources and environmental services. Local and international externalities become pervasive. There is a need to accommodate the economy to the environment, in a process that could be called ecological adjustment (parallel to the financial adjustment of stabilization programmes). This is the subject matter of ecological economics, which studies the ecological unsustainability of the economy. Ecological economics is transdisciplinary; it is not simply a branch of economics (on a par with agricultural economics or transport economics). It argues that it is impossible to give present-day monetary values to the myriad externalities, many of which are unknown and will have uncertain and perhaps irreversible future effects. When businessmen or politicians are advised to use phrases such as 'Getting the prices right', or 'We must include the full social environmental costs', this is impracticable advice. For instance, a calculation of the marginal external costs of nuclear power would require estimates, at present-day value, of the costs (or benefits) of radioactive waste for tens of thousands of years. At what rate of discount? A solution in terms of attribution of 'property rights' and subsequent market negotiations over radioactive waste and pollution would not really cope with today's uncertainties or solve the intergenerational question. Ecological economists argue that elements of an economy with pervasive uncertain future externalities are incommensurable.

Bringing equity considerations into the analysis of valuation leads to the conclusion that money values (in actual or fictitious markets) depend on distribution. Economists sometimes explain the existence of externalities or the rapid depletion of resources by the absence of property rights to the environment. But externalities can often be seen as 'cost-shifting', where 'cost' does not only mean money cost. Since not everything is in actual or fictitious markets, since 'the poor sell cheap' and future generations cannot come to the markets, other types of value (apart from money value) are also relevant. If we interpret externalities as successful cost-shifting rather than market failures, then the question is not so much how to internalize the externalities into the pricing system. The relevant question becomes which are the social movements that complain and act (or do not act) against the externalities? The word 'externality' itself, contaminated by its economic origin, is no longer appropriate.

Ecological economics argues that environmental limits (or targets, standards or norms) to the economy cannot in general be set through a process of comparison of private profits and social, external costs, but rather must be set, *and are set in practice*, through a process of social evaluation (how else?) after scientific-political debates.[1] Once such limits are set, the conventional economists may come back on stage, with their special competence in discussing instruments (for example, for a reduction of SO_2 emissions of X per cent, would a Pigovian tax be more cost-effective than a market in emission permits or vice versa?).

There have been proposals for monetary indicators on the state of the environment, such as a 'green' GDP. 'Weak sustainability' has also been proposed – that is, net investment should be at least equal to the depreciation of 'natural capital'. Weak sustainability is a synthetic monetary indicator. To assert that the economy would be weakly sustainable if net investment exceeded the sum of depreciation of renewable and non-renewable environmental resources implies faith in the substitutability of capital for environmental resources and in the possibility of measuring the depreciation of environmental resources in the same units as capital. Weak sustainability assumes we know how to value the services of non-appropriated, non-marketable natural resources and life-support systems in money terms. However, techniques of economic valuation are unable to give convincing updated value estimates on the use of natural resources or future, uncertain externalities. Therefore, monetary indicators are believable only to captive audiences of professional economists.

We are then left with physical indicators (or, equivalently, with 'satellite' accounts of variations in 'natural patrimony', not integrated in money terms within national income accounts). Behind a list of indicators would always be a history of scientific research and political controversy. Notice, however, that a list of indicators is far from being a list of targets for indicators, and moreover, that the list is always incomplete. Once an indicator has been constructed, and a target set, then the instruments used to reach such an objective could be discussed. This is the 'cost-effectiveness' approach. But, as ecological economists, we should also be interested in the processes of social perception of externalities, and in the processes of social evaluation linked to the selection of indicators and targets. For instance, an index of loss of natural biodiversity would be human appropriation of the annual biomass net production.[2] There is the well-known figure of 40 per cent for the terrestrial ecosystems of the whole world, which comes from the sum of direct human use (4 per cent), indirect use (26 per cent) and losses (10 per cent), which clearly indicates how the space for other species is narrowing. This would be an interesting indicator for different regions, some of which use more biomass than they themselves produce. How much biomass and space do other species need for conservation and future evolution? Are there social groups that make political use of such an index?

How could indexes of environmental impact be aggregated? Generally, some indexes improve while others deteriorate. The Wuppertal Institute is trying to develop one synthetic physical index, MIPS (material input per unit service) (Schmidt-Bleek 1994), in the expectation that the economy is moving towards dematerialization. In general, there have been inconclusive attempts to decide whether economic growth is bad (or good) for the environment, and in the wake of the Brundtland Report (WCED 1987), the fashion was to prove that poverty was the main enemy. True, the amount of energy used for cooking might go down with economic growth in poor countries (as kerosene or liquid petroleum gas kitchens are substituted for open fires burning woodfuels or dried dung), but in general economic growth goes together with environmental degradation, although selected indicators follow different trends. Studies of industrial ecology (Ayres and Ayres 1997) show that increasing efficiency in the use of materials and energy is sometimes overcome by the 'Jevons effect' – as unit costs become cheaper, there is a tendency to increase the scale of operations.

Are we on a good course if sulphur dioxide emissions go down while carbon dioxide emissions keep on increasing? While some indicators might improve, others deteriorate, and we would need to know the relative weight to give them to assess overall environmental impact. Thus, MIPS might improve while HANPP or the 'energy cost of obtaining energy' (Cleveland 1991) deteriorate. (Incommensurability of values is discussed in Martinez-Alier et al. 1997). Can we apply non-compensatory multi-criteria evaluation to the macro-economy? There is no bottom line in money terms that decides all issues. There are different, incommensurable, types of value. This is why ecological economics uses a variety of physical indicators.

Environmental Justice, Local and Global

As shown above, the relationship between economic growth and environmental impacts is much debated by ecological economists. In my view, environmental movements may be seen as the social expression of (some) non-internalized externalities (Leff 1994). The difficulty of giving convincing economic values to externalities opens up much space for environmental movements.

Environmental movements signal the conflicts between the economy and the environment – the so-called second contradiction of capitalism (O'Connor 1994). In other words, sometimes environmental movements acting outside the market push up the costs that firms (or governments) incur for their use of environmental resources and services. But which environmental movements? Local or global? In rich or in poor countries? Reliance on environmental movements (whether in rich or poor countries) might seem misplaced because they are mostly local, while environmental problems such as global warming or loss of biodiversity are seemingly beyond the reach or comprehension of local environmental movements.

'Ecological distribution' refers to the social, spatial and temporal asymmetries or inequalities in the use by humans of traded or non-traded environmental resources and services; that is, in the depletion of natural resources (including the loss of biodiversity) and the burdens of pollution (Martinez-Alier and O'Connor 1996). 'Political ecology' as used by anthropologists and geographers for some time (Schmink and Wood 1987; Peet and Watts 1996) refers to the study of such ecological distribution conflicts. For instance, unequal distribution of land and pressure of agricultural exports on limited land resources may cause land degradation by peasants pushed to mountain slopes (Stonich 1993). There is increasing discussion of 'ecologically unequal exchange' and also 'biopiracy'. Work has been done on the environmental space really occupied by industrial economies (both for obtaining resources and for disposal of emissions).[3] In the United States, the environmental justice movement was born from local complaints against the alleged disproportionate burden of waste dumping in predominantly Afro-American, Hispanic or Native American areas. We Europeans pay nothing for the environmental space we are using in order to dispose of our emissions of carbon dioxide and act as if we own a sizeable chunk of the planet outside Europe (cf. Opschoor 1995). The value of externalities depends on the allocation of property rights to the environment and the income distribution. Almost nobody is yet complaining, or trying to charge us a fee, but the occupation of an environmental space larger than one's own territory gives rise to an ecological debt with spatial and temporal dimensions (Azar and Holmberg 1995). Here I will give other examples, local and international, of ecological distribution conflicts.

Varieties of Environmentalism

The relationship between wealth and environmental degradation varies with each factor analysed. Water quality is lower in poor countries and improves with wealth, but water consumption also increases with wealth, and thus water reserves are overexploited in some rich countries and suffer salinization in coastal areas. Emissions of carbon dioxide increase with wealth. The production of domestic waste increases with wealth, and its composition makes it harder to recycle. Recently the relationship between wealth and environmental impact has been discussed in terms of the so-called 'inverted U relationship' (Selden and Song 1994; Opschoor 1995). Emissions of sulphur dioxide per head increase in the early stages of industrialization and then decrease as filters are installed in metal smelters and in power stations, or different fuel is used (gas instead of lignites). If one defines improvement in environmental quality by the decrease in emissions of sulphur dioxide, then rich industrialized countries are improving environmental quality. However, there is no evidence yet of a general relative delinking, much less of an absolute delinking (for sulphur dioxide emissions) between growth of the economy and environmental impact (De Bruyn and Opschoor 1994; Opschoor 1995).

What are the reasons for the growth of environmentalism (that is, the actions taken or the concerns expressed over the state of the environment due to human action)? Some authors believe that the growth of environmentalism in rich countries is explained mainly by a post-1968 shift to 'postmaterialist' cultural values. This optimistic position is known as Inglehart's postmaterialist thesis and explicitly leaves aside distributional conflicts. It assumes that the economy becomes dematerialized; hence postmaterial environmentalism is concerned with the amenity values of nature rather than with life-support systems or with the conditions of livelihood and production. I do not agree with this thesis, or rather it seems to me that it accounts for only one variety of environmentalism. Inglehart (1977, 1995) accepts that in the affluent countries there is worry about the deterioration of some environmental indicators and about the increasing share of GNP that must be spent on protective, defensive, corrective or mitigatory expenditures to make up for environmental damage (as shown by Leipert 1989). But, quite apart from objective environmental impacts and costs, Inglehart's thesis is that the cultural shift towards subjective, postmaterialist values is making some societies more sensitive to environmental issues. In trying to disentangle the sources of support for environmentalism in various countries, Inglehart (1995: 61) describes the environment of the Netherlands as relatively pristine, which is surprising since this is a country with a population density of 400 persons per square kilometre and nearly as many cows, pigs and cars as humans. This misrepresentation attributes Dutch environmentalism not only to objective environmental impacts but also, even more so, to postmaterial values. Meanwhile, the 1993 Friends of the Earth report on the Netherlands (Buitenkamp et al. 1993) showed that the Netherlands (such a clean country! with such a green awareness!) takes up an environmental space about fifteen times larger than its own territory.

The postmaterialist thesis explains environmental movements in rich countries in terms of a change in cultural values away from material consumption and towards 'quality of life' issues. The fact that economic distribution conflicts are no longer so acute has led to a generational shift towards new values, which include an increasing appreciation of environmental amenities because of the declining marginal utility of abundant, easily obtained material commodities. Indeed, conventional resource economists in the United States[4] had proposed that the demand for environmental amenities increases with income, and that, implicitly, the poor are 'too poor to be green'. Inglehart's thesis can be criticized if we take the position that economic growth goes together with environmental degradation. Hence in rich countries there exists a materialist environmentalism against dangerous or annoying 'effluents of affluence' (e.g. the environmental justice movement in the USA; Schwab 1994; Szasz 1994). The postmaterialist thesis has also been criticized because it is easy (through opinion polls) to find evidence for a strong interest in the environment also in poor countries (Brechin and Kempton 1994). There is indeed evidence for environmentalism of the poor in many social conflicts both in the past and present (Guha 1989; Martinez-Alier 1991). Sometimes such conflicts are identified as 'environmental' by actors themselves; at other times, conflicts have been expressed in non-environmental terms. Thus *seringueiros* in Acre in the late 1980s were members of a union, had links to some local Christian movements inspired by liberation theology, and became known as environmentalists, perhaps to their own surprise.

In poor countries, environmentalism is sometimes supposed to have been imported and organized by the postmaterial environmentalism of the North, inspired by people with incomes high enough to allow them to worry about postmaterial quality of life issues rather than about livelihood and survival. Hugo Blanco, a former peasant leader in Peru, wrote:

> At first sight, environmentalists or conservationists are nice, slightly crazy guys whose main purpose in life is to prevent the disappearance of blue whales or pandas. The common people have more important things to think about, for instance how to get their daily bread. Sometimes they are taken to be not so crazy but rather smart guys who, in the guise of protecting endangered species, have formed so-called NGOs to get juicy sums of dollars from abroad ... Such views are sometimes true. However, in Peru there are a very large number of people who are environmentalists. Of course, if I tell such people they are ecologists, they might reply, 'ecologist your mother', or words to that effect. Let us see, however. Isn't the village of Bambamarca truly environmentalist, when it has time and again fought valiantly against the pollution of its water from mining? Are not the city of Ilo and the surrounding villages which are being polluted by the Southern Peru Copper Corporation truly environmentalist? Is not the village of Tambo Grande in Piura environmentalist, when it rises like a closed fist and is ready to die in order to prevent strip-mining in its valley? Also, the people of the Mantaro Valley who saw their little sheep die, because of the smoke and waste from La Oroya smelter. And the population of Amazonia are totally environmentalist, for they die defending their forests against depredation. Also the poor people of Lima, when they complain against the pollution of water on the beaches.[5]

I have direct knowledge of similar cases in other countries. For instance, in Ecuador are not the poor and indigenous people of Zambiza environmentalist, who live around the valley in northeastern Quito where more than one million kg of domestic waste are dumped everyday and have unsuccessfully asked that this dumping ground be closed? And the population of Salango, on the coast, who complain about the pollution from a fishmeal factory, as in so many other places on the Pacific Coast of Chile (Talcahuano) and Peru (Chimbote)? Have the peasants of Salinas in Bolívar province not been ecologists who, without the support of the communal authorities, nevertheless prevented mining by Rio Tinto in their territory? And the Amazonian population who complains against oil spills? And the poor, black population of

Esmeraldas province on the coast, mainly women, who are in the forefront of the defence of the mangroves against the shrimp industry (Varea 1997)?

In Chile, were the poor urban inhabitants in Santiago who complained and complained until the waste-dump of Lo Errázuriz was closed not truly ecologists (Sabatini 1997)? Are the Huilliche communities of Compu and Güequetrumao in Chiloe island not environmentalists, despite their ignorance of such terminology, who have confronted the forest firm Golden Spring, in a case similar to so many others in southern Chile and elsewhere? And the population of Paipote, who complain against sulphur dioxide emissions from copper smelting, risking their own sources of employment? And the farmers of Huasco, some poor, some not so poor, their olive trees damaged by emissions of iron particles from the pellet factory in their valley?

Perhaps the most well-known instances of environmentalism of the poor have been Chico Mendes and the *seringueiros;* the Chipko Movement; the movement against the Narmada dams; and now the Ogoni struggle against Shell. But there are many more. In the Brazilian Amazonia, Acevedo and Castro (1993) describe the trouble that fell upon an ethnic group along the Trombetas River, reminiscent of *quilombos* of ex-slaves, who from the mid-1970s onwards tried to fight back against hydroelectricity and bauxite mining from Brazilian and foreign companies that threatened to destroy the Cachoeira Porteira waterfall, a sacred place to them. At the same time, this group confronted IBAMA, the Brazilian environmental agency, which designated the territory occupied by these *negros de Trombetas* as a 'biological reserve'. This was seen as a trick to dislodge them for the benefit of the mining companies. In the region around Santarem there is a conflict between *ribeirinho* fishermen, who fish in the *varzea* lakes that the Amazon leaves behind in the low water period from July to December, and industrial fishermen, called *geleiros* (ice men). Attempts are being made to institute legally a system of communal management of the lakes, to the benefit of local people, and for conservation of the resource (McGrath et al. 1993). The movement in defence of the babassu palm in Maranhao and neighbouring states in the Brazilian Northeast, based mainly on women, the *quebradeiras de coco* (Almeida 1995) is also becoming well known. Tens of thousands of people are involved over a wide area. Women who make a living or complement their meagre income by collecting and breaking coconuts and selling the oil-rich seed want to preserve the palm trees and protect them from the landowners. Furthermore, all over Brazil there are movements of *atingidos pelas barragens* (Magalhães 1994), similar to other movements against big dams around the world.

Table 10.1 classifies the varieties (and theories) of environmentalism. One criterion is the material/non-material dimension. Another is the environmentalism of affluence vs. the environmentalism of survival; the environmentalism of enhanced quality of life vs. the environmentalism of livelihood (Martinez-Alier and Hershberg 1992). Some situations cross the boundaries of the categories shown in Table 10.1. For instance, there are fights in poor countries

TABLE 10.1 Environmentalism

	Materialist	Non-materialist
In affluent countries	Reaction against the increased impact of the 'effluents of affluence', e.g. the environmental justice movement in the USA, the anti-nuclear movement.	Cultural shift to postmaterial 'quality of life' values and increased appreciation for natural amenities because of declining marginal utility of abundant, easily obtained material commodities (Inglehart 1977, 1995).
In poor countries	The 'environmentalism of the poor', i.e. the defence of livelihood and communal access to natural resources threatened by the state or the market (Guha 1989).	Biocentric religions as distinct from 'Western' anthropocentric religions (White 1967).
	Reaction against environmental degradation caused by unequal exchange, poverty, population growth. Also, social eco-feminism (Agarwal 1992).	Essentialist eco-feminism (e.g. Shiva 1989).

against toxic waste (imported or locally produced), while there are fights in affluent countries (Canada, New Zealand, United States) by native peoples to enforce territorial rights to protect access to their own natural resources or to protect themselves against waste dumping. Also, the defence of communities against the state or market sometimes rests in part on religious values – as in the belief in *pachamama* in the Andes. And, certainly there are cases that do not fit at all with environmentalism of the poor – for instance, the Amazonian *garimpeiros* who, in their search for gold, pollute rivers with mercury. The global vs. local dimension is still absent from Table 10.1 and will be discussed in the following sections.

International Externalities and TNCs

According to the doctrines of ecological modernization (or sustainable development or scientific industrialism, as Guha calls it) (Guha and Martinez-Alier 1997: 83), if the economy could grow without increased environmental impact, then movements such as environmental justice and the environmentalism of the poor would little by little lose their reasons for existence.

On the contrary, we are witnessing an increasing throughput of energy and materials in the world economy, increasing greenhouse effects and an increasing appropriation by humans of biomass production with a resulting decrease in biodiversity. Local cases of pollution often receive a local answer. But what kind of social answer is there for global depredation of resources, or global externalities such as loss of biodiversity or the enhanced greenhouse effect?

Reliance on the birth of environmental movements to signal the conflict between the economy and the environment seems misplaced when the issues are global. There are cases in which, despite the existence of an acknowledged externality (such as the destruction of the ozone layer), there have *not* been spontaneous grassroots environmental movements, and it was scientists who called attention to the issue. This absence of grassroots movements contrasts with their presence in other types of environmental conflicts, for instance against sulphur dioxide from power stations or smelters, or against the loss of access to common property resources by private enclosures or by state appropriation. After the Union Carbide chemical plant explosion at Bhopal there was some debate on compensation for externalities produced locally by transnational corporations, but it is sometimes noted that there is little response or interest from the South about planetary climate change. Beyond scientific uncertainties (which are very large concerning impact at the local level), it is believed that day-to-day struggles for economic survival prevent people from thinking about global ecology. Concern for climate change would be a luxury of the rich, not a necessity of the poor.

In the case of loss of biodiversity (certainly a new term for most people in the world), the situation is different. There is local involvement. There is a new perception of the appropriation of genetic resources without recognition or payment for peasant or indigenous ownership and knowledge of such resources. Biopiracy is a new word (introduced by Pat Mooney around 1993), but the practice itself is old. Even those companies that in principle are ready to compensate local knowledge (such as Shaman Pharmaceuticals) engage in exchanges that are very unbalanced (Reyes 1996). In agriculture there is now a worldwide movement of self-conscious peasant agro-ecology, which is not at all a postmodern fad but a route towards an alternative modernity based on the defence of agricultural biodiversity and sensible agronomic practices (Martinez-Alier 1994). Global environmental ideas are used for, and supported by, local struggles. In response to attempts through GATT negotiations to enforce intellectual property rights to 'improved' seeds, while nothing has ever been paid for traditional seeds or traditional knowledge (despite the FAO's support for so-called farmers' rights), there have been strong protest movements in India against firms such as Cargill. For another example, the opposition to NAFTA in Mexico could combine Mexican oil nationalism (*à la* Cárdenas in the 1930s) and the defence of *milpa* agriculture by pointing out that NAFTA means the intensification of ecological dumping. Cheap oil exports from Mexico to the United Sates (at prices that certainly do not internalize local and global externalities) will be exchanged for imports of maize at low prices. This will destroy the agriculture of southern Mexico despite the fact that maize agriculture in the United States is more wasteful of fossil-fuel energy, and biologically more fragile than in Mexico. Hence Victor Toledo's wish after the Chiapas uprising for *un neozapatismo ecológico*.

The fact that agricultural and 'wild' genetic resources have been appropriated gratis, and that in recent times intellectual property rights have been imposed on them, is animating a general discussion in the South on biopiracy and the merits and demerits of the merchandising of biodiversity. However, even if property rights to biodiversity are bestowed on poor people, there will be a tendency for prices to be low, according to the principle 'the poor sell cheap', which I also call Lawrence Summers' principle (*The Economist*, 8 February 1997). Everybody (except slaves) is the owner of his or her own body and health; however, poor people sell their health cheaply when working for wages in mines or plantations. There appear to be cases in some Southern countries in which poor children's sexual services (over which they themselves presumably have property rights) are sold cheaply to Northern tourists, and there are plausible rumours that body parts are carved up and exported cheaply for transplanting, which might be deemed an efficient allocation of such 'fictitious commodities' given the existing distribution of income.[6]

I shall now give some other examples of international externalities in order to insist on the following point: the economic values of externalities depend not only upon the social perception of physical realities, but also upon the institution of property rights and the distribution of power and income. International externalities may refer to transboundary pollution (as with acid rain in Europe, or radiation from Chernobyl), to the export of carbon dioxide to distant sinks, and to exports of toxic waste. There are some cases that arise from the practices of multinational corporations in the South. For example, there are at present a number of pending court cases brought against international companies for damage done in poor countries – what I call 'the internalization of international externalities'. Such cases show the influence of the institutional framework on the valuation of externalities. How are such externalities socially constructed? How do we count, for instance, damage to human health and to biodiversity from oil spills in Amazonia? How do we value them? Although such court cases can sometimes arise from lawyers' love of litigation rather than in defence of environmental and social justice, they are nevertheless a by-product of a trend towards increasing environmental impact on the industrial economy. Such damages are not surprises (techniques or new products gone wrong). They exist because of economic growth, disparities in power and income, and the absence of clear property rights for local people. I have good information on cases brought from Ecuador (class-action suits) against Texaco (in New York) because of oil spills in Amazonia, and against Dow Chemical and other firms (in Texas and Mississippi) because of sterility produced by the nematicide DBCP to workers in banana plantations. There is a case in Texas against the Southern Peru Copper Corporation for damages to health (because of SO_2 emissions) in Ilo (*New York Times*, 12 December 1995; Balvín 1995). There is a court case in New Orleans against the mining firm Freeport-McMoRan (partly owned by Rio Tinto) for damages in Irian Jaya (*The Economist*, 20 July 1996, p. 52; *Down to Earth*, 31 July 1996). If jurisdiction in US courts is refused (as in the case of Bhopal), then the externalities will be cheap. If jurisdiction is accepted, then the money awarded to compensate for damages might be abundant. Because of intensive exploitation of oil and timber, and the expansion of mining in the tropics, it can be expected that such conflicts will increase and may involve firms with headquarters in Europe, for instance Shell (Peru and Nigeria) and Elf (Ecuador).

Of course, multinational companies were not responsible for the disappearance of people and cultures in America from 1492 onwards. However, despite all the promises that improvements in technical efficiency will be matched by increasing incomes and increasing populations, the increasing environmental impact of the human economy is actually causing new international ecological distribution conflicts. Such conflicts, where oil, gas, minerals, the enhanced greenhouse effect, and human cultures and lives are all involved, cannot be solved by mere appeals to the internalization of externalities.

Uncertain science converted into the doubtful economics of present-value costs (at arbitrary rates of discount) is not really useful for guiding oil exploration and exploitation in the rainforest, or, on a smaller level, for deciding the disposal technique of the Brent-Spar drilling platform. While in some business (and political) circles a blind confidence in the simple plan of internalizing externalities into the pricing system still predominates, coupled perhaps with a good measure of what activists call 'greenwashing', experience teaches the value of a more participatory approach. Shell's spokesmen now say, 'we want to engage, not enrage', and according to *The Economist* (20 July 1996), Shell launched a Brent-Spar site on the Internet to encourage people to debate the issue. My view is that what is good for the North Sea goose should be good for the lower Urubamba (or the Ogoni) gander, not only on grounds of justice but also for the sake of the environment.

The Global and the Local in Greenhouse Politics

There is at first sight much distance between local movements and global issues. However, this topic is open to research. Let us turn to, for instance, international greenhouse politics and the issue of joint implementation. The enhanced greenhouse effect is not attributable to any single corporation or citizen, and there is no international jurisdiction (in my opinion) to which a country or group of citizens could appeal as plaintiffs against those who are responsible for climate change. Neither an international 'polluter pays principle' nor an international law of tort applies. This might change.

When firms or individuals produce negative externalities and are not held accountable, then they are acting as if they owned the environment, not in the legal sense but in an economic sense. This is the economic notion of property rights. Now, the economy is open to the entry of energy and materials, and produces residues, such as carbon dioxide, heavy metals and radioactive waste. Until about a hundred years ago, the social perception of carbon dioxide emissions caused by humans burning fossil fuels did not exist as an externality, and in fact until the 1950s the usual interpretation of scientists was that an increase in temperature would be good. Even today there is much uncertainty as to the local effects of the increased greenhouse effect. Attempts at a cost-benefit analysis are not convincing because of the arbitrariness of the discount rate (Azar and Sterner 1996) and because many items are not easily measured in physical terms, much less easily valued in money terms (Funtowicz and Ravetz 1994). Moreover, both property values and the economic value of human lives depend on social institutions. Internalizing externalities in money terms is not a minor technical exercise. When things are done this way, they can backfire, as happened to the IPCC application of cost-benefit analysis to climate change.

The discussion on joint implementation – in the sense of paying for reforestation projects in the South to offset excessive carbon dioxide emissions in the North – will perhaps give rise to a generalized claim in the South to property rights to the absorptive capacity of the earth, perhaps in terms proportional to population (following Agarwal and Narain 1991). Joint implementation is usually praised on grounds of cost effectiveness. It is cheaper to place carbon dioxide in the growing vegetation of tropical countries than to reduce emissions in rich countries. Indeed, were it not because of the absorption of human-produced carbon dioxide by 'natural' sinks – namely, new vegetation and the oceans – the greenhouse effect would be larger than it is at present. Approximately one-half of the carbon dioxide produced by burning fossil fuels does not accumulate in the atmosphere but is placed gratis in natural sinks. The rich therefore act as if they were the owners of a disproportionate part of the carbon dioxide absorption capability provided by the new vegetation and the oceans. The remaining carbon dioxide they dump into the atmosphere, as if they were also its owners. To allow excessive emissions to go on, until a still 'safe' concentration of 500 or 600 ppm of carbon dioxide in the atmosphere is reached, raises the scientific and political questions of 'safe for whom' and 'allowed by whom'. In this sense, joint implementation – exporting carbon dioxide to outside sinks, beyond one's own environmental space – has been going on for many decades. What is now being proposed is that, in specific cases, regarding a minute amount of the excessive emissions of carbon dioxide, a payment will be made for the use of one of the natural sinks: new vegetation. Such explicit reforestation proposals for joint implementation as exist at present put on the negotiating table the issue of property rights to the absorption capability of carbon dioxide. They also put on the table the issue of the ecological debt owed by the North to the South, on account of the environmental services of carbon dioxide absorption provided gratis up to now. Countries that are in a creditor position could give a sense of urgency to the negotiations on climate change by a generalized claim in the South to property rights to this absorptive capacity.

New 'down-to-top' movements attempt to connect local and global environmental issues. For instance, there is an Alliance for Climate, between COICA (an umbrella group for indigenous peoples in Amazonia) and many European cities, whose authorities at least pay lip-service to the cause of carbon dioxide reduction. Indigenous peoples oppose deforestation, but northern environmentalists may object to it only if a proposal is included for reductions. The global discussion on carbon dioxide is made locally relevant by linking it to campaigns in favour of poor people and good public transport, and against urban planning in the service of the motor car, an issue even more relevant in Bangkok or Mexico City than, say, in Bologna. Or, for instance, environmental groups in Venezuela (Orinoco Oilwatch) published an open letter to President Clinton on the eve of his visit to the country in 1997, complaining about American oil companies' operations in areas inhabited by Waraos and other indigenous groups, and pointing out the incongruity between Clinton's and Gore's well-publicized awareness and alarm at the increased greenhouse effect and Venezuela's plans, with American support, to increase oil exports to 6 mbd.[7] The use of global ideas in the service of local or national social and environmental aims is also present in debates on ecological trespassing, the ecological debt, ecologically unequal exchange and biopiracy.

The term 'toxic imperialism' has been used in struggles against the export of toxic waste. Such struggles could easily link up with the environmental justice movement in the United States. There are other cases in which the local is connected to the global, in a generalized movement of resistance. There are international networks against big dams (McCully 1996), for the defence of the mangroves, against impacts from the mining industry – all of them linking local environmental movements and global ideas. Indeed, the relevance of one global idea coming from Indian environmentalists (Agarwal and Narain 1991) – equal access to carbon sinks – has been explicitly acknowledged by US academics involved in the environmental justice movement.

Ecological Distribution Conflicts

Table 10.2 lists the names and definitions of some ecological distribution conflicts, and the related resistance movements, both domestic and international. The 'prices' that externalities might have depend on the outcomes of such ecological distribution conflicts.

TABLE 10.2 Ecological distribution conflicts and related resistance movements

Name	Definition	Main source
Environmental racism (USA)	Dumping of toxic waste in locations inhabited by African-Americans, Latinos, Native Americans.	Bullard 1993
Environmental justice	Movement against environmental racism.	Bullard 1993
Environmental blackmail	Either you accept LULU (local unacceptable land use) or you remain without jobs.	Bullard 1993
Toxic imperialism	Dumping of toxic waste in poorer countries.	Greenpeace c.1989
Ecologically unequal exchange	Importing products from poor regions or countries at prices that do not take account of exhaustion or local externalities.	
Raubwirtschaft	Ecologically unequal exchange, 'plunder economy'.	Ramoulin 1984
Ecological dumping	Selling at prices that do not take account of exhaustion or externalities. It occurs from North to South (agricultural exports from Europe or USA), and from South to North.	
Internalization of international externalities	Law suits against TNCs (Union Carbide, Texaco, Dow Chemical, etc.) in their country of origin, claiming damages for externalities caused in poor countries.	
Biopiracy	Appropriation of genetic resources ('wild' or agricultural) without adequate payment or recognition of peasant or indigenous knowledge and ownership over them (including the extreme case of the Human Genome project).	Mooney RAFI c.1993
Ecological debt	Claiming damages from rich countries on account of *past* excessive emissions (e.g. carbon dioxide) or plundering natural resources.	IEP Chile 1992, Azar and Holmberg 1995, Borrero 1994
Transboundary pollution	Applied mainly to sulphur dioxide crossing borders in Europe producing acid rain.	

Term	Description	Reference
National fishing rights	Attempts to stop open access depredation by imposing (since the 1940s in Peru, Ecuador, Chile) exclusive fishing areas (200 miles and beyond, as in Canada, for straddling stocks).	
Environmental space	Geographical space really occupied by an economy, taking into account imports of natural resources and disposal of emissions. Empirical work has been done.	Buitenkamp et al. 1993
Ecological trespassers vs. ecosystem people	Applied to India, but could be applied to the world. Contrast between people living off their own resources, and people living off the resources of other territories and peoples.	Gadgil and Guha 1995
Ecological footprint or appropriated carrying capacity	The ecological impact of regions or large cities on the outside space. Empirical work has been done.	Rees and Wackernagel 1994
Workers' struggles for occupational health and safety	Actions (in and outside the framework of collective bargaining) to prevent damages to workers in mines, plantations or factories.	Castells 1983,[8]
Urban struggles for clean water, green spaces, etc.	Actions (outside the market) to improve environmental conditions of livelihood or to gain access to recreational amenities in urban context.	
Indigenous environmentalism	Use of territorial rights and ethnic resistance against external use of resources (e.g. Crees against Hydro Quebec, Ogoni against Shell).	Geddicks 1993
Social eco-feminism, environmental feminism	Environmental activism of women, motivated by their social situation. The framework of such struggles is not necessarily that of feminism or environmentalism.	Agarwal 1992
Environmentalism of the poor	Social conflicts with an ecological content (now and in the past), of the poor against the (relatively) rich, not only but usually in rural contexts.	Guha 1989

Coda: Looking Back in 2025

Here I present some hopes for the next decades, based on favourable solutions to the conflicts identified. The environmental justice movement and environmentalism of the poor, together with eco-feminism, may help to change society and the economy.

The changes in the economy and society we have seen between 1997 and 2025 have been so exciting and moving that not everybody will share the dryness of my dissection of social trends and movements, or appreciate that I start this retrospective account with Paul Ehrlich, a maligned 'neo-Malthusian' who became known by his depressing book *The Population Bomb* in the otherwise optimistic year of 1968. Nevertheless ... as the social perception grew in the late 1960s and 1970s that there would be serious environmental impacts on the environment if economic (and demographic) growth continued, different causes were emphasized. Using Paul Ehrlich's 'equation', I = PAT (where I is environmental impact, P is population, A is affluence, T is technology), different solutions were proposed according to whether emphasis was put on the P, the T, or the A:

1. a population solution: drastic curtailment of population growth and indeed a decrease in the human population to make room again for other species;
2. ecological modernization: legal regulations, economic policies and a change in technologies towards dematerialization, estimated by economic instruments such as eco-taxes ('fiscal environmentalism') or markets in pollution permits, so as to be able to have ecologically sustainable economic development; and
3. social and environmental justice: decrease in incomes and consumption of the rich in order to avoid the 'effluents of affluence', such as radioactive waste or carbon dioxide, which have increased the greenhouse effect.

I shall look backward, from 2025, to some of the salient points in the discussions and events of the past 30 years on the three clusters of solutions. I shall consider first population, then technology and economic policies (i.e. ecological modernization), and finally the attack on affluence in the name of social and environmental justice.

Let us remember the growth of eco-feminism. Peasants, indigenous peoples and women in general had been seen as 'closer to nature' than industrial and post-industrial men, but, as Salleh (1997) argues, this belief could exist only because men had mistaken their own alienation for reality. All their activities depended on nature (on the throughput of energy and materials in the economy) and in most cases also on the unpaid services of women in the *oikonomia*. Marilyn Waring and other women had already pointed out at the time that feminists and radical environmentalists (and ecological economists) had many points of agreement on the importance of non-waged caring labour, on the view of the economy more as *oikonomia* than chrematistics, on the absurdity of the analogy 'women = nature/men = culture', as if men could really function outside and above nature in a postmaterialist, dematerialized economy. Such insights led to the combining of environmentalism and feminism into eco-feminism, a multi-issue, wide-ranging, all-encompassing set of ideas that now dominates the twenty-first century. But despite such favourable encounters, around 1995 environmentalists and feminists (including eco-feminists such as Maria Mies, Vandana Shiva and Ariel Salleh) still differed very strongly on the population question. By environmentalists I do not mean only awful social-Darwinists, but also sweet environmentalists who worked in networks such as 'Damn the Dams', 'Plantations are not Forests', and 'The Ecology of the Dispossessed'. All environmentalists (whether deep ecologists, ecological modernizers or believers in environmental justice) shared the view that it would be better to have a world with four billion people than with fourteen billion people. All environmentalists (especially the deep ecologists) watched the HANPP index, which roughly showed how much, or rather how little biomass was left for other species not associated with humans deteriorate year after year. Many environmentalists, particularly those of us who believed in environmental justice and the environmentalism of the poor, also emphasized the right of indigenous minorities to exist and prosper and keep their own languages. The rapid disappearance of languages (is Aymara the only pre-colonial language to survive in America?) was a topic discussed in the many conferences on globalization in the 1990s.

From the 1950s and 1960s onwards, birth control was indeed sometimes imposed brutally by governments and international organizations upon populations (usually women, sometimes even men, as with Indira Gandhi's policies in India) in what feminists called repressive 'body politics'. Women in poor countries often served as guinea pigs for industry experiments with new contraceptives. Many feminists (as well as many Marxists) had pointed out in the 1970s and 1980s that there was no correlation between population density and poverty, and that therefore poverty could not be blamed on population growth. Western Europe and Japan had far higher population densities than most Latin American and African countries. Also, why was there so little public debate in Northern countries about the hundreds, perhaps thousands of deaths each year of people trying to cross from the South to the North, through the Straits of Gibraltar and elsewhere? Why could oil from Mexico or gas from Algeria flow so cheaply and easily towards the North while the population could not? And this was not all. At the end of the twentieth century there were also exhortations to expand the base of the population pyramid in some Northern countries ('Will the Germans disappear?' asked Günter Grass in the 1970s), with the argument that a baby-boom was needed in order to finance in due course the health care and pensions of the old. (The argument was not convincing in its own terms, considering the 10 per cent rate of unemployment.) In Europe and Japan there was also the memory of the fascist state that had preached population growth, and kept men out of the kitchen and sent them into the battlefield. Population politics was abhorrent to the feminist movement.

After the year 2010, male and female children quite often took their maternal grandmother's name as their principal surname. The feminist movement was the most successful social movement of the twentieth century. It was certainly not a single-issue movement. It was also about men, about feelings, about abolishing the separation between public and private that was the refuge of the powerful and corrupt. It was about the real economy, about the inequalities of property and incomes. The fight for the reproductive rights of women, that is, the freedom of women to choose their partners and the number of children they wanted to have, had to be carried out against the opposition of churches and states, and often against the men in their own family (fathers, brothers, husbands). For instance, abortion was still criminalized in many countries in the year 2000. The feminist movement had made great advances by that year, but it did not know what to make of the population–environment conundrum. Slowly it came to realize that reproductive rights had to be exercised in an ecological context. The human species was destroying the environment to its own detriment and to the detriment of other species that had a right to exist. There was a renewed interest in the late 1990s in Europe and America (North and South) in the work and the beliefs of feminist and anarchist women such as Emma Goldmann and Maria Lacerda de Moura, who nearly a hundred years earlier had worked in neo-Malthusian circles. Perhaps neo-Malthusian had been the wrong name; they could have called themselves neo-eco-Verhulstians, but then many would have perhaps missed the point. In the first decade of the twenty-first century, other new questions were: how could the idea of reproductive rights in an ecological context spread in Islamic or Hindu countries and cultures? How could resentment at government imposition of birth control in China be turned into grist for the eco-feminist mill? Such questions had already been formulated before the turn of the century, but the answers came later.

Population was only one of the variables in the $I = PAT$ equation. Technology was another. How to 'delink' the economy from the flows of materials and energy? Such delinking seemed pure metaphysics, but industrial ecologists and students of industrial metabolism (such professions did not exist until the 1990s), riding the waves of ecological modernization, asked the following questions. Could the economy become dematerialized in relative terms (per unit of GDP)? Note that gross domestic product is how the production of goods and services was quaintly termed at the time – excluding precisely unpaid domestic caring services. What did they mean by domestic, really? The GDP also included, for instance, the money value of the production of oil, but what did they mean by production? Oil was produced long ago: they meant its extraction and burning.

Could the economy become dematerialized? While the forests of Sumatra and Borneo burned in the 1990s, making room for tree plantations for the export of paper pulp, some people were rightly asking whether the Internet would lead to forms of almost immaterial transaction as people downloaded information, news from nowhere and everywhere, conversations, entertainment, films, books and articles into their computers without any need to travel to a bookshop, a theatre or a classroom, without any need for paper. Certainly the introduction of photovoltaics has slowed down the greenhouse effect (nevertheless carbon dioxide in the atmosphere will inevitably reach a concentration of 600 ppm). Around 2005 these new forms of energy had become competitive in purely chrematistic terms with other sources of electricity (nuclear, gas, coal and oil), even without taking into account the negative externalities of such other sources. But were they a real substitute? Or were they rather a complement, given the rate of growth of energy expenditure as China and India followed the path (until a few years ago) toward economies based on car production, fully urbanized, with energy-intensive agriculture? Moreover, would not cheap energy lead to more use of materials, to a greater intensity of extraction of resources, to an increase in world trade in raw materials?

The eco-technological revolution, which was rather a series of innovations, is still working itself out in 2025. Experts in mass psychology now have a good hypothesis for how pseudo-inventions such as the 'cold fusion' of 1989 are sometimes generally taken in earnest, and we have also learned once and for all (after the experiences with nuclear energy and some bio-technologies, and of course the automobile) to tame our technological optimism. It seemed that the eco-technological revolution would be decisively helped by the introduction of environmental economic policies. Indeed, at the Rio de Janeiro conference of June 1992, the Business Council for Sustainable Development had solemnly proclaimed the need to 'internalize the externalities' into the pricing system, as if they knew how to count in present-value money terms the cost of future, uncertain externalities (such as plutonium from nuclear waste, or loss of biodiversity because of tropical timber exports). Some economists claimed to be able to 'capture the total economic value' of the environment, and a well-known ecological economist was understood to be saying in 1997 (probably with a subtle intention that escaped his contemporaries and still escapes us), that the environmental goods and services were worth US$33 trillion per year. Let us leave aside the vicissitudes of environmental money accounting (believe it or not, there is a group of people who, unaware of the march of history, still practise this *Glasperlenspiel* in 2025). In retrospect, what seems important was the new fiscal environmentalism of the 1990s. The share of direct and indirect taxes and social security payments in GDP in most Northern countries was between 30 and 40 per cent. A drastic change in the fiscal system towards resources and pollution could indeed change the economy. The fiscal system had moved relatively towards taxes on labour rather than on (increasingly mobile) capital in the 1970s, 1980s and 1990s (partly because of the triumph of neoliberalism, which paradoxically coincided with the ecological scepticism about the absence of long-term rationality of the market). Proposals were made for new eco-taxes, and indeed (despite the failure of Bill Clinton and Al Gore to introduce the BTU-tax in 1993, and despite the failure of Jacques Delors in the European Union in the same period to decrease taxes and charges on labour so as to increase employment and at the same time move towards taxes on energy and raw materials), there was a trend already in the 1990s towards a slight increase in fiscal revenues from taxes on pollution, on raw materials and the use of energy. However, there was a backlash – parties and movements arguing for tax-free car driving and air travel joined forces with the anti-feminist Men Movement (the MEMO, of such ugly memory), and together managed to downgrade and retard fiscal environmentalism. It was also realized that substantial carbon-energy taxes in countries depending on imported oil and gas (Japan, Western Europe, and increasingly the United States) would provoke international distributional conflicts of first magnitude with oil- and gas-exporting countries – some of them going through civil wars, or on the brink of revolution. The turmoil in Morocco, after the king's death and in the aftermath of the Algerian revolution of 2003, cut off the new gasoduct into Europe and pushed up fuel prices, while the Mexican Zapatista revolution was helped along by the obvious absurdity (from a Mexican point of view) of President Gore of the USA trying to fulfil once again in 2001 the promise of a substantial BTU-tax to be collected on oil imported (to a great extent) from Mexico.

In the 1990s, not only local but also international so-called 'externalities' (including carbon dioxide emissions) began to be discussed in a framework of 'environmental justice', that is, the equitable access to natural resources and the equitable distribution of the burdens of pollution. The environmental justice movement in the United States had been born in the 1980s out of many local fights against 'environmental racism' – the disproportionate allocation of toxic waste to areas inhabited by poor people who also happen to be Afro, Hispanic or Native Americans (such as the Navajo, who suffered the effects of uranium mining and radioactive waste). It came to be believed that in order to improve the state of the environment, the concern for environmental justice must be extended to the entire planet, including future generations. Demonstrations and mild riots by eco-feminist groups against the failure by governments to adopt effective greenhouse policies (the first one took place in Kyoto in December 1997) did more for the eco-techno-logical revolution (for instance, the spreading use of photovoltaics) than a hundred conferences of ecological economists or a hundred parliamentary projects on eco-fiscal reform.

However, the increasing success of the environmental justice groups gave cause for alarm, for the following reason. The promises of ecological modern-ization were not really fulfilled. The A in Ehrlich's equation continued to threaten the environment, and is a threat even now, when the rate of population growth is zero, and people are free to migrate throughout the world. Despite technical changes, the environmental impact of the economy has grown larger (measured by the physical indicators and indexes developed by ecological economists). Such indicators and indexes are of course controversial. Some indicators showed an 'inverted U' pattern early on, environmental impacts growing in the early stages of industrialization and decreasing later in absolute terms. This up-and-down pattern was much celebrated in the mid-1990s in Washington. The rich were greener than the poor! The poor were still too poor to be green! Other indicators showed the N pattern, or Opschoorian 'sideways inverted Z', up-down-and-up-again, which was also much celebrated at the time though not in Washington. Certainly, a strict thesis of global ecological limits would reduce economic growth to a zero-sum game, and this, it was feared – not without reason – could lead (in the rich North) not so much to feelings of guilt over the burden of the ecological debt as, on the contrary, to an aggressive *Lebensraum* reaction (such as the colonial war against Iraq in 1991, or the emphasis in NATO around the year 2000 towards the Southern Flank rich in oil and gas). Fortunately there was some scope for a little delinking, for some dematerialization and de-energization, without a decrease in living standards. More important than technological change, the Great Eco-Feminist Downsizing of consumption of commodities started at the time, in the rich countries. Large groups of young people (some of them claiming to have been influenced by the hippies of the 1960s) refused to have cars and became vegetarians. Courageous calls were heard from remote locations in the Rocky Mountains and from a place called Carnoules (where was Carnoules?), for a 'factor 4' or even a 'factor 10' reduction in energy and materials throughput in the rich economies. A factor 10 reduction without a decrease in welfare! Such ringing calls from ecological modernizers (one of them, the well-known professor Dr Mips, came straight from the ranks of the Technocrats of the 1930s and 1940s) were indeed meant in earnest and were useful for the cause of environmental justice because some precious time was gained to sort out ideas, and to stop the aggressive reaction from the governments of the ecological trespassing countries – if there is not enough for everybody, then 'we' have priority. True, to discuss again and again greenhouse economics and policies, from Rio to Berlin and to Kyoto and back again, and do nothing, was bad. In 2025, because of the accumulated greenhouse gases, it seems that the Gulf Stream could still change course and leave Western Europe shivering. Inaction by the rich was bad. Inaction was better, however, than claiming the right (not merely *de facto*) backed by military might to the whole atmosphere, the oceans and all new vegetation.

One idea that became popular in the early years of the twenty-first century, already presented by Dassman in the 1970s, was the contrast between 'eco-system people' and 'ecological trespassers'. Moreover, if increasing wealth meant (despite efforts at increasing efficiency in resource use), more use of undervalued natural resources from other territories, and also an increased production of residues, then there was an increasing ecological debt (admittedly difficult to quantify in money terms). Such ecological debt was owed not only to future generations, but also to the members of our own generation who used little environmental space. It also included a historical element, on account of the past occupation of environmental space. The annual meetings of the World Bank and IMF, where financial adjustment programmes were discussed that would make it possible to pay the external debt of indebted countries, were regularly disrupted from 1999 onwards by 'eco-debt' activists speaking for 'ecosystem peoples', led by a remarkable group of Latin American surnameless women belonging to the EPA network (the Ecology of the Poor of America): Silvia, Esperanza, Rayen, Ivonne, Alicia, Elizabeth, Cecilia, Margarita. They interrupted the meetings of the World Bank and IMF (i.e. the International Monetary Fundamentalists) to teach the delegates the principles of 'ecologically unequal exchange' – how aluminium from Ghana or northern Brazil or Venezuela was produced with cheap electricity, at great environmental cost, to the benefit of importing countries; how exports of bananas did not include in the price the loss of soil fertility because of loss of potassium as a nutrient; how tropical timber was exported at a speed much higher than its reproduction, and without accounting for loss of biodiversity. The 'Potosí Network' held a congress in Antwerp in 2007 that was a turning point in the discussion. Governments of countries that were debtors in external financial debt and creditors in ecological debt began to try to negotiate exchange of external debt for ecological debt, and (although the Third World debt was small compared to the large public and private debt in the rich countries) this unexpected threat of not paying, and claiming instead arrears from the North on account of the ecological debt, was a factor in the international financial crash of 2016. Financial debt, or 'virtual wealth', had grown in the South and especially in the North, far beyond what the productive economy could support. Moreover, a great part of the so-called productive economy (based on oil and other natural resources) was not productive at all, but was really a destructive economy.

Nowadays, the statistics on the 'ecological footprint' and 'environmental space' are taught in schools, but in 2000 they were really understood in all their complexities only by the members of the Society of Ecological Economists, a society that seems to have arisen at Louisiana State University (a wetland or a campus?) around 1980. In an urban context, the notion of the *ecological footprint* (implicit already in the 'organic' urban planning of Patrick Geddes and Lewis Mumford) had been developed in the 1980s and 1990s, showing how cities occupied hundreds of times their own territorial space in terms of the area needed to grow their food and their timber for paper, and to grow their energy sustainably or deposit their carbon dioxide safely.

The network REES (Real Ecological Economics for Society) published the landmark book *Green Cities of Today* in 2009. Subtitled 'A Practical Utopia', it provided a wealth of empirical material showing how urbanization could be combined with gardens and local recycling of waste, with local water collection, with intermodal walking-bicycling-public transport systems, with local supplies of energy and bioclimatic architecture, and with patterns of different sorts of local work and entertainment. Ecological economists became urban and regional planners in large numbers, displacing architects, economists and even geographers (who could have done better), but their ideas came too late to stop the disastrous growth of the large Asiatic conurbations (of 40 or 50 million inhabitants in some cases). We are now working hard on the change in land use, and in transport patterns everywhere in the world: this is perhaps the most important collective task of our age.

In the late 1990s, the 35-hour week in France and Italy, the LETS schemes, the defeat of plans for building incinerators of urban domestic waste (a scarcely noticed environmentalist success in Barcelona in 1997) and the new pride in composting and recycling, the campaigns against cars and in favour of bicycles (cars that killed cyclists were often destroyed and burnt on the spot, in the streets of Delhi and Shanghai and many other cities, after the drivers had been non-violently frightened away), the many movements for 'just and ecological trade' and for low-input or 'organic' agriculture (something of a misnomer since still in 2025 photosynthesis continues naturally to be the basis for all types of agriculture), all such movements and events had already announced the change. Instead of counting only in money, it was more sensible to count sometimes in calories and sometimes in hours of work, and sometimes not to count at all. Instead of working for the market, it was better to work for family, friends, neighbours and communities. Reciprocity and redistribution were preferable, socially and ecologically, to the unlimited expansion of the generalized market system. Was it Herman Daly or Leonardo Boff who in the bad old times had reminded us: 'Our blessings cannot be counted in money'?

In this way, the Eco-Feminist Alliance of Feminist Groups and environmentalism of the poor and environmental justice groups started to grow, linking up with the International of Hope, which the neo-Zapatistas had promoted in the late 1990s. They met in and outside the Web. They (us) are changing the world. We learnt to link up local and global issues, we were willing to use the intellectual resources and even some of the policies and technologies provided by the 'ecological modernizers', we introduced in the mainstream political and economic debate the notions of environmental space and the ecological footprint, ecological debt, biopiracy and ecological trespassing. All this, plus the financial crisis, gave us the triumph we are now enjoying in 2025. Marcos, the Sub, in his ripe old age, still dislikes the word 'ecology'; he claims that ecology is something for the Gringos. There are many Gringos in the Alliance, so perhaps he is right.

Notes

1. Cf. Funtowicz and Ravetz 1991 on 'post-normal science' and 'extended peer reviews'.
2. Human appropriation of the products of photosynthesis (HANPP) (Vitousek et al. 1986).
3. See the reports by the Wuppertal Institute, *Towards Sustainable Europe* (1995) and *Zukunftsfähiges Deutschland* (1995).
4. At least since Barnett and Morse 1963 and Krutilla 1967. See a critique in Norgaard 1990.
5. Article in *La Republica*, Lima, 6 April 1991. The words 'ecologist' (in the sense of not scientist but of social activist) and 'environmentalist' are used interchangeably.
6. 'Fictitious commodities' was Polanyi's term for land and labour in *The Great Transformation* (Polanyi 1944).
7. This letter is published in *Ecologia Política*, no. 14, 1997.
8. Castells is not explicitly environmentalist in his interpretation.

References

Acevedo, R. and E. Castro (1993) *Negros do Trombetas. Guardaes de Matos e Rios*, UFPA, Belem.

Agarwal, A. and S. Narain (1991) *Global Warming in an Unequal World: A Case of Environmental Colonialism*, Centre for Science and Environment, Delhi.

Agarwal, B. (1992) 'The gender and environment debate: lessons from India', *Feminist Studies*, 18 (1).

Almeida, A. W. (1995) *Carajas: a Guerra dos Mapas*, Supercores, Belem.

Ayres, R. U. and L. W. Ayres (1997) *Industrial Ecology: Towards Closing the Materials Cycle*, Edward Elgar, London.

Azar, C. and J. Holmberg (1995) 'Defining the generational environment debt', *Ecological Economics*, 14 (1): 7–20.

Azar, C. and T. Sterner (1996) 'Discounting and distributional considerations in the context of global warming', *Ecological Economics*.

Balvín Díaz, D. (with J. Tejedo Huamán and H. Lozada Castro) (1995) *Agua, minería y contaminación: El caso Southern Perú*, Ediciones Labor, Ilo, Perú.

Barnett, H. J. and C. Morse (1963) *Scarcity and Growth: The Economics Of Natural Resource Availability*, Johns Hopkins University Press, Baltimore, MD.

Borrero, J. M. (1994) *La deuda ecológica*, FIPMA, Cali.

Brechin, S. R. and W. Kempton (1994) 'Global environmentalism: a challenge to the post-materialism thesis?', *Social Science Quarterly*, 75 (2): 245–69.

De Bruyn, S. M. and J. B. Opschoor (1994) 'Is the economy ecologizing?', Tinbergen Discussion Chapters, TI 94–65, Tinbergen Institute, Amsterdam.

Buitenkamp, M., H. Venner and T. Wams (eds) (1993) *Action Plan Sustainable Netherlands*, Dutch Friends of the Earth, Amsterdam.

Bullard, R. (1993) *Confronting Environmental Racism: Voices from the Grassroots*. South End Press, Boston, MA.

Castells, M. (1983) *The City and the Grassroots: A Cross-cultural Theory of Urban Social Movements*, E. Arnold, London.

Cleveland, C. J. (1991) 'Natural resource scarcity and economic growth revised: economic and biophysical perspectives', in R. Costanza (ed.), *Ecological Economics*, Columbia University Press, New York.

Ehrlich, P. (1968) *The Population Bomb*, Ballantine Books, New York.

Funtowicz, S. and J. Ravetz (1991) 'A new scientific methodology for global environmental issues', in R. Costanza (ed.), *Ecological Economics*, Columbia University Press, New York.

Funtowicz, S. and J. Ravetz (1994) 'The worth of a songbird: ecological economics as a post-normal science', *Ecological Economics*, 10 (3): 189–96.

Gadgil, M. and R. Guha (1995), *Ecology and Equity: The Use And Abuse of Nature in Contemporary India*, Routledge, London and New York.

Gedicks, A. (1993) *The New Resource Wars: Native and Environmental Struggles against Multinational Corporations*, South End Press, Boston, MA.

Guha, R. (1989) *The Unquiet Woods*, Oxford University Press, Delhi.

Guha, R. and J. Martinez-Alier (1997) *Varieties of Environmentalism*, Earthscan, London.

Inglehart, R. (1977) *The Silent Revolution: Changing Values and Political Styles*, Princeton University Press, Princeton, NJ.

— (1995) 'Public support for environmental protection: objective problems and subjective values in 43 societies', *Political Science & Politics*. 57–71

Kuletz, V. (1992) 'Eco-Feminist philosophy. Interview with Barbara Holland-Cunz', *Capitalism, Nature, Socialism*, 3 (2)

Krutilla, J. V. (1967) 'Conservation reconsidered', *American Economic Review*, LVII (4).

Leff, E. (1994) *Green Production*, Guilford, New York.

Leipert, C. (1989) *Die heimlichen Kosten des Fortschritts*, Fischer, Frankfurt.

Magalhaês, S. B. (1994) 'As grandes hidroeléctricas e as populaçôes camponesas', in Maria Angela d'Incao and Isolda Maliel da Silveira, (eds), *A Amazônia e a crisi da modernizaçâo*, Museo Emilio Goeldi, Belém, pp. 447–56.

Martinez-Alier, J. (1991) 'Ecology and the poor: a neglected issue in Latin American history', *Journal of Latin American Studies*, 23 (3).

— (1994) 'The merchandising of biodiversity', *Etno-ecologia*, 3.

— (1995) *De la economía ecológica al ecologismo popular*, 3rd edn, Icaria/Nordan, Barcelona/Montevideo.

Martinez-Alier, J. and E. Hershberg (1992) 'Environmentalism and the poor', *Items*, Social Science Resource Council, 46 (1)

Martinez-Alier, J. and M. O'Connor (1996) 'Ecological and economic distributional conflicts', in R. Costanza, O. Segura and J. Martinez-Alier (eds), *Getting Down to Earth: Practical Applications of Ecological Economics*, ISEE, Island Press, Washington, DC.

McGrath, D. et al. (1993) 'Fisheries and the evolution of resource management in the lower Amazon floodplain', *Human Ecology*, 21 (2)

O'Connor, M. (ed.) (1994) *Is Sustainable Capitalism Possible?*, Guilford, New York.

Oilwatch (1996) 'Los desastres del petroleo en la Amazonia peruana', *Ecologia Politica*, 12.

Opschoor, J. B. (1995) 'Ecospace and the fall and rise of throughput intensity', *Ecological Economics*, 15 (2): 137–40

Peet, R. and M. Watts (eds) (1996) *Liberation Ecology*, Routledge, London.

Polanyi, K. (1944) *The Great Transformation*, Beacon Press, Boston, MA.

Raumoulin, J. (1984) 'L'homme et la destruction des ressources naturelles: la Raubwirtschaft au tournant du siecle', *Annales E.S.C.*, 39 (4).

Rees, W. and M. Wackernagel (1994) 'Ecological footprints and appropriated carrying capacity', in A. M. Jansson et al. (eds) *Investing in Natural Capital: The Ecological Economics Approach to Sustainability*, ISEE, Island Press, Covelo, CA.

Reyes, V. (1996) 'El valor de la sangre de drago', *Ecologia Politica*, 11.

Sabatini, F. (1997) 'Chile: conflictos ambientales locales y profundización democrática', *Ecología Política*, 12.

Salleh, K. Ariel (1997) *Ecofeminism as Politics: Nature, Marx and the Post-modern*, Zed Books, London.

Schmidt-Bleek, F. (1994) *Wieviel umwelt braucht der mensch? MIPS–Das Mass für ökologisches wirtschaften*, Birkhauser, Basle.

Schmink, M. and C. Wood (1987) 'The political ecology of Amazonia', in P. D. Little and M. M. Horowitz (eds), *Lands at Risk in the Third World*, Westview Press, Boulder, CO, pp. 38–57.

Schwab, J. (1994) *Deeper Shades of Green: The Rise of Blue-collar and Minority Environmentalism in America*, Sierra Club Books, San Francisco.

Selden, T. M. and D. Song (1994) 'Environmental quality and development: is there a Kuznets curve for air pollution emissions?', *Journal of Environmental Economics & Management*, 27: 147–62.

Shiva, V. (1989) *Staying Alive: Women, Ecology and Development*, Zed Books, London.

Stonich, S. (1993) *I am Destroying the Land! The Political Ecology of Poverty and Environmental Destruction In Honduras*, Westview Press, Boulder, CO.

Szasz, A. (1994) *EcoPopulism: Toxic Waste and the Movement for Environmental Justice*, University of Minnesota Press.

Varea, A. et al. (1997) *Ecologismo Ecuatorial* (3 vols), Quito, Abya-Yala.

Vitousek, P., P. Ehrlich, A. Ehrlich and P. Matson (1986) 'Human appropriation of the products of photosynthesis', *Bioscience*, 34 (6): 368–73.

WCED (1987) *Our Common Future* (the Brundtland Report), Oxford University Press, New York.

White, L. (1967) 'The historical roots of our ecological crisis', *Science*, 155 (3767): 1203–7.

11

Feminist Futures

AZZA M. KARAM

Feminism has been with us for a significant amount of time. It has coexisted with wars, peace, national, ethnic and religious mobilizations. While some ideologies and movements have risen and fallen, feminism in its many forms has remained and in some parts of the world continues to flourish. As we approach a new millennium, prophecies of doom and gloom are coterminous with those that predict more spirituality and development of the faculties of the human mind. Many questions are being posed as to where we will be as human beings, in a world for which global is a byword, ten or twenty years from now. How does feminism (some would call it a way of life, a mode of thinking and existing) fare today and how will it fare tomorrow? What will feminism mean in and for the next millennium? This chapter far from attempts to answer these considerable questions. It also does not look at every single dimension of feminism and therefore does not boast a comprehensive overview. These are reflections, many of them personal, by no means definitive, and intended to be provocative. The emphasis here is on what feminism means and the organizational practicalities it may entail, rather than on questions of political economy or sexuality.

The journey begins with a look at the current state of feminism, from the standpoint of someone who remains a 'conditional feminist', who is 'non-Western', but also non-anything else definable and quantifiable, but more a product of the 1960s to 1990s and looking forward to being a product of the 2020s as well. The second part of the journey attempts to map out the most pressing concerns that a future feminism will have to contend with, while the last section looks briefly at what feminism can do for the future, in the belief that some things are best left unsaid, perhaps because the feminism that lies ahead simply cannot and should not be anticipated.

Feminism and Diversity

The most pressing question, it seems to me now, is not just about going beyond a singular identity for feminism, since it has become all the more pressing to speak of feminisms in the plural, but about levels of identification among different generations of women with the bodies of feminist knowledge which have emerged in the last twenty-five years. (Deepwell 1997: 152)

Katy Deepwell's question is pressing for women anywhere in the world. But there are some slight qualifications. It should be added, for example, that what is at issue is not only 'levels of identification among different generations' but also different feminist convictions and ideas. While the need for different feminisms is perceived to be more or less a reality today, much the same way (i.e. not without controversy) that pluralism and hybridity are features of contemporary theoretical articulation, the diversity of feminist strategies also means that there are different priorities. These priorities may well render the question of feminist *identity* either redundant or secondary to other concerns (national, communal, religious or economic or a combination of all), deemed to be more pressing.

Julia Kristeva characterizes three moments of feminism that exist simultaneously: equal rights, advocacy for a separate women's culture, and a total re-evaluation of the notions of 'masculinity' and 'femininity' (1982: 36–8). These moments are certainly true of North American and European feminisms, but they are difficult to extrapolate in their entirety to other feminisms practised and conceptualized in different parts of the world.

'Western feminisms' have long been engaged in critiquing the Enlightenment and its offshoots in modernity. Such theoretical contestations have been the standard battleground for much of today's social, political and social science rhetoric and the site of substantial theoretical exchange and deliberation. But these contestations have also been ridiculed by many activists as 'elitist', 'removed from reality' and 'the stuff of luxury' – the latter referring specifically to the fact that working in the field often does not entitle one to the luxury of theoretical deliberations, no matter how relevant that may be. Some of those who share these feelings have tended to include feminists from the South (the Middle East, Latin America and the Indian subcontinent, among others), who are busy with traditional charitable work (soup kitchens, sewing classes, small-scale income-generating projects, mothers of prisoners and combatants in conflict situations, etc.). These women (and some of their male colleagues) will still maintain that the project of organizing and obtaining women's human rights is intimately connected to ensuring a better life for men and women in societies characterized by poverty and lack of freedom and democratic norms. Moreover, any re-evaluation of femininity and masculinity may well be undertaken as a side activity by others in these same societies, but the fact remains that the kind of feminism alluded to by all manner of feminist theorists (e.g. Judith Butler, Catherine MacKinnon, Julia Kristeva, Luce Irigaray, Naomi Wolf, Kate Millet and others) is seen as largely removed from the exigencies of daily life of many of these women.

Added to the ever-present gap between largely Western feminist theory and the practical needs of women globally is another feature of the state of today's feminisms: namely that of enduring sexism and its godfather, patriarchy, as well as the tendency to veer towards 'agonistic politics and strategic intervention' (Butler and Scott 1992; Braidotti 1995). The former applies almost universally and will be elaborated upon below, while the latter, in the contexts of the Middle East and elsewhere in the South, could also be described as the politics of reaction to incidents. This is intimately connected to the gaps that exist between feminist theory and practice in different parts of the world. For while the theories may critique subjectivities and offer alternative meta- or mini-narratives of emancipation, or critique the critique of the critique, women's realities are undergoing constant objectification in a number of open and subtle manners. The latter render it difficult to write about altering subjectivities, and more opportune to act out the symbols and means of reacting to this objectification on a daily basis.

An example of this manner of reacting to objectification can be found in the practice of veiling carried out in the Muslim world. While theorists would have it that 'the veil' is grounded within a history and practice of the objectification of woman's body, and general subordination and oppression, practice has indicated that veiling is also a form of consenting opposition, and in some cases, outright resistance to the objectification of the female body (cf. Macleod 1991; Karam 1996). This is intimately connected to a strategy that deems it necessary to defend oneself in a manner that would be acceptable and understood by others, or at least to attempt to use tools that are indigenous to the discourse of the situation and of that particular socio-political and historical moment. It is therefore in many ways a means of reacting, as well as a calculated intervention, to resist actively while revamping and recreating existing symbolism.

This strategy would remain anathema to many Western feminists, and indeed has its own indigenous opponents within the Muslim world. Yet it is a strategy that espouses so many feminist ideals: liberation, alternative subjectivities, contextuality and historicism, the right to choose, difference as positive, and most important of all, deconstruction (understood here in the broad sense of a consistent revision of the intersection between power and knowledge to counter strategies of marginalization) and reconstruction of meanings. The latter is best adjudicated by Braidotti:

> Some notions need to be deconstructed so as to be laid to rest once and for all: masculinity, whiteness, classism, heterosexism, ageism. Others need to be deconstructed only as a prelude to offering positive values and effective ways of asserting the political presence of newly empowered subjects: feminism, diversity, multiculturalism, environmentalism. (1995: 186)

Hence, in reacting to diverse situations, feminism is liable to be deconstructed in such a manner that it no longer follows a known pattern, which brings us back to the need for future feminisms to come to terms with diverse strategies and ideologies. But how can that take place when feminism still rallies around unity in collective action, and indeed, when postmodern hailing of difference as positive continues to receive angry and assertive negations from radical feminism as well as other dogmatic feminists who strongly maintain that stressing 'difference' is the death of feminism? More pertinently, what form of inclusion is feminism really when some feminists, in the pursuit of power, still follow exclusionary tactics of positing 'the other' – tactics that are supposed to be 'male', and would seem to stab at the core of collective feminist action?

It is ironic that the very methods that are critiqued by many feminists, such as those of nationalist movements ignoring women's concerns until 'national' unity is achieved, are also being used by some feminists against others who espouse a different set of priorities and/or concerns. It is even more ironic that the same methods of dismissal and delegitimation of arguments are being used by some feminists against others: either they are illogical (read irrational), or superfluous (read there is no problem), or are mean and nasty attempts aimed at destabilizing a growing force (read who do you think *you* are?). These are issues that will have to be dealt with in the coming years in order to achieve some kind of consistency and, indeed, in order to empower and enrich feminism.

Feminists and 'Others'

Another example of where Western feminisms have fallen short of taking into account the different experiences of 'others' – even though this experience is essential to comprehending and conceptualizing feminist realities (or imaginaries) – is in the domain of the public–private dichotomy. A large part of the feminist body of literature is dedicated to criticizing the dichotomy between public and private, arguing that it devalues women's contribution to society, and that it has been used to confine women and inhibit their input. A major problem with this kind of sustained criticism is that it ignores the fact that some feminists in other parts of the world have argued that the private domain does indeed exist separately from the public one, but that both domains are needed and are actually political. In other words, instead of motherhood being a private occupation forced on some women, which limits women's political inputs or contributions, it is actually reconstructed as a chosen political occupation with important social and economic repercussions (see Karam 1998).

Some Islamist feminists (some of the women who have joined movements of political Islam and argue for women's rights from within an explicitly Islamic framework[1]) have argued that it is necessary to maintain the two domains because each entails its own kind of politics, and that this difference in sites and diversity of strategies is an important and enriching tactic to empower both men and women – particularly in contexts where repressive state structures necessitate multiple means of countering power and creating discursive spaces. In a similar vein, the Argentinian Mothers of the Disappeared movement had explicitly political tones and repercussions, but relied on and derived legitimacy from a 'private' function – that of motherhood. In these contexts, a cry against the public–private dichotomy, and arguments that this dichotomy demeans women's work, may well run the risk of being characterized by the same ahistoricity and lack of context and universalism that feminism is meant to counter.

Yet another context in which today's feminisms operate revolves around the persistence of patriarchy and sexism, both evidenced in the stereotypes associated with feminism/ists. Elaborating on some of the stereotypes in the 1990s, Deepwell maintains that:

> Popular assumptions about feminism are used to close down on discussions of more complex issues by stereotyping anyone who raises feminist issues along the lines of: 'feminists just hate or have problems with men' ... Feminism can, then, be presented as a form of essentialist, separatist feminism dated from the seventies, associated with bra-burning, male-hating castrating viragos, or a monstrous female superiority identifiable ... as part of a radical 'outdated' politics. (1997: 158)

The idea that feminists hate men, and that consequently feminism entails that women's issues are separate from men's, is one that is, ironically, almost universal. The other stereotype associated with feminists as cyborgs and/or masculinized women of some sort is more relevant to the part of the world where women's choice to counter the femininity screamed by advertisements has become, to a large extent and relatively speaking, the norm (mostly in the Western world). In other words, in contexts where commercialized femininity is still seen as the ideal by some (which incidentally happens to coincide with situations where homosexuality remains an illicit and largely underground activity), and only gets vehemently criticized by 'those mad feminists', the stereotype rarely applies.

What does apply, however, with different emphasis and in diverse stages and doses according to the context, is the negative imagery associated with independent women = working women = morally loose women. Among some in the non-Western countries, feminism indeed carries the above associations, which are sometimes linked to overall Western norms and values in general. Among conservatives and traditionalists in many parts of the world, the notion that women should insist on being independent remains anathema, and the tendency is to connect this wish to women wanting to be wanton and uncontrolled. To that end, witness the supposedly 'Islamic' concept of *fitna* (chaos supposedly caused by women when/if they are too self-willed and thus uncontrolled), and the associations the 'Latino' concept of *machismo* has of 'controlling their women' and/or impacting on them (sexually and otherwise).

In the context of the persistence of patriarchy, Gayatri Spivak critiques the Subaltern Studies group by pointing towards this trend:

> Through all of these heterogeneous examples of territoriality and the communal mode of power, the figure of the woman, moving from clan to clan, and family to family as daughter/sister and wife/mother, syntaxes patriarchal continuity even as she is herself drained of proper identity. In this particular area, the continuity of community or history, for subaltern and historian alike, is produced on (I intend the copulative metaphor philosophically and sexually) the dissimulation of her discontinuity, on the repeated emptying of her meaning as instrument. (Guha and Spivak 1988: 31)

Another site where feminism has made an impact over the last 20 years is arguably one of the most important in terms of ensuring continuity in thinking and awareness-raising. It is also the site where knowledge is to be produced, shared and articulated: the university. As Maggie Humm indicates, 'Feminist politics and feminist theories of the 1990s have a fresh set of priorities including ... a renaissance of feminist culture ... in teaching' (1992: 60). It is no small feat that most universities in the Western world have included women's studies as a discipline in its own right, or a subject of study in the curriculum. It is a testament to the efforts of those who pioneered and argued for this as well as to the seriousness with which the issue is taken and the impact of long, hard years of feminist struggle on Western academia. Taking into account the criticisms that black feminists in particular have articulated regarding the exclusionary tactics of white feminism, constant reflection on the creation and production of knowledge remains important. As bell hooks notes, 'If we do not interrogate our motives, the direction of our work, continually, we risk furthering a discourse on difference and otherness that not only marginalizes people of color but actively eliminates the need for our presence' (1990: 132).

Women's studies have yet to be institutionalized in academia all over the world. And it would not be illogical to assume that as the credibility of reclaiming women's history and acknowledging the legitimacy of women's experience and their contribution grows, so will 'the permission' (indeed, one would think of 'the need', but it is important to be pragmatic enough to realize that academia in many parts of the world remains male-dominated and male-controlled; witness the Taliban in Afghanistan's first moves to bar women from education) to create a specialized space within the process of the production of knowledge. Today, even in the Western world, which pioneered the first women's studies centres, discussions are still going on regarding the need to have separate 'women's studies' within academia and the potential benefits of integrating that approach within other disciplines. These discussions often ignore the fact that women's studies are in themselves an integration of various disciplines and are therefore not detached and separate in substance, but are creating the discursive space where such integration is a focus rather than a by-product.

Keeping all these elements/problems/strengths of feminism in mind, the question remains what would/should feminism entail, ideally speaking, in the new millennium? And what would feminisms do for the new millennium?

Feminist Futures[2]

Global feminism enables women worldwide to see themselves as a part of a larger movement for change and to acknowledge and accept diversity of perspectives, opinion, and priority. Furthermore, a global feminist movement can respond to increased state repression of women, as governments that have lost control over economic systems try to increase control over social and cultural systems, particularly women and families ... The movement must bring women's ideas into society at large and must bring more feminists into the arena where decisions are made about women's lives. These are the challenges of the feminist future (Leslie Wolf and Jennifer Tucker, in Basu 1995: 457–8).

While the above are indeed challenges for the feminist future, the image portrayed nevertheless deserves caution. Global feminisms will be not one movement but many and hence there will be not one future, but many, each reflecting the different aspirations and priorities set by the different women. Furthermore, the assumption that 'women's ideas' are unique may not be shared by others in any given society. Whereas most women's life experiences are different from those of men, and hence their outlook and needs are different, it is also true that the mélange of different experiences is equally important to change a system of thinking and managing.

This is what Nederveen Pieterse refers to in terms of the necessity to have 'wider fields of negotiation' of interests in order to arrive at some kind of global regulation – a feature of global futures (see Chapter 1). Future proposals, he argues, must 'also be interactive multidimensionally ... and global futures thinking must turn in intersectoral synergies'. Issues that have been argued for many years to be 'women's issues', and to which many an international convention has catered, have to be seen in the future in terms of societal and global issues, that is, issues that touch all sectors of most societies. It is common to hear that 'women are half the population', that 'poverty and war affect women the most', and so on. But these have tended to be seen as issues separate from 'more major' concerns, or as demands that require specialized attention – witness discussions on women and/in development, or gender and development. In many respects, discussions concerning the *special* needs of women in development processes reflect the widening of discursive space. Today, most development agencies and literature have shifted from arguing for specialized projects/programmes for women in development towards arguing for *mainstreaming* gender into every aspect of policy-making and institutional development.

Mainstreaming, which can be seen as ensuring that what is unique becomes normal, constitutes one of the biggest challenges facing feminisms worldwide. For this widening of discursive space and practice is not only part of any attempt to ensure synergies, but can also be dangerously threatening to the specificities of any discipline or thought. The question that needs to be asked is whether feminism, as it has been understood up to now, is ultimately willing to risk losing its position as the only means of arguing for women's rights and developing a more just society. But before this question is asked, the widening of discursive space argued for requires that a more fundamental aspect be dealt with – the need for more futuristic modes of conceptualization. Rosi Braidotti argues for the need for 'visionary modes of intellectuality':

> This is the challenge of our immediate future: how to avoid the pitfalls of relativism (dismissing the universal as redundant) and of essentialism (nostalgic reassertion of essentialised identities), while asserting the accountability of our gender. ... This process is in no way nostalgic. Instead it is forward-looking. It does not aim at the glorification of the feminine, but rather at its actualisation as a political project of alternative female subjectivities. Its object is not to recover a lost origin, but to bring about modes of representation that take into account the sort of women whom we have already become. (1995: 188)

What is being pointed out here is to be distinguished from theory as currently understood.[3] What is called for is a way of thinking that takes as its point of departure the need to be grounded in local contexts. Such a feminism would indeed not be unilinear and may well be far from theoretical, but will no doubt acknowledge difference in tactics, perceptions, rationales and priorities. What it needs to do is to go beyond quantitative analysis. For many years the number of women who have been aware, educated, knowledgeable, involved, in development, in power, in environment, in, in, in, has been a central concern – rightly so. Future feminisms should show concern for the impact of those feminists already in positions of substance, that is, the qualitative dimension of feminism. Criteria for this kind of assessment, which would take into account the different contexts and prioritization that have been made and the rationale for doing so, have yet to be developed. This need not be seen as a means of evaluating feminism *per se*, but is rather a means of documenting, practically and with a view towards the future, best practices and lessons learned.

This feminism needs a forum for debate and one is provided by educational establishments, including universities. Future forums should include governmental as well as non-governmental organizations and organizations involved in the kind of work around such *en vogue* terms as 'development', 'democracy', 'human rights' and so on – enter the inter-sectoral synergies.

These institutions should further their efforts towards indicating that feminist endeavours should be seen as integral to overall attempts towards achieving a more just and equitable world. This can be done through practical cases that highlight successful endeavours and compile best-practice indices of use to others in the field.

Although it comes fully 20 years after Adrienne Rich's *Towards a Woman-Centred University*, the need for that forum remains and will continue to exist for some time. In Rich's words, 'women's studies programs, where they are staffed by feminists, will serve as a focus for feminist values even in a patriarchal context. Even where staffed largely by tokenists, their very existence will make possible some rising consciousness in students' (in Humm 1992: 392). While the need for awareness-raising within a diversity of forums is ongoing, what we may take into account is awareness-raising to whom and how? In the past, the emphasis on awareness-raising was largely tailored to women and was dominated by an emphasis on the 'weaknesses' (for lack of a better word) and problems that women face(d). Future tactics, however, will need to take into account that feminism can no longer afford to prioritize women as a target group and needs to include men as a prime constituency. Men should be included in the planning stages of all projects. Nor should 'men' be generalized and homogenized in the way some feminists say women have been themselves. There is no single category of men, and programmes designed for women should take this into account. Men have not exactly been enthusiastically included in feminist strategies (whether in classrooms, books or general discourse). Even if this is understandable in the light of mechanisms of exclusion and delegitimation that men in and out of power continue to use, it may be time for a change of strategy, such that men are seen as a target group to which many programmes, ideas, strategies and literature are directed.

Much feminist discourse tends to take as its starting point the weaknesses that women share. Indeed, a great deal of feminist literature addresses how women can empower themselves, and yet more of that in plain language needs to be carried out. The histories of feminisms so far have been a litany of complaints that seem to encourage discourse in a similar vein. Yet, after more than a century of modern feminism, it would seem to be wise to introduce a litany of successes – not because women should become complacent, but because it is high time that women and men be subjected to a barrage of success stories of how women actually overcame, in addition to how difficult it was, is and will be.

Feminism has been grounded in, and in many respects is about, a politics of power. That it is a fallacy that women do not care for power is by now an acceptable aspect of feminist discourse. What is less acknowledged and needs to be consciously addressed is the need to feel special and superior that many women still wish to feel. To this day, talk of how women can do a better job at politics, economics, global relations, etc., is rife. It is not in any way a novelty to advocate that traditional dichotomies of superior/ inferior, male/female need to be not reversed, but rejected. However, this can take place only when feminists themselves actively seek to eject policies of exclusion from among their own ranks. Deconstruction of feminism is to occur not only on the level of theory but also on the level of actual events. What is meant here is deconstruction as questioning and revamping the categories, frameworks and strategies that determine some things as 'natural', 'better', 'successful', etc. Deconstruction of dichotomous thinking should enable a thorough reworking of the way we view our lives and the meanings we attach to all forms of interaction.

A further consideration concerns feminism as a linkage between the global and the local, and featuring within future projects of emancipation. Feminism has been able to withstand a great deal of rupture and to use that positively to grow, largely due to a politics of resistance. Politics of resistance does not mean delinking or opting out (Nederveen Pieterse 1997: 84), but rather engagement on feminism's own terms. Resistance, as Foucault reminds us, is power: 'when there is power there is resistance, and yet, or rather con- sequently, this resistance is never in a position of exteriority in relation to power' (1978: 95). Since power politics is crucial to feminist endeavours, it follows that any future agenda cannot afford to be detached from that form of resistance.

By resisting Enlightenment legacies, feminist theory developed and was refined and used in such a way that it became instrumental in the formation of other theories and approaches to dominant paradigms. Moreover, it is by resisting today that feminism is no longer a singular, homogeneous movement but one that has become enriched in the plural. And it is by resisting that inclusiveness – or what some feminists have termed 'a politics of difference' (Lourde 1984: 115) – has been possible. Resistance has entailed a process whereby difference is queried, analysed, turned around and, in the process, acknowledged. Since resistance is an act of power it cannot be ignored – witness the latest feminist trends whereby feminism entails thoughts and ideas that, just five years ago, would have been anathema to mainstream feminism (and still are to some extent; cf. Karam 1997).

Resistance has been part and parcel of what has defined feminism. Implicit in resisting was the process of creating 'the other' – one has to resist something. This is where the widening of discursive space, of the terrain of negotiation, plays an extremely important role, for the challenge then becomes resisting the politics of othering through creating a politics of difference. Widening the space of inclusion is not synonymous with homogenization – although it may often be taken as such. It is precisely through developing a politics of difference, and a politics of inclusion, that feminist networks have managed to create the bridges and 'multilevel connections from local organizations to international networks'. The latter has been argued by Nederveen Pieterse (1997: 91) and others to be the core of emancipation in the context of globalization. Emancipatory futures are inextricably linked to making the connections between local events and global ones, and doing so through resistance and accommodating difference, thus sharing in the kaleidoscope of power.

Here we return to the question posed earlier: what can feminisms do for the future? As long as women feel oppressed/subjugated/unequal/discriminated against *as women*, feminisms will retain their *raison d'être*. Yet, once the discursive space is widened and enriched with the entry of other disciplines, other regional narratives, with the mainstreaming of gender concerns into each dimension of work and thinking, with multidimensional interaction, and synergies between different sectors, groups, ideas, experiences, then the specificities of feminisms may well appear problematic. Feminisms have an important role to play as long as there is a need (or perceived need) for their goals and their ideal of existence. As long as this need exists the futures imagined can still do with improvement. Once improvements take shape it will be the turn of another politics of resistance. The latter realizations are a prelude to coming to terms with the fact that, like language, feminism will vary from one family to another; like bridges, connections will be endlessly made; and like life, they will never be boring.

Notes

1. I make distinctions between different types of feminisms operating in the Muslim world: secular, Muslim and Islamist. The secular and the Islamist are seen as two extremes in a continuum, while the Muslim feminists are those who advocate a feminism based on harmonizing and bridging perceived gaps between Islamic principles and secular ones. For more elaboration see Karam 1997.

2. The following section, to reiterate, is not so much everywoman's dream as it is a personal reflection. As such, it has obvious limitations of general applicability, but remains a hopeful articulation.

3. Judith Grant, in a similar vein, argues that: 'A revitalised feminist theory must be, in some ways, a theory against feminist theory. There can be no democratically determined, universally applicable values, but they must be derived in practice by local struggles in order to avoid setting up abstract notions of humanity that recapitulate problems of exclusion endemic to older humanist models. It must be a feminism that talks about women's freedom and self-determination and that iterates the need for feminists to defend the rights of women to make bad choices. It cannot advocate a priori a "politically correct" standard of sexual or any other behaviour' (1993: 15).

References

Basu, A. (ed.) (with C. E. McGrory) (1995) *The Challenge of Local Feminisms: Women's Movements in Global Perspective*, Westview Press, Boulder, CO.

Bell, D. and R. Klein (eds) (1996) *Radically Speaking: Feminism Reclaimed*, Zed Books, London.

Benhabib, S., J. Butler, D. Cornell and N. Fraser (1995) *Feminist Contentions: A Philosophical Exchange*, Routledge, London.

Braidotti, R. (1995) 'Afterword: forward looking strategies', in R. Buikema and A. Smelik, *Women's Studies and Culture: A Feminist Introduction*, Zed Books, London.

Butler, J. and J. W. Scott (eds) (1992) *Feminists Theorize the Political*, Routledge, New York and London.

Deepwell, K. (1997) 'Bad girls? Feminist identity politics in the 1990s', in J. Steyn, *Other Than Identity: The Subject, Politics and Art*, Manchester University Press, Manchester.

Foucault, M. (1978) *The History of Sexuality*, Vol. 1 (tr. R. Hurley), Pantheon, New York.

Grant, J. (1993) *Fundamental Feminism: Contesting the Core Concepts of Feminist Theory*, Routledge, New York

Guha, R. and G. C. Spivak (eds) (1988) *Selected Subaltern Studies*, Oxford University Press, New York.

hooks, b. (1990) *Yearning: Race, Gender and Cultural Politics*, South End Press, Boston, MA.

Humm, M. (ed.) (1992) *Modern Feminisms: Political, Literary, Cultural*, Colombia University Press, New York.

Karam, A. (1996) 'Veiling, unveiling, and meanings of the veil: challenging static symbolism', *Thamyris: Mythmaking from Past to Present*, 3 (2): 219–36.

— (1997) 'Feminisms in Egypt', *People's Rights*, Cairo, August.

— (1998) *Women, Islamisms and the State: Contemporary Feminisms in Egypt*, Macmillan, London.

Kristeva, J. (1982) 'Woman's time', in N. O. Keohane, M. Rosaldo and B. Gelpi (eds), *Feminist Theory: A Critique of Ideology*, Harvester Press, Brighton.

Lourde, A. (1984) *Sister Outsider: Essays and Speeches*, The Crossing Press, New York.

Macleod, A. E. (1991) *Accommodating Protest: Working Women, the New Veiling, and Change in Cairo*, Columbia University Press, New York.

Nederveen Pieterse, J. (1997) 'Globalisation and emancipation: from local empowerment to global reform', *New Political Economy*, 2 (1): 79–92.

Steyn, J. (1997) *Other Than Identity: The Subject, Politics and Art*, Manchester University Press, Manchester.

Wolf, L. and J. Tucker (1995) 'Feminism lives: building a multicultural women's movement in the United States', in A. Basu (ed.) (1995), pp. 435–62.

III

Culture: Economics, Technology and Cities

12

Culture and Economic Growth: The State and Globalization[1]

KEITH GRIFFIN

It is commonly argued in economics that growth and human betterment can best be achieved by the accumulation of physical capital, that attempts to reduce inequality are likely to reduce economic efficiency and the rate of growth, that government can contribute most by doing least, and that culture has little or nothing to do with improving the material well-being of people or promoting human development. All four of these propositions have recently been challenged anew, and this chapter should be seen as part of that challenge, albeit a small part. In addition to challenging ancient ortho-doxies, however, I wish to look forward and consider briefly the policy implications of the revisionist views and the outline of a possible alternative future.

Inequality and Growth Revisited

There is a long tradition in economic thought that postulates a conflict between efficiency and equity, growth and equality. Indeed, this conflict sometimes is described as the 'great trade-off' (Okun 1975). The conflict has its origins, depending on the author, in the historical role of the capitalist class, in the importance for investment of a high share of profits in national income (Kaldor 1978) or in the propensity of the rich to save a higher proportion of their income than the poor (Haq 1963). Whatever the precise formulation, the conclusion inevitably reached is that any attempt by the government to reduce inequality in the distribution of income is highly likely to impair efficiency in the allocation of resources or lower the rate of growth, and probably both.

The human development perspective challenges these propositions and casts a different light on these issues.[2] For example, one implication of the human development approach is that the more equal the distribution of income is, the easier it is for the fruits of growth to be transformed into human development. It is equally plausible that under some circumstances, the greater the degree of equality, the faster the rate of growth is likely to be. Why might this be the case?

First, the perpetuation of inequality can be costly. Severe inequality produces resentment, discontent and unruliness, even rebellion. Containment of unruliness or suppression of discontent requires resources in the form of expenditure on the police and armed forces, the judiciary, prisons and the penal system – resources that could otherwise be used to promote economic expansion. In extreme cases inequality can make a society ungovernable and cause serious disruption of the economy.

Second, even in less extreme cases, inequality can undermine the legitimacy of the political regime. Inequality, and the avarice and ruthlessness that often are required to sustain it, weaken the rule of law, sever the bonds of trust that enable a society to function properly and destroy the social solidarity necessary for an 'imagined community' to operate as an effective state.[3] Moreover modern technology has destroyed the monopoly of the state over the means of violence. Crime, terrorism and insurgent movements have become banal; violence has become democratized; the victims of injustice have explosive means to vent their anger. And all of this can lower the rate of economic growth. One need look no further than Africa, the Middle East or American ghettos for evidence.

Third, the other side of this coin is that measures to reduce inequality can simultaneously contribute to faster growth. For example, there is much evidence that small farms are more efficient than either large collective farms of the Soviet type or the capitalist latifundia one finds in Latin America and elsewhere (e.g. Griffin 1974; Berry and Cline 1979). A redistributive land reform and the creation of a small peasant farming system can produce performances as good as, if not better than, those of other agricultural systems. The experience of such places as China and South Korea is instructive.

Fourth, what is true of small farms is equally true of small and medium industrial and commercial enterprises. An egalitarian industrial structure, as Taiwan vividly demonstrates, can conquer world markets (Fei et al. 1979). Large enterprises do not in general enjoy competitive superiority – the importance of economies of scale is much exaggerated – and often in developing countries large enterprises depend on the state for protection from foreign producers, for subsidized bank credit, for tax favours and for guaranteed sales to the public sector under state procurement policies. Industrial p licy thus often encourages both inequality and inefficiency. Small enterprises in contrast often face numerous official barriers, the removal of which would reduce inequality while encouraging faster growth.

Fifth, investment in education, particularly at the primary and secondary levels, is a highly effective way to reduce inequality in the distribution of income. It is also, as is becoming widely recognized, an effective way to stimulate growth. Even if one remains an unreconstructed advocate of growth and is unpersuaded by arguments that human development is the ultimate objective, there is a strong case for supporting large public and private expenditure on education. There probably is no easier way to combine equality and rapid growth. The whole of East Asia is testimony to the veracity of this proposition (e.g. Birdsall et al. 1995).

A final example of the falsity of the great trade-off is the liberation of women. Equal treatment of women would release the talent, energy, creativity and imagination of half the population. As it is, women already do more than half the world's work, but they have little control over resources (and often over their own bodies); they have restricted opportunities for education, employment and participation in political life; they are engaged in sectors such as the household economy, which are severely undercapitalized compared to other sectors, and which therefore condemn them to low productivity labour and low returns on their effort; and they are denied opportunities for advancement.[4] The subjugation of women produces inequality, inefficiency and a slower rate of growth than would otherwise be possible. The removal of discrimination, in contrast, would reduce inequality and promote growth, while of course raising the level of human development.

The old conflict between equality and growth thus turns out to be a shibboleth. Under some circumstances greater equality actually can accelerate economic growth, and greater equality almost certainly would contribute to human development. Thus intervention by the state to reduce inequalities in opportunities, income and wealth, if properly designed and implemented, can have very beneficial consequences.

Culture and the State

Although in principle the state can introduce policies to reduce inequality, increase the pace of economic growth and enhance human development, in practice states are often weak or use such power as they have to benefit particular classes, groups or factions in society rather than the population as a whole. This can occur in both democratic and authoritarian states, as the experiences of, respectively, Brazil and the Sudan attest. There are many possible reasons for this, but one neglected explanation – and possibly an important one – has to do with the role of culture.

Defining culture broadly, as is most appropriate in this context, as 'ways of life' helps to highlight several notable features of the contemporary world. First, there are of course a great many ways of life that one can observe. Some ways of life are geographically restricted while some cultures cover a large terrain. Indeed, there are more ways of life – that is, more cultures – than there are states. One obvious implication of this is that cultures and states do not coincide; the jurisdiction of territorial states does not 'map' the space occupied by distinct cultures. There is a disunity of coverage and this lack of coincidence creates a possibility of conflicting allegiances, divided loyalties and contested claims for primacy of affection.

Second, the cultures that one observes today are almost always older than any existing state. In fact the contemporary state is a relatively recent institutional innovation, dating roughly from eighteenth-century Europe, and the majority of actual states were created in the twentieth century after the disintegration of the worldwide imperial system. Most cultures antedate the emergence of the state system and the nationalism and patriotism associated with it. This does not imply that cultures are necessarily ancient, traditional or static, much less that they are timeless. On the contrary, cultures should be seen as changing, dynamic, fluid, in a constant state of flux. Thus cultures, paradoxically, are simultaneously young and old; they represent distinctive ways of life yet they are influenced by other cultures with which they come into contact.

Third, cultures often are transnational phenomena. Geographically, cultures frequently transcend the boundaries of territorial states. This obviously is true of Arab culture in the Middle East, of many African cultures divided by arbitrary boundaries during the colonial period, of 'Western' culture, of Kurdish culture in Turkey, Syria, Iraq and Iran, of Chinese culture in East and Southeast Asia, and so on. Cultures thus pose, or are perceived to pose, both an external challenge to some states and a risk, perhaps only a latent risk, of internal subversion. States often respond to these threats, real or imaginary, either by suppressing transnational cultural minorities (for example, the suppression of the Kurdish minority by the Turkish state) or by half-hearted obeisance to ideals of transnational economic and political union (as in the various, and unsuccessful, pan-Arab, pan-African and pan-Latin American movements). Only in western Europe, with the formation of the European Community, have strong supranational institutions been created within a relatively homogeneous cultural space.

Fourth, virtually all states include within their boundaries a multiplicity of cultures. Indeed, the term 'nation-state' is a misnomer. Modern states include a large number of national groups, ethnicities, 'tribes', languages and religions – that is, ways of life. The modern state is irreversibly a multicultural institution. Pluralism is a fact of life of the contemporary world, a fact that has yet to be properly digested by analysts and policy makers alike. Some states (Israel, Pakistan, Iran) behave as if they contained a homogeneous population of uniform religious belief; few states (Switzerland is an obvious exception) have constructed institutions that explicitly take into account the linguistic, religious and ethnic diversity of citizens.

Many states have made attempts, of varying degrees of effort and success, to reduce discrimination against minority groups, to integrate those of different 'race' into the mainstream and to assimilate the foreign-born, the indigenous population and other minorities into the dominant society. Diversity, pluralism and multiculturalism within states, however, raise issues that go beyond assimilation, integration, affirmative action, anti-discrimination and the like. They raise questions of access to resources and institutions, participation in the wider life of the polity and society, as well as issues of fairness and equity. Cultural diversity raises the questions of how best to protect the interests and rights of minorities, how to avoid the tyranny of the majority, and how best to secure adequate representation of minorities in decision-making institutions.

How one approaches these questions depends in part on how one views the role of multiculturalism within states. At one end of the spectrum of opinion are those who view pluralism as a disadvantage. Diversity is a source of conflict: it often leads to violence and bloodshed; it results in political instability; and it makes it hard for people to get along together in their daily life. Multiculturalism is something that must be contained or managed, preferably by making 'them' as much like 'us' as possible. Far from contributing to economic growth and human development, cultural diversity is an obstacle that in one way or another must be overcome or got around.

At the other end of the spectrum are those who regard cultural diversity not as a liability but as an asset. Different ways of life, different ways of looking at the world, different ways of thinking are indeed challenging and a source of dissonance and tension that can lead to conflict and violence. But those challenges and tensions are also a source of creativity (in all its forms) and it is creativity (not capital in any of its forms) that is the fountainhead of economic growth and human development. That is, it is new knowledge, new technology and new institutional arrangements that are the ultimate sources of growth and development[5] and it is a plausible hypothesis that cultural diversity acts as a stimulus to innovative activities of all sorts. That is, one can view cultures as 'experiments' that are sources of knowledge. The more experiments humanity conducts, in other words the greater the cultural diversity, the more knowledgeable and innovative we are likely to be.

It has long been recognized that minorities often are highly innovative in business and account for a disproportionate number of entrepreneurs. Think of the Chinese in Southeast Asia, the Lebanese in west Africa, the Indians in east Africa and the Quakers in the United Kingdom. The claim being made here, however, is more general: namely, that pluralism contributes to creativity in all fields of endeavour. If this is true, then over the very long run multicultural states have more potential than states with a relatively homogeneous population. A potential for human and material progress does not of course imply that the potential inevitably will be realized. The translation of potential into actual achievement depends on whether in a particular time and place the advantages of pluralism can be brought into play and the disadvantages minimized. At any given moment some culturally homogeneous societies (e.g. Japan, South Korea) may appear on balance to be less divisive and more dynamic than some pluralist societies, but given a longer time horizon, pluralism is likely to be more advantageous than homogeneity.

Globalization and Cultural Interchange

Cultural diversity is of course much greater at the global than at the country level. It might have been possible once upon a time to imagine cultures as being separated from one another – with room to breathe and to develop independently – but technological change in transport and communications has for centuries been dissolving time and space, breaking down the barriers that surround even the most isolated cultures. This process has accelerated dramatically in the last 50 years and is part of a wider tendency towards globalization. One consequence of globalization is that cultures are coming into increasingly close contact with one another. The Chinese culture rubs against the Indian culture. The Indian culture rubs against the European culture. The European culture rubs against African cultures, and so on.[6]

The 'rubbing' of cultures is not a question of physical proximity and, indeed, strictly speaking cultures do not have fixed boundaries. They interpenetrate and for this reason cultures are not homogeneous; they are, rather, hybrids (Nederveen Pieterse 1994c). It is thus particular cultural attributes that rub against one another and not one particular reified culture (much less a singular national or state culture) that rubs against another.

Be that as it may, this 'rubbing' has been going on for a long time and before considering the implications for the contemporary world, it is worth glancing back at history. It would be fatuous to claim that technological change and the cultural interchange that follows it have been universally beneficial. Development has been uneven and, more important, the impact of cultural interchange has often been asymmetrical, some groups and cultures losing absolutely, not just relatively. Central Asia, for instance, long occupied a strategic position on the caravan trade routes connecting China with the eastern Mediterranean and Europe. Its cities of Samarkand, Bukhara and Khiva (now in Uzbekistan) were centres of economic, political and cultural activity where the arts and architecture, the natural sciences and mathematics and theology flourished. Beginning in the fifteenth century, however, the development of transoceanic transport made overland transport through Central Asia unprofitable and the region fell into a steep decline. The maritime regions of Asia were brought into closer contact with Europe while parts of the interior of Asia became increasingly isolated.

Closer contact, however, has been a mixed blessing. Whether one considers the explosive conquests of Islam beginning in the seventh century, which from the epicentre in Arabia covered the whole of the Middle East, all of North Africa and the Iberian peninsula in Europe, or the westward migration of the Mongol 'hordes' of the thirteenth century, which ended at the Danube river and the outskirts of Budapest, or the unrelenting expansion of western Europe from the fifteenth century onwards to virtually every corner of the globe, cultural interchange often seems more like a one-way street than a dual carriageway. Cultural contact has often been a by-product of military encounters and has been associated with violence, pillage, war, enslavement, conquest, colonialism and imperialism (Elsenhans 1991). It has led to the introduction of alien diseases to those who had no natural resistance to them, and in some cases to the decimation of indigenous populations. It has helped to spread racism;[7] occasionally it has resulted in genocide; more often it has led to the destruction of pre-existing social structures and the system of beliefs that sustained them.[8] Historically, globalization has often had a fatal impact.[9]

Yet there is another side to the story: cultural contact was indeed a mixed blessing. The initial effects of cultures rubbing against one another may well be accurately described by the phrase 'a fatal impact',[10] but the longer-term effects were more positive. Contacts between cultures led to a myriad exchanges and adaptations that were of benefit to all parties. Consider foodstuffs and primary commodities. Latin America gave us maize, potatoes, the tomato and natural rubber; Ethiopia and Yemen gave us coffee; China gave us tea and noodles (which the Italians transformed into pasta), and so on. The world's pharmacopoeia similarly draws on botanical products from many different regions. The same is true of our domesticated animals.

Early Chinese science led the world and in the field of technology, China gave us paper, porcelain (or fine 'china'), the compass, gunpowder and much else (Needham 1954). The Arabs gave us our system of numerals. The Central Asians gave us algebra and taught us how to measure the motions of the heavens. India gave us Buddhism, the Arabian peninsula Islam and Palestine Christianity. Mutual influences in art and architecture, music and dance, crafts and household technology are too numerous to recount. All our cultures have been immeasurably enriched by contact with others.

Similar processes can be observed today. Indeed, whatever may have been the case in the past, today no culture, no society is completely closed.[11] The questions revolve around the degree of openness and the terms on which a culture interacts with other cultures – that is, whether the relationship is one of subordination, domination and exploitation or one of equality, mutual respect and beneficial exchange. The difference today is that globalization has made cultural interchange more frequent than in the past, deeper and more rapid. Some have speculated that we are witnessing the emergence of a 'global culture' with local cultures being submerged under an irresistible tide of Western influence. Culture worldwide is becoming more homogeneous: Coca-Cola, blue jeans and North American popular music rule the roost. Local dialects and entire languages are disappearing by the hundreds, local cuisines are being replaced by Western-style fast foods, traditional ways of life are being abandoned in favour of pale images of the American way of life.

While there is some truth to this, cultural interchange in the modern world is a two-way exchange. Capital, technology and even labour circulate globally. Science is universal and accessible to all to a greater degree than ever before. Ideas, information and knowledge are transmitted much more rapidly and more widely than in the past. The result is an increase in diversity: greater heterogeneity, not greater homogeneity. This is true at any given location, as more and more ways of life learn to coexist, and it also is true globally, as cultural interpenetration multiplies the number of permutations and in the process creates new ways of life, new cultures. This increased diversity, in turn, has led to an acceleration in creativity and innovation. There has been an explosive growth of knowledge and technology in the last 50 years and this has greatly contributed to the rapid advances in human development that have occurred and to the rapid economic growth we have enjoyed, a pace of growth worldwide that is unprecedented in human history. Cultural interchange has indeed been a mixed blessing, but the positive contribution of interchange has been extraordinarily large.

Intrinsic and Instrumental Values of Culture

Culture (or the communal aspect of life) is analogous to human development (which focuses on the individual) in that culture is valued in itself and also as a means to obtain other things that are desired or valued. That is, culture possesses both intrinsic and instrumental value. The intrinsic value of culture has long been recognized and is reflected in many ways: in concerns to preserve cultural heritage, to respect our traditions and the preceding generations who passed them on to us, to record spoken languages before they disappear, to conserve, restore and maintain historical monuments, art objects and ancient artefacts. Culture as our way of life is something most of us treasure and wish to preserve in a recognizable form; it contributes to our sense of self or who we are and to our sense of satisfaction or well-being.

In addition, however, culture as a means is becoming widely recognized. Increasingly the instrumental value of culture is being used by leaders in various areas of life to achieve economic, social and political purposes. This includes the appeal to tradition to forge new alliances based on ethnicity or nationality, sometimes with the objective of creating new, culturally homogeneous states, as with the Serbs in Bosnia. It also includes the revival of religious and other traditions in an attempt to re-establish an old order, to re-create a 'golden age' and to impose ancient, fundamental values on a society regarded as immoral and godless. The Christian, Jewish, Islamic and Hindu 'fundamentalist' movements can be interpreted in this way.

Thus culture has been used in places for sectarian and reactionary purposes and as a weapon to preserve or create a particular way of life. These uses of culture reflect 'a politics of nostalgia' (Nederveen Pieterse 1995). These uses of culture, however, are only part of the global picture. As argued above, globalization has led to an intensification of cultural interchange and this, in turn, is transforming local cultures without necessarily producing cultural uniformity. For example, culture is being used to create new forms of expression: English is becoming the *lingua franca,* yet spoken English is evolving in different directions in different regions of the world and taking on a separate identity, while at the same time the number of people who are bilingual or multilingual is increasing rapidly. Similarly, cultural interchange has led to new ways of communicating (such as the fax and Internet), new types of music, new ways of doing business (the transnational corporation), new forms of political organization (such as the European community), new channels of international crime and even new ways of finding a spouse (for example, by advertising in the international media). This burst of cultural creativity or cultural vitality, although uneven across space, is very widespread and indeed is reshaping the world, simultaneously creating elements of a 'global culture' while strengthening many features of 'local culture' or, better still, 'popular culture'.

One can think of culture as the glue that binds people together and enables them to interact. But cultures may not be equally successful in enabling people to live well, in peace and harmony, and to exercise their creativity. A culture of peace and harmony, for instance, is something that must be created, not just taken for granted. Genocide, ethnic cleansing, civil conflict, repression of minorities, domestic violence – today as in the past, nationally and internationally – are a reproach to our political cultures. Far too many people on this planet experience violence as an undesired aspect of their 'way of life'. Indeed, for many, violence or the threat of violence have become routine, a commonplace.

Yet at another level the glue provided by culture makes human development and economic growth possible. At this more profound level, culture is the most valuable instrument of all. Culture gives people a sense of identity and helps to define one's place in the world. It provides a degree of psychological security by enclosing each person within symbolically visible cultural boundaries. It fosters trust and cooperation within the group and thereby facilitates collective agreements, working together and market exchange. It makes people's behaviour and reactions more predictable than otherwise and this, too, facilitates cooperation, exchange and economic transactions in general. It inhibits (or at least contains) interpersonal, interkinship and intercommunity conflict while at times accentuating conflict with those of other cultures, particularly when 'the other' is sharply defined or differentiated.

Globalization is bringing cultures into increasingly close and frequent contact with one another. This 'rubbing' produces friction and the possibility of conflict,[12] which in turn require further cultural adaptation and institutional innovation. But cultural contact also leads to cultural exchange, to mutually profitable borrowing and lending, and to cultural adaptation. These, in turn, result in cultural vitality for all concerned, in aesthetic, scientific and technological creativity and in economic expansion. Indeed, it is quite possible that cultural exchange is one of the roots, perhaps the principal root, of global dynamism and the ultimate source of human creativity, human development and economic growth.

If one adopts a culture-centred rather than a state-centred view of the world, things look rather different. Culture seen from a global perspective can be regarded as human 'software' (Banuri 1990). This is a global asset that in principle is accessible to all, although in practice some groups have much greater ease of access than others. Access to this 'software' takes place when cultures interpenetrate, a historical process that goes back as far as one can see. Today, however, cultural interpenetration is more frequent, more rapid and more pervasive than ever before. This aspect of globalization may ultimately be more significant than other features of the process that receive so much attention, namely, the rapid growth of international trade, the investments by transnational corporations, the huge flows of financial capital, the migration of labour and the political and institutional transformations occurring at supra-national levels. The reason cultural interpenetration is so important is that it implies cultural exchange and this, in turn, implies diversity, heterogeneity and a breaking down of mental and conceptual boundaries. That is, cultural exchange can be understood as 'a translocal learning process' (Nederveen Pieterse 1994c: 177) that stimulates creativity and is the fountain-head of material progress and human development.

An Alternative Future

A reassessment of the four propositions with which we began has implications for an alternative future. This alternative future could be constructed around the nexus of equality, growth, human development and culture. I have argued that for any given increase in output, the greater is the degree of equality in the distribution of income and wealth, and the greater the increase in the average level of human development. That is, the impact of growth on human development depends in part on the distribution of income. At the same time, however, the greater the degree of equality, the faster the rate of growth of output is likely to be. That is, the direction of causality runs from equality to growth, and not the other way round. There are thus good reasons to give greater prominence to policies to reduce inequality than has been common in recent policy debates.

Technical change in the armaments industry has led to the democratization of violence. The state no longer has a monopoly on the instruments of warfare or the means to control the civilian population, and hence its ability to maintain law and order has been eroded. Recognition of this fact will result eventually in greater recognition by the state that it must seek to reduce the justifications or pretexts for violence adduced by those who oppose the established order. If the state is increasingly unable to control the supply of the instruments of violence, it will have little alternative but to diminish the desire for violence. This implies the creation of a 'culture of peace', nationally and internationally, based on respect for human rights, participation in political life and a celebration of cultural diversity and pluralism. Equality in this sense is likely to be high on future global agendas.

Greater public expenditure on education (especially at the primary and secondary levels), and greater investment in human capital in general, would almost certainly result in a reduction in inequality and, simultaneously, in an acceleration of the rate of growth of incomes and output. The denigration of the welfare state, so fashionable today, has gone much too far, and an alternative future consistent with the arguments of this chapter is bound to include a prominent role for public expenditure on human development.

The liberation of women – and specifically the provision of greater educational opportunities for girls, the creation of opportunities for paid employment by women, the removal of discrimination and barriers to occupational mobility, the provision of greater access to credit, and the equal treatment of women by the legal system, including inheritance laws – would obviously do much to redress pervasive inequalities. By releasing the talents, energy and creativity of half the population, greater equality for women also would stimulate economic growth.

These changes require action by the state. No desirable alternative future can be based on a withering of the state. The contemporary state, however, requires considerable adaptation. The point of departure is recognition that modern states are inescapably pluralist and multicultural institutions, and this implies that the legitimacy of states in future will have to rest on the foundation of wide participation in political, social and economic institutions; unhampered access to resources by those who can use them productively; fairness and equity in all spheres of life, including for instance language policy in multilingual societies; and constitutional or other mechanisms to ensure that the rights of minorities are protected.

The reconstruction of the state on a multicultural foundation would reflect not only the reality of pluralism as a social fact of life but also recognition that pluralism is a collective asset, a public good that can yield benefits to all. Cultural heterogeneity is a source of creativity and dynamism and arguably the ultimate source of economic growth and human betterment. Openness to ideas and to alternative ways of life, to the 'other' and to 'them', is a more secure and more fruitful foundation for future states than an attempt to construct a community around a homogeneous 'nation', at least in the long run. Indeed, the aspiration to create 'nation-states' is little more than a will-o'-the-wisp.

Just as one must recognize that states contain a multiplicity of cultures, so too one must recognize that individual cultures often cross state boundaries. This fact of cultural geography rarely is reflected in our political institutions. In future, however, we may well see the growth of supranational institutions that embrace transnational cultures and which provide a layer of organization somewhere between the state and the global level. Seen in this light, the European Community may be a harbinger of things to come. The Association of South East Asian Nations (ASEAN) may be another.

Globalization in the realm of culture is, however, a very powerful force, no less powerful than economic globalization. Moreover, cultural interchange globally is as valuable as commercial interchange, and ultimately perhaps more valuable. The interpenetration of cultures at the global level that we are now witnessing will, in my judgement, lead not to a 'world culture' but rather to the creation of new hybrids, new permutations and greater diversity. That is, globalization will spawn new cultures, and these new cultures – like the old ones – will be a source of dynamism, creativity and increased well-being. We must use our imagination, however, to ensure that cultural interpenetration is genuinely a two-way street, that is, that exchange rather than domination characterizes cultural globalization.

Rules of the game will have to be established and enforced concerning, for instance, trade in valuable cultural artefacts, the preservation of treasured sites and monuments, the recording of languages threatened with extinction, and the use by transnational media of the airwaves and space (part of our global commons) for transmission of cultural material. Some progress has been made already, but we have a long way to go.[13] If cultural interpenetration is to be a two-way street, then the rules of the game must be based on principles of equality and mutual respect that, in turn, reflect widespread recognition that cultural interchange is mutually advantageous.

Notes

1. I am grateful to Steven Helfand, Azizur Rahman Khan, Prasanta Pattanaik and Jan Nederveen Pieterse for helpful comments on an earlier version of this chapter. This chapter is a much shortened version of Griffin 1997.

2. For statements of the human development approach see Sen 1990 and UNDP 1990: Ch. 1.

3. The phrase 'imagined communities' is borrowed from Anderson 1983.

4. A great deal of evidence is assembled in UNDP 1995.

5. This idea is nicely captured in Joseph Schumpeter's statement that 'add successively as many mail coaches as you please, you will never get a railway thereby' (1959: 64, n1).

6. Indeed, it can be argued that European culture was constituted historically by non-European (namely Asian and African) influences and is a product of cultural mixing that goes back at least to ancient Egypt. See e.g. Nederveen Pieterse 1994a.

7. For an analysis of how scientific and technological achievement became a measure of the value of a civilization in the eighteenth century, justifying the right to 'civilize' inferior 'races' and to dominate the world, see Adas 1989.

8. For a study of how this continues today in the Amazon, see Lewis 1988.

9. The phrase is borrowed from Moorehead 1966.

10. The effects of European expansion and the 'development of underdevelopment' are discussed in Griffin 1969: Ch. 1 and Frank 1966.

11. In the late 1960s to the early 1980s some analysts advocated policies of semi-autarky and 'delinking' underdeveloped countries from the global economy (e.g. Amin 1982). It is

obvious today, however, that neither involuntary delinking (as in Iraq and North Korea) nor voluntary delinking (as in Myanmar and Cambodia) is a promising avenue for economic growth or human development (see Nederveen Pieterse 1994b).

12. Samuel Huntington (1993) has argued that in future the 'principal conflicts of global politics' will be dominated by the clash of civilizations or cultures.

13. See the report of the World Commission on Culture and Development 1995.

References

Adas, M. (1989) *Machines as the Measure of Men*, Cornell University Press, Ithaca, NY.

Amin, S. (1982) 'Crisis, nationalism and socialism', in S. Amin, G. Arrighi, A. G. Frank and I. Wallerstein (eds), *Dynamics of Global Crisis*, Monthly Review Press, New York.

Anderson, B. (1983) *Imagined Communities: Reflections on the Origin and Spread of Nationalism*, Verso, London.

Banuri, T. (1990) 'Modernization and its discontents: a cultural perspective on theories of development', in F. Appfel Marglin and S. A. Marglin (eds), *Dominating Knowledge*, Clarendon Press, Oxford.

Berry, A. and W. Cline (1979) *Agrarian Structure and Productivity in Developing Countries*, Johns Hopkins University Press, Baltimore, MD.

Birdsall, N., D. Ross and R. Sabot (1995) 'Inequality and growth reconsidered: lessons from East Asia', *World Bank Economic Review*, 9 (3).

Elsenhans, H. (1991) *Development and Underdevelopment: The History, Economics and Politics of North–South Relations*, Sage, New Delhi.

Fei, J., G. Ranis and S. Kuo (1979) *Growth with Equity: The Taiwan Case*, Oxford University Press, Oxford.

Frank, A. G. (1966) 'The Development of Underdevelopment', *Monthly Review*, 18 (4).

Griffin, K. (1969) *Underdevelopment in Spanish America*, Allen and Unwin, London.

— (1974) *The Political Economy of Agrarian Change*, Macmillan, London.

— (1997) 'Culture, human development and economic growth', UNRISD–UNESCO *Occasional Papers on Culture and Development*, no. 3.

Haq, M. ul (1963) *The Strategy of Economic Planning*, Oxford University Press, Karachi.

Huntington, S. P. (1993) 'The clash of civilizations?', *Foreign Affairs*, 72 (3).

Kaldor, N. (1978) 'Capital accumulation and economic growth', in N. Kaldor (ed.), *Further Essays on Economic Theory*, Holmes and Meier, New York.

Lewis, N. (1988) *The Missionaries*, Secker and Warburg, London.

Moorehead, A. (1966) *The Fatal Impact: An Account of the Invasion of the South Pacific, 1767–1840*, Hamish Hamilton, London.

Nederveen Pieterse, J. (1994a) 'Unpacking the West: how European is Europe?', in A. Rattansi and S. Westwood (eds), *Racism, Modernity and Identity: On the Western Front*, Polity Press, Cambridge.

— (1994b) 'Delinking or globalisation?', *Economic and Political Weekly*, 29 January.

— (1994c) 'Globalisation as Hybridisation', *International Sociology*, 9 (2).

— (1995) 'The cultural turn in development: questions of power', *European Journal of Development Research*, 7 (1).

Needham, J. (1954) *Science and Civilisation in China*, Cambridge University Press, Cambridge.

Okun, A. (1975) *Equality and Efficiency: The Big Tradeoff*, Brookings Institution, Washington, DC.

Schumpeter, J. (1959) *The Theory of Economic Development*, Harvard University Press, Cambridge, MA.

Sen, A. (1990) 'Development as capability expansion', in K. Griffin and J. Knight (eds), *Human Development and the International Development Strategy for the 1990s*, Macmillan, London.

UNDP (1990) *Human Development Report 1990*, Oxford University Press, New York.

—— (1995) *Human Development Report 1995*, Oxford University Press, New York.

World Commission on Culture and Development (1995) *Our Creative Diversity*, UNESCO, Paris.

13

Technologies of Post-Human Development and the Potential for Global Citizenship

MIKE FEATHERSTONE

The invitation to speculate on what one would like to see in the year 2020 has to be set against a particular horizon of possibilities. One is the discourse of technology-led change, which assumes that the possibilities new technologies offer for empowerment, for economic gain and 'worlding' will mean that they are sought out and implemented. In effect, all our cultural practices and the majority of our modes of association and social and human reproduction are potentially mediated through these future technologies. How these technologies are mediated and regulated by the various collectivities and agencies on the global level (nation-states, corporations, NGOs, etc.) is another question – a vital question that relates to our capacity to act and make a difference. We need to theorize about the possibility of developing a global public sphere with new forms of global and technological citizenship that can mobilize critical publics. We need to understand the potential for greater flexibility of communication and association to create new alliances that have the potential to work through once rigid institutional forms and help to de-monopolize existing modes of exclusion and power structures.

One powerful and influential image of our global future comes from the cyberpunk novels of William Gibson. In his first novel, *Neuromancer* (1984) Gibson coined the term cyberspace to refer to the global communication network, which has been extended beyond the current Internet into a parallel virtual reality world – a vast digital data construct in which one can move and interact with the full range of sensory involvement. Cyberspace is a vast three-dimensional city of data containing every book, text, image, picture, movie, TV programme – all human culture is there. It is also a space for corporate power struggles, with one of the main aims to maintain an edge over one's competitors by stealing data (hacking into corporate databases, which are consequently protected with electronic counter-measures). It is this description of cyberspace, as a three-dimensional dataspace through which one can fly through cities of data, that has caught the imagination of the information technology community. At the same time, it has been remarked that cyberpunk fiction often has a *cinema noir* quality to it, a combination of 'hi-tech' and 'low-tech' 'mean streets struggles'. William Gibson has had a creative interchange with Mike Davis, whose influential book on Los Angeles, *City of Quartz* (1990), presents LA as a divided city with a ghettoized lower class who lack access to public space and are excluded by private policing and surveillance from the middle- and upper-class fortress enclaves.

In Gibson's world, and in novels like Neal Stephenson's *Snow Crash* (1992) and Bruce Sterling's *Islands in the Net* (1988), the current phase of global economic deregulation and marketization is extended into the future. Not only do we have the roll-back of the state, but large corporations dominate the world and have taken over many state functions, as in Stephenson's account of early twenty-first-century Los Angeles in *Snow Crash*. LA has succumbed to balkanization with districts of the city franchised off to Uptown, Narcolumbia, Caymans Plus, Metazania, Nova Sicily, New South Africa, Mr Lee's Greater Hong Kong and The Clink. Each unit operates its own security and legal system and admits only certain people. Even the US Navy has been sold off and 'Uncle Bob's Defense Force' runs its largest remnant.

But it could well be the case that in the year 2020 nation-states will not have disappeared, and an intensification of the globalization process does not preclude a new global phase of increasing regulation with global institutions and movements towards regional bloc, superstate and even rudimentary global state formation. The Gibson *Neuromancer* trilogy and other cyberpunk novels written in the 1980s are set against the backdrop of continuing USA–USSR superpower conflict. Neither the cyberpunk novelists, nor left-wing critics, nor sociologists for that matter, predicted the revolutions in Eastern Europe of 1989 and the break-up of the Soviet Union (Turner 1990).

From this perspective the new technological developments may open up a prospect of a post-human world, in which human values are totally eclipsed, as more powerful artificial and cyborg entities carry out work and interaction. This may open up not merely increased possibilities of 'super-panoptic' surveillance by the state and corporations through closed circuit television and databases (Poster 1995), but also possibilities for democratization and the extension of citizenship. While new technologies are becoming increasingly pervasive globally, we need to see them as a new cultural framework that, of course, contains dangers and problems, but that can also be transformed from within (Feenberg 1995). We need to get beyond seeing technology through the binary opposition of dystopian nightmare or Utopian saviour. Rather than making a strong opposition between technology and society, in which the former somehow invades or saves the latter, we need to see technology as intertwined with social codes that maintain hierarchies of power, codes that are increasingly becoming subject to reflection and critique. The public is increasingly sceptical about the authority of scientific experts. In Europe, there has been a decline in trust in politicians and experts over public health matters (in Britain the BSE and genetic modified food crises have been important). The green movement has also raised awareness about risks, which Ulrich Beck (1993, 1996) has linked to the development of technological citizenship and the potential to construct 'another modernity'.

If the current tendency is for all forms of cultural production (even poetry, or singing) to be filtered through technological systems, then we need to try to understand what this 'technoculture' combination entails. If technology is increasingly embedded in our everyday activities, from means of physical communication involving movement, to mediated forms of communication at a distance (telephone or Internet), then technology is part of the material structure of everyday life in the sense that it provides a familiar range of objects with which we associate and that our bodies have become accustomed to feeling at home with. We cannot assume that this is a negative or alienating process *per se* without investigating the specific social uses of technology, how particular groups seek to direct and channel the potential of new technological forms. New technologies may well extend our field of possibilities and capacity to relate to others in humane and non-violent ways. It may therefore be limiting to harbour too strong a suspicion of post-human development. Human beings have always been involved in social relationships mediated by technologies. The idea that we should at all costs seek to preserve some pure essence of the human, which is found in some forms of humanism, is a dangerously nostalgic reification that leaves the unfolding of the social implications of technologies in the hands of establishments and powerful groups who have always been confident that their specific interests amount to the public interest.

The Construction of Technological Worlds

How are we to understand technology? At its simplest level, it entails the extension and replacement of human organic capacities by devices fashioned from nature. Here technology is conceived as instruments and tools. But it can also become autonomous self-governing systems with regulated automated machines carrying out tasks that were formerly performed by human labour. In a further stage of development it can enable the creation of independent animal and human life forms, along with computer-simulated artificial life and a range of hybrid combinations of these elements. Post-human systems could develop their own independent evolutionary momentum.

One way to conceptualize this process is to view technology in relation to a series of different 'natures' that encompass, constrain and act as fields of possibilities. It is possible to identify four forms of nature that have acted as time–space environments or worlds and as horizons that delimit and structure the possibilities for social life. The first nature is the original nature, the ecological biosphere that envelops and resists us. Here nature is 'that which cannot be produced'. The second nature is the technosphere, the anthropogenetic domain of the built environment and material urban land-scape that human beings have created and inhabit. The third nature is the cybersphere/telesphere, a second anthropogenetic domain, but in this case the structure is built from 'bits', not atoms, to produce the digitalized information world (Internet, cyberspace, virtual reality) (Luke 1995). The fourth nature is the sphere of artificial life, a post-anthropogenetic domain, still the subject of considerable speculation – a domain in which the genetic structures of life forms are reduced to an information code that can be replicated, manipulated and engineered to reproduce and make new life, first in computer environments and then, allegedly, in the real world. These new life forms, once fed back into the life world, will inhabit and introduce complexities into any of the three previous domains of nature (new plants, animals, eventually humans, and computer-generated electronic organisms) – new systems that could potentially create different worlds and become self-replicating and self-mutating post-human systems, in which the originating traces of the human species that initiated the process become surpassed and eventually erased.

We can now turn to examine some of the implications of the third and fourth natures in more detail. One of the features that makes both possible is digitalization. Digital computing means not only that numbers can be reduced to a binary code, but that more and more forms of information can be reduced to bit-strings that can be rapidly accessed, stored and modified (Fidler 1997: 71f; Negroponte 1995: 11–21). Digital language does not dis-tinguish between texts, images and sounds; as Negroponte remarks, 'bits are bits' and all forms of information can be reduced to them, the only difference being the volume of bits different cultural forms demand. All forms of information, then, be they text, images, sound, music, paintings, photographs, television, movies, can be digitalized and stored and accessed in computers. The new generation of multimedia computers will facilitate the combination of all previous forms, enable the development of ease of passage between the arts and further the development of new genres.

It is not only the accelerated delivery of large amounts of data, but the capacity for flexible navigation through the data in a variety of ways and the ability to reshape data that is becoming significant. This means the end of a linear path through the data, as in narrative formats where we read a text from beginning to end, in favour of hypertext links where one can jump around within the text, or jump out of the text into other texts or sites. We can therefore see a move away from the more traditional narrative forms found in novels, drama and movies. This means that texts, images and movie forms are deliberately constructed in discrete units that permit a range of recombinations and different pathways through data. In part this is made possible by the move from analogue to digital formats: the former are more suitable for time narrative flows, whereas digital formats permit ease of segmentation and recombination of the broken-down units, as in hypertext fiction and interactive cinema that feature interactive modifiable storylines.

The capacity to copy and recompose cultural forms is not merely the capacity for montage, the ability to cut and jump. The shift from analogue mimetic modes, such as photography, to computer-generated digitalized modes means that it is possible to morph and recompose data from photographs, film, television, art and other sources to make simulacra, as was the case with *Jurassic Park*, *Terminator 2* and other recent movies (Clark 1997). Some films of the 1990s have involved the construction of digitalized simulations of actors (because they have died or the scene involved physical risks). Special effects, once a minor part of cinematography involving the construction of models and special sets, now involve digital computer generation and are becoming an essential part of film-making (Tudor 1995). Morphing replaces montage and pastiche as the key compositional technique.

Digitality will enable a seamless composition and transition between current cultural forms. It will enable the coding of all forms of sensory data, which can be simulated and combined to weave data-worlds that possess a high order of believability and immersive qualities. Virtual reality offers a further intensification of this process in its capacity to replicate realistic and hyperrealistic environments, which permit movement (flying through) and interaction with other simulated puppet-like entities that are operated by other people in different locales.

We are in the process, then, of seeing the formation of a new digital world. The Internet, with increasing use of multimedia and hypertext links along with greater use of virtual reality sensory-immersive environments, points towards a new parallel digital world that has the potential to provide dramatic changes in the fabric of work, interaction and everyday life. These changes have their critics. Virilio (1999) has drawn attention to the implications of the speed of electronic transmission of data, arguing that as we become plugged into the electronic apparatus we develop into the catastrophic figure of the 'citizen terminal'. Our cybernetically modified bodies make us the equivalent of the motorized and wired disabled person. The implications of this build-up of speed and mobility as information and people shift across a vast range of environments are the dangers of overstimulation and the production of multiple decentred personalities suffering from neurasthenia, psychasthenia and visual dyslexia (Olalquiaga 1992; Turkle 1995; Simmel 1997; Armitage 1999; Virilio 1999).

Artificial Life and the Post-Human

According to Paul Virilio (1999) there have been a series of revolutions in technology: the first entailed transport (the steam engine, electric motor, etc.); the second was transmission (electronic media such as radio, television, the Internet); the third involves miniaturization and entails the colonization of the human body through implants (Armitage 1999). The third revolution opens the potential of going beyond the human. As biology becomes more technological and technology becomes more biological, biotechnological syntheses offer the prospect of a new form of evolution, in which digital codes and life forms are converging. Extreme technophiliacs see this as leading to a new phase of evolution and envisage humans and machines merging into new cyborg systems and the emergence of machine systems with sensory capacities (such as the cruise missile, which can see and target through the use of elaborate shape-recognition technologies). Ultimately, it is argued, sustainable artificial life will be created, moving from the current forms of computer-generated artificial life to self-replicating, evolving life systems. This post-human potential, whereby the human will be relativized, excites many commentators. Michael de Landa (1992) remarks that in long-term evolution human beings may well have only minor significance – a status similar to that currently accorded to the butterfly in the chain that leads up to human beings.

The simplest post-human form is the cyborg, a combination of animal or human and machine, a hybrid in which devices are fitted onto or into the body to act as supplements to enhance or regulate the body's sensory apparatus and organic functioning. In using prosthetic devices –if I wear a pair of spectacles or insert false teeth – in a basic sense, I am a cyborg (Wilson 1995). If we follow this process through and move beyond wearing – an artificial lung, heart or liver that is either implanted or functions by the body being linked up to a machine – then we have a human–machine hybrid. If we move to a hybrid being that is more machine than human, then we enter the realm of the post-human. Now our images of human–machine hybrids are confined to playing off the human form, in particular the male warrior form (e.g. *Robocop*). Yet there is no reason why cyborgs could not be a vast machine, like a building site earth-mover, or a battlefield tank, aircraft or ship into which parts of the human are integrated – one of the long-held dreams of military strategists. It can also be related to another dream found in science fiction, that of downloading human consciousness into a computer (Hayles 1995: 334).

Shifting from the potential to change the form, structure and coding of bodies to the potential to employ representations of the body, or body-puppets on the Internet, one aspect that has received a good deal of attention is the capacity for deception on multi-user domains (MUDS) and there are a number of interesting case studies of 'computer cross-dressing' (Feather-stone 1995b; Featherstone and Burrows 1995). A further variant is that one's interactant may appear human but in actuality be a programmed artificial entity. Currently on the Internet there are 'bots', which inhabit MUDS, that are programmed to respond and hold a conversation, perform certain tasks and appear human within this textual domain (Turkle 1995: 16–17). Another variant is the construction of 'agents', which can operate either as search engines programmed with one's own set of tastes, or in interactive computer fiction, in which characters are programmed with knowledge and preferences and have the capacity to pick up knowledge and learn from interactions.

At the end of the continuum, we have independent artificial life capable of reproducing in self-replicating systems. It is argued that computer-generated, or digital, artificial life is a crucial step in this process as it is constructed to enable self-replication and evolutionary development; in effect, able to function like a living organism. Hence for computers to use digital coding to replicate genetic coding is not a massive qualitative leap. Digital artificial life can be created which has the equivalent of a genetic programme for its operation and reproduction. As Terranova (1996: 75) argues, 'If natural life is information which circulates in a system, and machines are increasingly based on the same circulation of information in a self-sustaining system (the definition of a cybernetic machine), what difference is there between the two?'

When artificial life research is combined with nanotechnology, there is the prospect of miniature machines building other machines that create and alter life forms in experimentally constructed life-worlds, or in the real world of nature and living things, all programmed and directed by computer-generated artificial life systems (Clark 1996). This offers the vision of totally efficient and ecologically correct industrial production coupled with the capacity to control technically disease, viruses and other threats to bodies and living organisms. Such systems, when they are scaled up, offer new levels of risk – especially so when one increases the level of complexity as one moves from closed to open evolving systems that are able to adapt to conditions too complex, turbulent, rapidly changing and multidimensional to be handled by human beings. On the one hand, this is reassuring; on the other, it is replete with risk. It is reassuring because this is the prospect of the long-hoped for benign guardian of humanity and the planet, and risky because we cannot predict the direction that self-evolving systems, artificial life and artificial intelligence will take.

This shift from the understanding of life in terms of closed-system, predictable models towards open, self-organizing processes clearly entails a relativization of the human dimension. For some, the post-human is to be welcomed as a move beyond the conceit of human uniqueness, our alleged all-seeing creativity and empowerment, which necessarily downgrades our similarities and communality with other life forms and machines. Yet for some technophiliac post-humanists these anthropocentric conceits slip in through the back door as their world becomes an aggressive warlike struggle of the survival of the fittest. There is also a strong sense of aggrandizement in cyberpunk fiction, where the body becomes a prosthetic we learn to manipulate, as we desperately want to leave behind 'the meat' for the empowerment of unimpeded pure mind ('data made flesh') that can fly, summon up data, change form (Hayles 1999: 5). Post-humanism, then, often entails a contradictory denigration of the liberal subject while at the same time retaining some of its dreams of control, domination and aggrandizement coupled with a distaste for the 'imprisonment of the flesh'.

The form of post-humanism that developed out of French theory, in particular the poststructuralist writings of Foucault along with Deleuze and Guattari (1982; see Ansell Pearson 1997) stands in marked contrast. Michel Foucault developed a strong critique of the separation of the subject from the object and the subject's capacity to stand outside the object and know it in an objective manner. The subject can work only through discourse, through systems of knowledge that structure the object and produce truths that are temporary, contingent and impossible to separate from their embedding in discursive formations and power relations. Hence humanism with its over-elevation of the human subject was one of his targets. In an oft-quoted passage, Foucault (1971) completely relativized the human subject, arguing that 'man is like a face drawn in sand at the edge of the sea'. The era of the human is an effect of a particular *epistème*, or complex of knowledge, whose emerging fault-lines threaten to crack the whole edifice and reconfigure it into a new structure of knowledge where the space once occupied by the human will no longer exist. Likewise Deleuze and Guattari, through their use of the term 'machine system' with regard to human beings and nature, take us beyond the separation of culture and society from nature and technology, which has been central to Western modernity with its emphasis on human distinctiveness and capacity to dominate and build. Hence critics speak of 'the terminal crisis of classical humanism' (Braidotti 1997: 10) and the need to rethink the relationship of human beings with nature and technology in a less grandiose manner.

We are no longer able to work off the same strong separation that assumes that we as human subjects are necessarily formed in a totally different way from, or are inherently superior to, natural or mechanical objects. We may be wrong to place all the emphasis upon individualization, the development of the human subject as it moves along the road towards maturity and responsibility. Rather, we need to also become interested in the process of 'objectualization' (Knorr Cetina 1997): that objects have a right to exist and develop, to membership and respect. What rights do living processes have, be they natural, or artificial life in the real world, or computer simulations? It may well be a limited perspective to fear the penetration of the life-world by the system, with the spectre of an instrumental rationality out of control, as Habermas has persistently argued. Rather, we already have technological objects integrated into our daily lives at many levels and need to think in terms of networks of humans and objects, and the responsibility and ethics that objects are capable of generating (Latour 1992, 1993).

Technological objects mediate our social relations and we should not preclude the positive normative possibilities that their capacity for reliability can generate. We should not see technology as automatically eroding good normative consensus and tradition, or having a negative effect upon morality or citizenship. This, of course, will depend upon the specific social and cultural context of use of technological objects and systems. Too often intellectuals and critics have worked off a strong opposition between techno-logy and culture in which the former is seen as somehow invading the latter. As we move towards post-human forms, it is important to dwell on the social framework of power relations within which technology is embedded. Techno-logical changes may offer possibilities not only of increasing centralization and control but also of democratization and participation, as is the case with radio, television and the Internet. The Internet has great potential for public communication and participation. Here technology should not be seen as something left to corporations and government experts: an active public sphere is also in the process of formation that has the potential to extend the range of rights to non-human forms and also for technological and global citizenship.

Developing Technologies for Global Citizenship

There is a strong tendency to focus upon the assumed logic of technology and to play down the social and cultural context of implementation. It is often assumed that the technology will drive the social world or pull it in its wake, with the demand for mastery closing off alternatives. Such assumptions often miss the way social processes structure the normative consequences of technological choices. This sociotechnical coding can be opened up to public discussion, as the movement of AIDS patients to gain access to medical decision-making in the United States has recently shown (Feenberg 1995).

One of the lessons from computer simulations of artificial life is the unpredictability of self-regulating systems: we need to face the possibility that we have constructed levels of complexity that make it exceedingly difficult for humans to steer social life. Hence the emergent qualities of self-replicating artificial life are much more open-ended and unpredictable than previous systems theory models. A small perturbation can send a complex racing out of equilibrium into completely unforeseen directions. This suggests a non-linear world in which it is important that there is a greater appreciation of the complexities and diverse emergent properties of the new forms of order that spring from disorder and contingency (Clark 1997). Given the capacity that computer-based artificial life evolutionary simulations will generate for self-steering through constructs that will act as guidelines for real world social processes, questions about human intervention to evaluate and steer may be more important. At the same time, given the instability of open systems and their sensitivity to minute fluctuations that have major un-predictable evolutionary consequences, the results of intervention cannot be guaranteed, and indeed could well become more dangerous. Hence the grounds for a centred modernity and postmodernity become more open and less easy to predict in terms of their social consequences and the mechanisms whereby technological changes are translated into sociocultural life. At the same time, the impotent acknowledgement that things are best left beyond our control in open chaotic systems echoes all too readily the global New World Order rhetoric that we should deregulate, step back and let the efficiency of the free market system work out its consequences (Terranova 1996: 81).

A further challenge to the logic of modernity and postmodernity occurring from within is the emergence of global risk society, discussed in the influential work of Ulrich Beck (1993). Beck's theory clearly comes out of the German 'centred modernity' tradition, with its high level of generality and assumption of universality. In contrast to many previous accounts, Beck envisages a new stage of modernity, reflexive modernity, which develops as a counter-tendency. Drawing on the experience of green politics in Germany since the 1960s, Beck argues that the development of big science and technology has led to an accumulation of ecological and health risks, which an informed public are increasingly coming to reflect upon and demand political changes. Beck (1996) has addressed the global dimension and 'world risk society', which essentially continues the same argument about the hidden cost of global consumer goods, the global 'bads', the waste and pollution that are not always evident when we purchase commodities. These 'bads' often take time to accumulate and become apparent. Our consumer societies in effect give massive hidden subsidies to multinationals and other corporations, because we have to pick up the bill for the damage their goods cause. Many of these 'bads' (such as global warming) do not stop at frontiers and have a transnational dimension. The global media now form the stage on which the struggles to expose the 'bads' are played out, with the activities of Greenpeace and other ecological groups often depicted as heroic 'David and Goliath' struggles against governments and corporations. A global public opinion is developing that can be rapidly mobilized, as the Greenpeace protests against the French nuclear testing on Mururowa atoll, or their occupation of the Brent Spar oil platform, indicate.

One might optimistically assume that this represents a big step forward in the development of a global public sphere around questions of technological responsibility that will help develop a strong notion of technological citizenship. Yet Beck's theory is still very much based upon a world view that is constructed from the point of view of the North. There is little sense that there may be public spheres and social movements in the South with different agendas and priorities. Different nations and cultural traditions may have developed different notions of nature and risk, and one can by no means assume that the plight of planet earth will strike everyone in the same way. Indeed Beck's account may be very much embedded within the German tradition, with its own particular cultural construction of nature (Alexander 1996; Heimer 1997).

Reading the critiques from within, such as Beck's, within a larger global framework of the global postmodern, takes us to the critiques of the centredness of modernity discourse from without. This perspective is sensitive to the interactive and dialogical formation of modernity. It refuses to talk about modernity in an abstract higher-level manner, but seeks to locate its processes spatially and grounds the analysis in the more substantive level of social practices and processes of cultural formation. While parts of the world in the North are concerned with avoiding risks from out-of-control technological processes, in the South, in the cases of people faced with starvation and poverty, the risk that plastics could cause hormone changes and lower the sperm count, or that meat could be contaminated with BSE, or that cigarettes cause cancer, are perceived from a very different base-line. From such a perspective, the Northern discourse of ecological enlightenment could well seem to be the ruminations of narcissistic over-pampered neurotics.

A discourse that has a potential to connect with the alternative discourses trying to decentre and re-think modernity and that, like Beck, seeks to reconceptualize modernity, but now from the perspective of the South, is the discourse of human development (Haq 1995). Both reflexive modernization and human development discourse embody a critique of Faustian develop-ment, the archetypal image of the Enlightenment modernizer that Goethe developed in *Faust Part 2*, where Faust absolves his sins by engaging in massive public health and building projects to tame nature and extend the benefits to humanity (Berman 1982). Both reflexive modernity and human development discourse are much more people-centred. For Beck, an educated public in Western societies is developing that has the reflexivity to question the experts, corporations and governments about the unintended consequences of techno-logical change, the hidden costs of the consumer society's institutionalized wastefulness. The bad modernity on rails that seemed to be heading for the technocratic nightmare outlined by the Frankfurt School, George Steiner (1971) and other cultural critics has imminent a mechanism that ensures a reverse thrust and the potential of a reflexive modernity based upon an active public.

Ul Haq and other human development thinkers move beyond seeing development in terms of abstractions such as 'the poor' and collectivities such as the nation-state, to the recognition that people are the end of development. Ul Haq was centrally involved in the development of the UNDP's Human Development Index (Haq 1995: Ch. 4). Unlike GNP, in which money serves as the common measuring rod of a nation's progress, this index combines a range of socioeconomic factors: life expectancy, knowledge (adult literacy and mean years of schooling) and income. A country's human capital, its investment in health and education, while import-ant ends in themselves, can also be the target of investment and the basis of economic growth (Haq 1995: 54f; Nederveen Pieterse 1997: 84–5).

It is now possible to consider these two positions – that of Beck, approaching the global from the perspective of the North, and ul Haq, who tackles global inequalities from the point of view of the South – and their relationship to post-human development and the possibilities for the world in 2020. Both are aware of the need to check runaway technological and economic processes. Both point to the need for human intervention and action; both are optimistic about the possibility of achieving greater human control. Beck's perspective has been criticized for overestimating the reflexivity of lay people and their capacity to distrust and criticize big science and the experts, as something akin to a rational choice model (Wynne 1996: 47). To assume that people now develop reflexive mistrust is also to assume that they were more trustful in the past and masks the ambivalence about public trust that people have often held. Beck also assumes a fundamental divide between nature and culture that tends to place human beings outside nature and technology, a central assumption of many theorists of modernity (Wynne 1996: 75).

Ul Haq is positive about global reform and challenges some of the myths of the inability of the South to achieve development. While the income gap between North and South is still very large (average income in the South being 6 per cent of that in the North), human gaps are closing fast, with average life expectancy in the South now 80 per cent of that in the North, adult literacy 66 per cent and nutrition 85 per cent (Haq 1995: 26). Many would temper ul Haq's optimism by referring to the continuing growth of global inequalities. One in five persons alive in the world (over one billion people) lives in conditions of absolute poverty (with an income of less than $1 a day) (Miller 1995: 127). Of the anticipated doubling of the world population by 2050, 90 per cent will occur in the South, especially in cities (ibid.: 128). The 300 largest multinational companies control around a quarter of the world's $20 trillion stock of productive assets. The sales figures of the largest 20 companies exceed the total GDP of 80 of the poorest developing countries (ibid.: 130). Or to put it another way, of the top 100 economies in the world, 47 are corporations, each one of which has more wealth than 130 countries (Brecher and Costello 1994: 18).

A host of proposals for global reform focus on regulation of transnational financial flows. The Tobin tax is based upon the need, in the words of James Tobin, to 'throw some sand in the well-greased wheels' of the world's financial markets (in Felix 1995: 195; cf. Chapter 6, this volume). Around 80 per cent of the daily flow of this volatile 'global casino' is speculative or linked to money laundering (Miller 1995: 131). A tax on international transfers of money at the rate of 0.003 per cent (the Walker tax proposal) would finance all UN operations, and a tax of 0.5 per cent (the Tobin proposal) would yield around $1,500 billion a year (ibid.: 136). This could be collected by nation-states taxing flows across their borders and used to finance welfare and other state-led reconstruction programmes. Coupled with other innovative suggestions such as a global carbon tax, debt-for-nature swaps and taxes on heavy users of the global commons, it would be possible to build a 'new Bretton Woods' and develop forms of global regulation that would lead to the reconstruction of the South (ibid.: 137). Small steps in this direction could lead to the realization of the dream of the elimination of poverty (Udavakumar 1995).

A discussion of global media and the Internet is essential if we are to understand the potential for new forms of global citizenship and public participation, yet too often these areas are looked at with an anti-technological bias and puritanical attitude, or at best indifference to new media developments. We need to examine the interface between the new information technology, the public sphere and global technological citizenship in relation to these changes.

Property, Cultural Rights and Global Citizenship

The division of the world into North and South is a device to highlight patterns of inequality, yet this divide is itself constructed in a very general way, especially if one breaks down data for countries in the South by region and district. Postcolonial theory argued that 'there is a third world in every first world and vice-versa' (Minh-ha 1989). It is not just uneven development within nation-states that is significant, but also the fact that in the postwar era the rate of global migration has been the most intense ever recorded (Gungwu 1997). One cannot seriously talk of a blanket Third World in which everyone is part of 'the excluded'. There is much greater segmentation, and within global cities in particular middle-class enclaves of advanced financial, business, media, cultural industry and other services are springing up (Featherstone 1999).

New information technology and the move towards what some refer to as 'global network society' (Castells 1996) speeds up the ability of parts of the network to communicate. This occurs not only within firms but between them, as companies develop new alliances on a global level. This gives rise to greater spatial mobility and travel, as many of these agreements have to be cemented by face-to-face contacts, hence within global cities there are burgeoning entertainment areas with hotels, clubs, restaurants, boutiques, galleries and museums. These themselves draw in a secondary migration of low-paid service workers, many of them women from poor countries. The global flows of information and people are, therefore, changing the contours of the North/South divide towards a more complex regional and intra-city mosaic of inequalities. At the same time, many countries do not have global cities and cannot aspire to join the group of NICs. For such countries the network society has the potential for greater isolation, especially since market processes will drive down the aggregate cost of telecommunications along those routes that are most highly used.

The new forms of mobility can also be seen to provide hopeful possibilities for the South. Northern states increasingly seek to regulate the growing flows of migrants from the South and are reluctant to consider granting adjunct rights, or implementing dual or multiple forms of citizenship (Sousa Santos 1999). Yet for Santos, the image of the migrant can be related to that of the frontier and the baroque and points to more fluid, chaotic, hybrid and mobile forms of subjectivity and sociability. This privileging of mobility and of the migrant and stranger resonates with the privileging of nomadism in recent cultural studies (Featherstone 1995a). It contains a danger of romanticizing the aesthetic of the traveller, which artists and intellectuals have long been engaged in, to the neglect of those who cannot travel, who remain fixed and rooted in a locale. Many travellers may wish to settle. The 4.5 million landless in Brazil do not seek to flow but want to settle. Such groups may want the benefits of rootedness and travel, of localism and global connectedness, which currently only the middle-class cosmopolitan professionals and upper-class elites are able to enjoy. In this respect, the Internet and new media, if made available and suitably priced, would represent a massive gain in direct democratic potential and human development for many in the South, not least by addressing one of the central aspects of human development: that it enlarges people's choices. Access to information and the capacity to interact and network with distant others can clearly increase choice and empowerment.

The third and fourth natures, the emergent information simulational sphere and sphere of artificial life discussed above, cannot easily be discounted by those in the South, for the global information revolution and the post-Fordist disaggregation of functions in corporate production already bring them into the South, not just as distant effects, but as real processes. From the perspective of the South it may be easier to dismiss the type of scenarios we discussed for 2020 as science fiction developed out of a technologically driven modernity, and to neglect the mediation, the intervening time in which the various threats and opportunities can be addressed and struggled over.

A consequence of economic deregulation and the GATT has been to increase the concentration of power and wealth in this sector in the North. The market for telecommunications services, broadcasting, cable and film industries has expanded two to three times in the past five years (Winseck 1997: 231). There has been an attempt to globalize US-style commercial freedom of speech, the free flow of information doctrine, to allow greater deregulation and cross-ownership. The advent of multimedia – telecommunications, pay-per-view television and film services, video-on-demand, audio-text-services and archive facilities – makes it increasingly difficult for nation-states to operate with a restricted definition of culture and to protect particular cultures against market forces (Winseck 1997: 238). The new international agreements and legal frameworks have extended corporate rights with the assumption that this is somehow coterminous with freedom of information and democratization. Yet the debate needs to move beyond questions of state versus corporate power in the field of communications and seek greater guarantees for the public sphere function of the media. Some of the new forms of communication with interactive qualities, such as the Internet, seem well suited for this function. State or regional intervention to provide Internet linkages and modems and extend networks among the excluded in the South could have important implications for education, empowerment, democratization and citizenship participation.

The emerging struggle to define people as citizens and not merely con-sumers is also manifest in struggles around intellectual property rights. There are continuing cases of Internet servers and others trying to establish vast cultural databases (photographs, paintings, art, movies, newsreels) that can be encrypted and brought into copyright. The US government's infamous Clipper Amendment sought to impose censorship on the Web and was eventually defeated by the US Supreme Court. Currently Internet material is not copy-rightable and people can download free, yet there are many corporate and other interests who seek to establish conventional property rules. Tim Berners-Lee, the founder of the World Wide Web, saw the Web not merely as a mechanism for information retrieval from a global archive, but emphasized its potential for a new inventive relationship to knowledge using hypertext links. The current commercialization of the Net seeks to institute Internet selling in which interaction is limited to the 'click' of purchasing, or pay-per-view. Yet the Internet has the potential to become a collective medium with the 'ability to annotate, to interact, to up-date information' (Caygill 1999: 9). The potential of the Internet is to redefine the nature of intellectual property rights and institute a much more democratic and creative relationship to information (Barlow 1996). The danger to the Internet is the commercial-ization and the power of transnational corporations to continue to build restricted-access fire-walled 'intranets' (Sassen 1999).

That the current phase of global deregulation favours private ownership can be illustrated with regard to the way in which the Uruguay Round of GATT sought to extend patent enforcement in the pharmaceutical and agrochemical sectors. This is an important example to connect to the previous discussions of nature and artificial life. From a legal point of view nature has traditionally been classified as a *res communis* (Frow 1997: 92). The structure of natural substances or natural species has been seen as existing independent of human beings, something we can discover, but not something we can claim authorship for, or to have invented, according to the criteria of patent law. The biotechnological revolution has blurred the line between invention and discovery and allows patents for products of nature, 'so long as the inventor has changed the product to conform to the novelty, utility and non-obvious requirements of patent law' (ibid.: 93). Human beings, who once were themselves seen as part of nature, have now risen above it to the extent that they can become rivals to it by producing hybrid plant species or genetic material that count as inventions and can therefore be patented (ibid.). We therefore have a range of patented life forms, from genetic material to single-cell organisms, genetically engineered seeds and plants, oysters and transgenetic mice. This means that the 'genetic commons' is up for grabs. To use the superior yielding and pest-resistant varieties of genetically altered plants, farmers must purchase their seeds from American companies and are not permitted to collect and use their own seed corn. This increases the asymmetry between the agriculture of the North and South, not just through the flow of seeds from North to South, but in the way the South is perceived as a vast commons of natural biodiversity to copy, modify and patent, with companies then extracting royalties for the use of seeds in their country of origin (ibid.: 97). Information, then, becomes a form of property and the rich indigenous knowledge of plants and animals in the South is up for grabs to be exploited by a new generation of bio-anthropologists working for agrochemical and pharmaceutical companies.

Many critics argue that the current logic of marketization and deregulation reduces citizens to customers. At best, corporations can grant 'customer charters', aiming to offer good-quality service, or a form of pseudo-citizenship in which membership in a collectivity becomes the act of purchase. One becomes a 'McCitizen' with the right to a standard-quality burger (Probyn 1998). On one level the corporate view of pseudo-citizenship has a progressive dimension that goes beyond conventional notions. The origin of the term 'citizen' takes us to a particularly restricted spatial location, initially the European city-state and eventually the nation-state. A citizen, then, was a member of a restricted collectivity with specific rights and duties. On the other hand, the McCitizen or Denizen has the advantage that his or her albeit limited rights are guaranteed whatever the spatial location. One can expect the same quality Big Mac or Coca-Cola wherever one is in the world. This global dimension is something to build on as it points beyond the nation-state, the traditional guarantor of citizenship rights (Turner 1996). Yet corporate global citizenship would hardly seem to be the answer, because it is product-specific and contains no rights of representation to alter the policies of corporations, whose limited mode of representation is through their shareholders and owners. If one seeks to stop McDonalds producing burgers, which have the ecologically damaging effect of turning rainforest into beef cattle-grazing land, then one can only organize a consumer boycott – which now seems to be impossibly idealistic.

The global mass media and new information technologies such as the Internet may well have potential for the development of global citizenship. This may generate levels of consciousness beyond narrow local or national interests. A global public opinion, then, could be in the process of formation, with a sense that it is proper for me to take an interest in other countries' treatment of their citizens and nature – if only in the sense that their fate impinges on mine, as the examples of the Chernobyl radioactive fallout and the problem of global warming show. There may be possibilities to develop a global public sphere through the dialogical qualities of the new information technology and interactive multimedia, which can lead to the development of a virtual institutional nexus that features good practice and polices violations of human rights and ecological abuses. Such a programme at the current time can advance only on an experimental basis. But there are encouraging signs from the South through the use of the Internet to date, and evidence that in certain fields, such as academic life, it is leading to a shift in power balances, drawing academics from the South more into dialogues, as information becomes more readily available.[1]

How are we, then, to understand the prospect for global citizenship? Citizenship rights have generally been limited to membership of a nation-state. States have been premised upon the monopolization of the means of violence and taxation within a territorial area and are therefore able to legally enforce citizenship rights. The corollary is that if we are to establish global citizenship we must first establish a global state – as yet an unlikely prospect. The long-term elimination contest between nation-states, each concerned to establish their own hegemony within a regional and then a global reference group, may now be relatively under control and we may be moving beyond the Hobbesian security discourse, which has been central to much international relations thinking. One variant of this, the imperial absorption model, seems to have been superseded: since the 1980s the counter-trend of the break-up of the Soviet bloc, the fragmentation of Yugoslavia and other nation-states, balkanization (Mestrovic 1994), ethnicity and regionalism has come to the fore. At the same time we see moves to establish larger blocs: in particular the European Union, along with other trading blocs in the North American, the South American cone and East Asia-Pacific regions. Yet apart from the EU, these blocs are largely interested in trade and show little interest in broadening citizenship rights.

The impetus for global citizenship, then, needs to come from below, and an important part of this process is the development of global cultural citizenship. There is, of course, a range of 'third cultures', over and above the level of the nation-state, which are already developing. One thinks of UN agencies, the International Court of Justice, human rights organizations such as Amnesty International, alliances of indigenous people, women's movements, Christian Aid, ecological organizations such as Greenpeace and a range of other organizations who refuse to halt their concern at the borders of nation-states. One assumes that with the Internet and development of a global public sphere, such organizations will grow, develop and consolidate alliances. One key aspect of the development of global cultural citizenship is the move to extend cultural rights: the right to information, representation, knowledge and communication (Murdock 1994: 158, cited in Stevenson 1997: 57). It can be argued that these rights assume a much greater importance with the coming information order, and the more agencies trying to promote human development and global citizenship are aware of the potential of the Internet, multimedia and other developments, the more they will be able to make alliances and reach more people. As mentioned above, this process must take place on an experimental basis. But there are already many examples of good practice, such as the move of Bologna to give all its residents free Internet access. A number of regional movements and indigenous peoples, such as the Zapatistas in Chiapas, Mexico, are beginning to explore the use of the Internet to publicize their cause. The important work in the next 20 years is to create spaces for interaction (the virtual spaces of the Internet) for such groups in the South to exchange information with groups in the North who are engaged in ecological and risk politics and work from a centred modernity perspective. Issues such as bio-agriculture and pharma-ceutical patenting and property rights are clearly potential points for the construction of alliances, as are broader questions of copyright, freedom of information and access to the Internet. Here there is potential to develop an alternative, more multicultural and multicentred, global public sphere, through public–private flexible alliance, to provide an alternative to the spread of global marketizaton. This model could well draw upon a successful institution of public life that flourished with the development of strong nation-states in the nineteenth century: the library.

The library model, and we can add to this the database and many new multimedia forms, is based upon what Marcel Mauss called 'prestations', gifts that return without conferring any rights of ownership or permanent use (Frow 1997: 101ff). Prestations are not commodities to be bought and sold and therefore to be freed from the market constraints flowing from the price mechanism, restricting access and use. To move the library model from information use into the sphere of informationalized objects, the genetic material, plants and seeds that are products of the biotech revolution as it speeds along towards nanotechnology and artificial life systems would be little short of revolutionary. Libraries involve classificatory systems and cataloguing and they can of course to some extent be policed. One thinks here of the ambitions to construct exhaustive libraries of humankind: the Library of Alexandria or the encyclopaedic schemes of the Enlightenment philosophers and the Saint-Simonians. Of course, public libraries are now only a shadow of their former selves and have been victims of the dismantling of the welfare state in the 1980s and 1990s. Yet it may well be that as we enter the new millennium the pendulum will swing back to reregulation, not necessarily on the state level, but in the transnational and global dimensions.

Some theorists of the Internet are already arguing that one of the major problems with it is how to gain money for information that flows freely like conversation. It could well be that these developments could point us beyond the value-form associated with commodities and signal a return to new forms of patronage, certainly for large sectors of cultural specialists and inter-mediaries who may become unemployed as the old markets of the print culture give way to the newer electronic forms (Barlow 1996). The library model based upon some form of collective ownership for humanity, with freedom of access and use, with a just form of payment to authors and inventors, would be a possible development in the direction of realizing a global public sphere and cultural citizenship.

Note

1. The *TCS Virtual Institute* is being proposed as one small step in this direction and we are developing a network to explore the politics of global citizenship and the potential to develop new alliances between academics, social movements, the excluded, business and local politicians. There is currently a space developing in the wake of processes of de-institutionalisation in the spheres of work, the family, the state and religion for experimental programmes in network and virtual institution-building. We are seeking to direct our efforts towards those who will be excluded from the new global information order in the South. See document on the TCS Centre Website: http://tcs.ntu.ac.uk.

References

Alexander, Jeffrey C. (1996) 'Critical reflections on "reflexive modernization"', *Theory, Culture & Society*, 13 (4): 133–8.

Ansell Pearson, K. (1997) *Viroid Life: Perspectives on Nietzsche and the Transhuman Condition*, Routledge, London.

Armitage, J. (1999) 'Interview with Paul Virilio', special issue on Paul Virilio, *Theory, Culture & Society*, 16 (5–6).

Barlow, J. P. (1996) 'Selling wine without bottles: the economy of mind on the global net', in L. H. Leeson (ed.), *Clicking In: Hot Links to a Digital Culture*, Bay Press, Seattle.

Beck, U. (1993) *Risk Society*, Sage, London.

— (1996) 'World risk society', *Theory, Culture & Society*, 13 (4): 1–32.

Berman, M. (1982) *All that is Solid Melts into Air: the Experience of Modernity*, Simon and Schuster, New York.

Braidotti, R. (1997) 'Meta(l)morphoses', *Theory, Culture & Society*, 14 (2).

Brecher, J. and T. Costello (1994) *Global Village or Global Pillage*, South End Press, Boston, MA.

Caygill, H. (1999) 'Meno and the Internet: between memory and the archive', *History of the Human Sciences*, 12 (2): 1–12.

Castells, M. (1996) *The Information Age, Volume 1: The Rise of the Network Society*, Blackwell, Oxford.

Clark, N. (1996) 'Creativity unbound: engaging with the molecular revolution of nano-technology', mimeo.

— (1997) 'Panic ecology', *Theory, Culture & Society*, 14 (1).

Davis, M. (1990) *City of Quartz*, Verso, London.

De Landa, M. (1992) 'Non-organic life', in J. Crary and S. Kwinter (eds), *Incorporations*, Zone Books, New York.

Deleuze, G. and F. Guattari (1982) *A Thousand Plateaus*, Athlone Press, London.

Featherstone, M. (1995a) *Undoing Culture: Globalization, Postmodernism and Identity*, Sage, London.

Featherstone, M. (1995b) 'Post-bodies, ageing and virtual reality', in M. Featherstone and A. Wernick (eds), *Images of Ageing*, Routledge, London.

— (1999) 'The global city, information technology and public life', in C. Davis (ed.), *Identity and Social Change in Postmodern Life*, Johns Hopkins University Press, Baltimore, MD.

Featherstone, M. and Burrows, R. (1995) 'Cultures of technological embodiment', in M. Featherstone and R. Burrows (eds), *Cyberspace/Cyberbodies/Cyberpunk: Cultures of Technological Embodiment*, Sage, London.

Feenberg, A. (1995) *Alternative Modernity*, California University Press, Berkeley.

Felix, D. (1995) 'The Tobin tax proposal', in H. Cleveland, H. Henderson and I. Kaul (eds), *The United Nations: Policy and Financing Alternatives*, The Global Commission to Fund the United Nations, Washington, DC, pp. 195–208.

Fidler, R. (1997) *Mediamorphosis*, Sage, London.

Foucault, M. (1971) *The Order of Things*, Tavistock, London.

Frow, J. (1997) 'Information as gift and commodity', *New Left Review*.

Fuchs, C. J. (1995) 'Death is irrelevant: cyborgs, reproduction and the future of male hysteria', in C. H. Gray (ed.), *The Cyborg Handbook*, Routledge, London.

Gibson. W. (1984) *Neuromancer*, Fantasia Press, New York.

Gungwu, W. (1997) 'Introduction', in W. Gungwu (ed.), *Global History and Migrations*, Westview Press, Boulder, CO.

Hayles, N. K. (1995) 'The life cycle of cyborgs', in Gray (ed.).

Hayles, N. K. (1999) *How We Became Posthuman*, Chicago University Press, Chicago.

Haq, M. ul (1995) *Reflections on Human Development*, Oxford University Press, Oxford.

Heimer, J. (1997) 'A comparison of the German and English green movements', PhD thesis, University of Teesside.

Knorr Cetina, K. (1997) 'Sociality with objects: social relations in postsocial knowledge societies', *Theory, Culture & Society*, 14 (4).

Latour, B. (1992) 'Where are the missing masses? The sociology of a few mundane artefacts', in W. Bijker and K. Law (eds), *Shaping Technology/Building Society: Studies in Sociotechnical Change*, MIT Press, Cambridge, MA.

— (1993) *We Have Never Been Modern*, Harvester Wheatsheaf, Hemel Hempstead.

Luke, T. (1995) 'New World Order or neo-world orders? Power, politics and ideology in the informationalizing global order', in M. Featherstone, S. Lash and R. Robertson (eds), *Global Modernities*, Sage, London.

Mestrovic, S. G. (1994) *The Balkanization of the West*, Routledge. London.

Miller, M. (1995) 'Where is globalization taking us?', in H. Cleveland, H. Henderson and I. Kaul (eds), *The United Nations: Policy and Financing Alternatives*, The Global Commission to Fund the United Nations, Washington, DC, pp. 125–44.

Minh-ha, Trinh T. (1989), *Women, Native, Other Writing: Postcoloniality and Feminism*, Indiana University Press, Bloomington.

Nederveen Pieterse, J. (1997) 'Globalization and emancipation', *New Political Economy*, 2 (1).

Negroponte, N. (1995) *Being Digital*, Hodder and Stoughton, London.

Olalquiaga, C. (1992) *Megalopolis*, Minnesota University Press, Minneapolis.

Poster, M. (1995) *The Second Media Age*, Polity, Cambridge

Probyn, Elspeth (1998) '*Mc*-Identities: food and the familial family', *Theory, Culture & Society* 15 (2): 155–73.

Sassen, S. (1999) 'Electronic space and power', in M. Featherstone and S. Lash (eds), *Spaces of Culture: City, Nation, World*, Sage, London.

Simmel, G. (1997) 'The metropolis and mental life', in D. Frisby and M. Featherstone (eds), *Simmel on Culture*, Sage, London.

Sousa Santos, Boaventura de (1999) 'Toward a multicultural conception of human rights', in M. Featherstone and S. Lash (eds), *Spaces of Culture: City, Nation, World*, Sage, London.

Steiner, G. (1971) *In Bluebeard's Castle*, Faber, London.

Stephenson, N. (1992) *Snow Crash*, Bantam Books, New York.

Sterling, B. (1988) *Islands in the Net*, Century Hutchinson, New York.

Stevenson, N. (1997) 'Globalization, national cultures and cultural citizenship', *Sociological Quarterly*, 38 (1): 41–66.

Terranova, T. (1996) 'Digital Darwin: nature, evolution and control in the rhetoric of electronic communication', *New Formations*, 29: 69-83.

Tudor, A. (1995) 'Unruly bodies, unquiet minds', *Body & Society*, 1 (1): 25–41.

Turkle, S. (1995) *Life on the Screen*, Simon and Schuster, New York.

Turner, B. S. (1990) 'The end of organized socialism,' *Theory, Culture & Society*, 7 (4).

— (ed.) (1996) *Postmodernism and Citizenship*.

Udavakumar, S. P. (1995) 'The futures of the poor', *Futures*, 27 (3): 339–51.

Virilio, P. (1999) *Polar Inertia*, Sage, London.

Wilson, R. R. (1995) 'Cyber(body)parts: prosthetic consciousness', in M. Featherstone and R. Burrows (eds), *Cyberspace/Cyberbodies/Cyberpunk: Cultures of Technologial Embodiment*, Sage, London.

Winseck, D. (1997) 'Contradictions in the democratization of international communication', *Media, Culture & Society*, 19 (2).

Wynne, B. (1996) 'May the sheep safely graze: a reflexive view of the expert–lay knowledge divide', in S. Lash, B. Szersynski and B. Wynne (eds), *Risk Environment and Modernity*, Sage, London.

14

Cities: Contradictory Utopias

ANTHONY D. KING

Before addressing the issue of a critical Utopia for the world's cities there are some important prerequisites to tackle, not least occasioned by the theme of this collection, global futures. In the first half of this chapter, therefore, I shall proceed with caution, examining some presuppositions. In the second half, I shall throw caution to the winds.

Having worked for many years in sociology and urban studies (including the field of 'development'), I moved some time ago into the realms of art history and cultural theory. A disciplinary change in mid-life is hardly as revolutionary or as liberating as a change of sex – but it does open new perspectives. If words such as 'development' or 'globalization' didn't figure ten years ago in most art historians' conceptual vocabularies, art history does, nevertheless, have a number of important conceptual concerns pertinent to the discussion here, two of which I shall first briefly explore: positionality and representation.

Positionality

The problem of position – the space from which we speak, whether political, spatial/geographical, ideological, dominant or subaltern – is not unknown to scholars in the field of development studies. At least some of the apparent insights of postcolonial criticism (to which I refer below), audible from the mid- to late-1980s, have a certain similarity with debates between a Third World intelligentsia and 'development' scholars in the 1960s (who had their own pre-poststructuralist insights). Questioning the assumption that history begins and ends with Europe, as reiterated by Chakrabarty (1992), Prakash (1990) or even Said (1978, 1993), in a (relatively) new postcolonialist discourse in the humanities, has its precursors among historians and social scientists of India (Romila Thapur), Egypt (Anouar Abdel Malik) and Sri Lanka (Susantha Goonitilake) in the 1960s, to cite only a few. The perspective of 'the Other', seen not just from a (subaltern) below, but from what? – from a Eurocentric 'centre' – was seen as the margins, was often more clearly exposed in the contested inter-cultural encounters of 'development studies' (as often as not in the postcolony) and in the social sciences, 20 or 30 years before it emerged, in the 1990s, in the postcolonial humanities textbooks of the metropole (Williams and Chrisman 1993; Ashcroft et al. 1995; Dirlik 1996; King 1997c).

What difference have the realities, as well as the discourses, of globalization made to the issue of positionality? The question is not simply whether the subaltern can speak (Spivak 1992) but whether she (or he) can set the agenda. If so, where, and how, is it set and what is to be discussed, not least in regard to 'global futures'? Have 30 years of apparent 'time–space compression' (Harvey 1989) made the question of position redundant? It is precisely these political and epistemological concerns, and the need for sensitivity towards them in regard to anything so momentous as 'global futures', that I shall briefly engage with some of the assumptions found in this collection.

'Global Futures'

Having in the last 15 years made considerable use of the terms global or globalization, I have subsequently become increasingly cautious (though not sceptical) about their application. I am concerned, especially, about their viability in particular contexts. This is not the occasion to elaborate on my reservations, some of which I have spelt out elsewhere (King 1997a, 1997b); nevertheless, some points need mentioning.

Global can be used in at least two senses: metaphorically, referring to the total whole or, especially since the 1960s (and particularly the 1980s), more literally as referring to, or encompassing, the entire terrestrial globe. In certain cases, global/globalization seem entirely appropriate – aspects of economic globalization in the 1980s (24-hour trading in the financial services industry, property marketing), the reach of satellite broadcasting, global production and marketing of products or, in the realm of ecology, global warming. I am less convinced about its application in the realm of the human, social and cultural, for a variety of reasons. As a term used to further a particular economic and ideological agenda, and one that assumes that which requires to be interrogated, it is at once both too broad and too narrow. Because all 'global' discourses 'stress the importance of transnational forces, the practices of coding and decoding everyday practices that disrupt, disturb, and even deny the identity of the global are not revealed' (Kusno in King 1997a). Above all, the discourse on the global – as here, and now – is positioned, understandably enough, in the place not only from which it emanates but from where the global discourse can be fuelled, disseminated and consumed, and from where, because of the absence of other discourses (on politics, religion, famine or war), it can expand to occupy a space in the public sphere.

In brief, the very concepts of the global and globalization have depended

on the material conditions that have produced and given access to them –
satellites, telematics, electronic communication, air travel, the production and
distribution of globally marketed commodities, the wealth of economic and
human resources to produce these, as well as the global mobility, intellectual
capital and networks of knowledge that keep the ideas in circulation. It is
hardly necessary to point out that relatively few have access to these resources,
that globalization, wherever it touches down, is a highly partial, very uneven
process (McGrew 1992; Scott 1997). Unless we recognize this, we may as
well assume that as much is known about Hinduism, and acted upon, in The
Hague as in Hardwar, or about space travel in Cape Town as at Cape
Canaveral.

Talking about the global is a highly economically and socially privileged
discourse for some, and for others, is totally irrelevant (O'Byrne 1997). As
a metaphor (and what else can it be?), the term global – with its connotations
of the singular, unitary, total – is, in many ways, the most ineffective metaphor
to identify what we are looking for, namely, the desires, wishes and aspirations
for the future of individuals and groups in a myriad different sites all over
the world. It comes as no surprise that the discourse on globalization
emanates overwhelmingly from the West; even when scholars from outside
are persuaded to enter, the tendency is to resist being incorporated into it,
to reject the West's definition of the situation, whether this is 'global' or
'international' (Kapur 1995). What this suggests, therefore, is a 'hermeneutics
of suspicion', a stance not of speaking to a situated audience, but of straining
to hear excluded voices outside.

Representing the City

In the context of these issues, therefore, writing a critical Utopia for the
world's cities assumes that we have some adequate theoretical tools to do so.
What can we say of those that already exist? How, in fact, is 'the city'
represented?

By far the dominant paradigm for over two decades has been a somewhat
tired urban political economy, though with some recent moves into the realms
of the postmodern (Harvey 1989; Watson and Gibson 1995). While the
predominantly economic discourse of world and global cities initiated in the
early 1980s (Knox and Taylor 1995) and the collapse of Eastern European
regimes both offered new analytical spaces, this largely structuralist theoretical
paradigm has simply not been able to handle the new concerns with identity,
representation and cultural difference that have arisen in relation to the city.
Nor has that particular discourse been very adept in addressing the questions
of meaning in relation to spatial and architectural symbolism that are central
to these concerns. On the other hand, much literature in cultural studies
dealing with representation as 'the production of meaning through language,
discourse and image ... of how visual images, language and discourse work

as systems of representation' (Hall 1997) has not had as its object of study the built and symbolic spaces of the city. The exception to this is the burgeoning field of postcolonial theory and criticism, which, having been largely concerned with literary studies for a decade, has in recent years been linked more closely to urban and architectural studies. The essays in *Postcolonial Space(s)* (Nalbantoglu and Wong 1997) are offered as 'a reminder of the colonial past and a salutary gesture towards the future'. Postcolonial space is seen as an intervention into those architectural constructions 'that parade under a universalist guise and either exclude or repress differential spatialities of often disadvantaged ethnicities, communities, or peoples'. In this case, however, the Marxism (whether 'old' or 'neo') that has sustained the urban political economy paradigm for 20 years has been relegated to obscurity. Capitalism is so taken for granted as to be absent from the debate. Of more interest here is the work of Yeoh (1996), which reasserts the agency of indigenous peoples in the cultural translation process that gave meaning to colonial space.

These strategies of postcolonial cultural and spatial de-centring, out of Euro-America, have been taken up by Spivak (1997) and others, not least in critiquing the narrowly focused (Western) obsession with the city and the urban, which is seen as the typical and paradigmatic cultural and spatial sign of the rich and postindustrial West.

> Let us not artificially exclude the rural from Indian urbanism; let us not look upon the villages as repositories of dead tradition. Let us look at them as the locus of hard core economic resistance where the binary opposition between economy and culture is broken down every day. Where initiatives for local self government immediately confront the global: as the area where the devastation of women's bodies and of land as the dumping ground of international pharmaceutics, of the displacement of peoples, destruction of the eco-biome, the destruction of traditional knowledge and means of production ... that rural is the new dynamic front against exploitative globalization ... you should teach [students of planning] to ask not merely what should this city be but why this emphasis on urban development, here, now; where should we build, with what task, today? The rural is not just a depository that provides ethnic chic. (Spivak 1997: 13)

Representations of the World

Thinking about a critical Utopia for the world's cities poses difficult questions. Does the world, as such, actually 'have' any cities? The answer is clearly no. We would be better off by asking, 'In what *ways* does the world have cities?' In that sense, we might be better served by speaking of French, Chinese, Dutch, Nigerian or Brazilian cities, prioritizing the possibilities of state intervention, regulation, longer or shorter traditions of urban policy-making, and other questions.

Even prior to this question, we might ask what we mean by *the* world. Which – or better – whose world? The now commonly used category of 'world' or 'global city' represents the world primarily (perhaps only) as an anonymous, and in some views, increasingly stateless world economy (Sassen 1991; Friedmann 1995), even though large parts of the world's population are effectively excluded from this. The economic calculations from which the concept, as well as designation, of such cities is derived does not necessarily accord with more cultural, social or political readings of 'globalization'.

For others, the world is primarily the home of the world's religions, although, in fact, religions clearly do not inhabit the same world (or worlds); they are rather involved in world-making. (The same is true of the worlds of gender.)[1] To think of specific cities – Kabul, Belfast, Bombay, Quebec, Jerusalem, or Beirut and others – either with reference to their sociopolitical, cultural, legal and spatial conditions, or the state of their civil society, without having recourse to mentioning Muslims, Protestants, Hindus, Jews, Catholics or Maronite Christians, among others, hardly makes much sense.

There is also, of course, the inter- or transnational world of the United Nations and the free market world of the World Bank and IMF. Most pertinent here is the UN Center for Human Settlements (Habitat), its various reports (United Nations Center for Human Settlements 1996) and what it sees as the world of 'basic needs'. While few would argue with their objectives (providing clean water, basic shelter, transportation, and other infrastructural facilities), each of these agencies operates with powerful ideological, political and economic agendas, providing the ground for the contradictions that I mention below. All of these representations assume the unproblematic existence of something referred to as 'the city'. Yet to quote James Donald:

> To put it polemically, there is no such *thing* as a city. Rather, *the city* designates the space produced by the interaction of historically and geographically specific institutions, social relations of production and reproduction, practices of government, forms and media of communication and so forth. By calling this diversity 'the city' we ascribe to it a coherence or integrity. *The city* then is above all a representation. (Donald 1992: 422)

Yet despite, or perhaps because of, Donald's hesitations, cities have been categorized – by geographers, planners, administrators, historians, novelists, film producers, poets and others – into any number of categories (King 1994). Such taxonomies are clearly hegemonic; they assume a false objectivity, external to the object itself. Our discourses about the city produce that which we want to address.

There are no cities without representations of them, no representations without the cities to which they apply. The times and spaces within which cities exist (the Ottoman city, the Victorian city) are quite different from the way the city is lived – written by Michel de Certeau (1988), Walter Benjamin (1986), or Salman Rushdie (1988). The experience of a place – Delhi, London

– is often closer to the textual representations of novelists Vikram Seth or Hanif Kureishi than those of academics (Durrschmidt 1997: 15).

Utopias

It might also be useful here to remind ourselves of the basic features of the 'Utopia' of Sir Thomas More (1477–1536), as well as the conditions prevailing at the time his book was published (1516). More's imaginary society was founded on the basis of a belief, or ideology – a passionate religious (Christian) belief for which its originator was ultimately to pay with his life; a society where people practised a form of Christian communism, participating with complete equality in all activities relating to housing, clothing, food, education, government, war and religion. What was common for full citizenship for all Utopians was a belief in a good and just God who ruled the world. Such an overriding commitment to a religious faith has characterized many, if not most, Utopian experiments, from that of the Pilgrim Fathers to the followers of Joseph Smith and the Latter Day Saints.

In the second place, Utopia was envisioned as a society and not a city. In early sixteenth-century England a city was a much more distinctive, and different, part of the society than it is in our own day (in the West, at least), when a lifestyle outside the city is not too different from that within it. Third, the actual space and territory of Utopia was represented by More as an *island* located at the limits of what, in 1516, was still a world without boundaries, though close enough to a New World which suggested everything the imagination made possible. Since then, by and large, the history of Utopian settlements has been one of *fleeing from* the social and political disasters created by humankind and attempting to establish *new* societies and settlements in some near-to-pristine environment. We need hardly remind ourselves that the conditions of More's time no longer prevail; the collective abandonment of social, political or environmental chaos is neither a socially responsible option, nor even – except at an individual level – a practical possibility.

Indeed, of the contradictory meanings implicit in the contemporary use of the term Utopian – 'a place or state of ideal (social and political) perfection', as against 'an impractical scheme for social and political improvement' (*Penguin English Dictionary* 1982) – neither really addresses the conditions and material results of five centuries of capitalism, imperialism, colonialism, environmental degradation, namely, *not* how to abandon existing settlements and establish new ones, but how to improve the ones we actually have. Such an agenda, of the improvement and development of both societies and cities, is much less romantic than More's Tudor dreams; much more akin to aiming at the 'satisficing' criteria of management guru Herbert Simon, i.e. not to attempt perfection but rather, considering all circumstances, to attempt what is attainable and satisfactory.

In this context, we need to have a much better historical understanding of the historically contingent concepts with which we try to understand, explain and, above all, order and decide our worlds, including different worlds of the city and the cities of the world. In thinking of Utopias we need knowledge as much as imagination. Much more needs to be known and understood of the *history* of so-called 'Third World' and colonial cities. As I've suggested elsewhere, 'the culture, society and space of early twentieth century Calcutta or Singapore pre-figured the future in a much more accurate way than did that of London or New York. "Modernity" was not born in Paris but rather in Rio' (King 1991: 8). If, after the collapse of the great social experiments of the twentieth century, we are now witnessing a 're-feudalization' of society in Europe and America, with an increasing retreat into suburban fortresses (Ellin 1997), we could benefit by knowing more about feudalism. City-states of the past may well offer visions for the future.

Contradictory Utopias

The 'contradictions' of my title are inherent in the understanding of the project. Utopia is the first, based as it is on a series of oppositions: between the imagined and the real, between harmony and conflict, between the communal and the individual.

As Marx took pains to point out, the city historically results from a contradiction between itself and the countryside; at the local level, the powers that form the city organize their hinterland and live off the surplus the non-urban realm provides. At the global level, existing cities organize the surplus of their own society as well as that of others. As the massive growth of cities since the sixteenth and especially in the nineteenth centuries is a direct outcome of worldwide capitalism (Harvey 1973), ideas for Utopia – depending on our different outlooks – can be based on a striving for anti-capitalism or a perfect capitalism, on being anti-urban or perfecting urbanism. The conventional wisdom emerging from urban studies is that cities are products of the societies in which they exist. This insight was extended to the concept of the world, or global city. To know what it was, how it worked, what it represented, we had to understand (especially) the world economy, and presumably also something of world society, world polity, transnational communications and cultures. The notion of the global city assumes the globalization of capitalism which, given its inherent nature, functions on assumptions of uneven development (Smith 1984); that it will always be possible to produce commodities more cheaply, and/or with greater exploitation of labour, in some parts of the world rather than others. The logic of the global city, therefore, is the persistence of uneven development. Yet rather than stating my vision of Utopia in terms of 'proposals and implementations' as requested, I shall adopt the style of an imaginary narrative.

A Critical Utopia for the World's Cities?

It was conventional wisdom that, over the last four decades of the twentieth century, First and Third World cities had, in certain specific ways, and to varying degrees, become increasingly similar. The ever-widening gap between the rich and poor, the potential of some to earn astronomically high salaries (or in other legal and illegal ways, to accumulate vast wealth) and others to become permanent members of an unemployed, impoverished underclass; the simultaneous production of luxurious high-rise apartments and office towers and low-rise street-level poverty and homelessness; the spread of fortress-like enclaves of residential privilege alongside the increase in street crime and social marginalization; socially, the existence of ethnic, racial and cultural diversity and spatially, ethnic, racial and cultural segregation; the heights and depths of conspicuous consumption as well as the heights and depths of crime, disease, burglary and drugs. In terms of social, racial and spatial segregation, cities in the First World as well as the Third increasingly took on the characteristics of historic colonial cities (King 1976).

The logic of the market, left unchecked, simultaneously reduced and exacerbated the scale of economic and social divisions between different spatial categories. In the last 30 years of the twentieth century, in what at the time were the Third World countries in Asia, differences were reduced between cities and the countryside, as had happened historically in the West – yet were simultaneously exacerbated within Asian Third World cities. Differences between the rich and poor in other Third World as well as First (and previously Second) World cities also became more extreme. Finally, through the same logic of the market and the processes of global capitalism, as economic, social and spatial differences in all cities increased, the differences between the various cities themselves, worldwide, in fact became reduced. Put another way, the economic, technological and social profile of cities worldwide became increasingly similar, although cultural differences remained.

Spatially – by which I refer to their architecture, urban design and physical and spatial form – cities also, in some ways, became increasingly alike (at least in the gaze of the globalized population who moved between them), the result of the international transfers of construction materials, consumer products, architectural and planning ideologies and transportation technology. In other ways, however, partly because it was in the interests of capital – which 'lives and works through difference' (Hall 1991) – to make them different, partly because of the tendency of globalization to 'exacerbate the concern with identity' (Robertson 1992), and partly due to the inherent lasting effects of cultural difference (Nederveen Pieterse 1996), they also stayed, or even increasingly became, different.

These tendencies had become more evident in the last decades of the twentieth century – but they were also much older than that. For what had long been globalized (yet Western-centred) professions of city planning, architecture and urban design, now invariably seeking to retain, or give their particular city, a distinctive visual and spatial image, the extent to which they could make each of them different was a measure of the degree to which all of them became the same – though again, only in the gaze of the 'external' observer. In the gaze of the international traveller, 'real' difference was evident only in cities where there was no local consciousness of their global existence.

In the realm of the spatial (as people were reminded, in the summer of 1997, by the global transmission of a funeral-as-spectacle) the visual exposure of particular city sites offered through the lens of aerial television cameras, deity-like in their vertical surveillance of the affairs of mortal man, increasingly directed the attention of those responsible for policing the city's visual image. A fourth, and hitherto neglected, dimension of the built environment was made visible, namely, the aesthetics of the ground, the horizontal surface of roads and streets. This exposure of public space through the eye of the camera – television, cine, video, as well as the traditional model – probing every corner, exposing the façades, the forms, the spaces and edifices of the city to a critical global gaze, came to have a major impact on the appearance of the city, increasing yet further a concern with the production and consumption of visual culture that had characterized the end of the twentieth century (Walker and Chaplin 1997). Already in the de-industrialized landscapes of the 1970s, public art had begun to impact on the appearance of the city. Blackened for decades, even centuries, many buildings had either been demolished, cosmeticized, or had given way to the plasticized postmodern. In reviving such cities in Europe and America, vast murals, inspired by images of the Brazilian rainforest or of scenes of Alpine meadows taken from *The Sound of Music*, were painted on the outsides of redundant factory walls (Miles 1997). Green activists dug holes in the asphalt surface of overused highways as well as aircraft runways, reducing the flows of traffic and cutting by half the impact of aircraft noise. Trees and shrubs were planted, their chlorophyll-filled leaves helping to clean up the still polluted air. Empty spaces were filled with people's sculpture and flower and vegetable gardens, or made available for musicians, acrobats, performance artists. By 2010, every city had a state-sponsored Centre for the Development of Carnival Arts, the directors of which had been recruited in Trinidad, Rio or Cologne.

The Rise of Urban Government

Given the degrees of difference between cities, and the imperative (see above) that each society or community had as much control as possible over its own agendas and desires, in and for the future, powers of government and control previously developed and implemented at world, state or regional levels were gradually, yet massively, shifted to the level of each individual city.

By the middle of the twenty-first century, cities, as the principal loci of population worldwide, and the centres (especially) of intellectual labour, cultural production, information processing, politics, communication and consumption, were in a far better position to take over many functions, and also services, previously provided and delivered at the level of the nation-state. Even in the 1980s, certain cities were already conducting their own foreign policies, particularly as far as these concerned their economic well-being (Kirby and Marston 1995). Despite the near universal access to electronic communication that was to develop by the mid-twenty-first century, cities, as social units, and their governments were still to be far more spatially accessible to their citizens than nation-states and their governments had been to their subjects. As much smaller social units of population, cities provided much greater possibilities for different political and constitutional choice: where the majority took the form of city republics, a number of others (especially in what was previously the USA) chose to be monarchies; others (especially in what was once the Soviet Union, and in other one-time colonial states) preferred to be bureaucracies; still others, theocracies or enlightened dictatorships.

This shift to the city as the organizing space of social and political life can best be understood as part of a larger historical trajectory. In ancient times, the social, political and spatial organization of people had been in empires, a system that had been revived in more recent memory. The dismantling of over large geopolitical units of authority had begun in the mid-twentieth century with the collapse and subsequent disintegration of the major European empires. The outcome of this disintegration, the tripling of the number of nation-states (from 67 to 186 between 1945 and 1990), had been a major phase in the nation-forming phase of humankind. Prior to the French Revolution there had been some 20 of what we would now recognize as nation-states. Between the Congress of Vienna (1815) and the formation of the United Nations (1945), the number had tripled, from 23 to 67 (Birch 1989).

This organization of people along 'national' territorial lines had largely, though not entirely, been governed by geographical factors – peoples, widely distributed across territories, were divided by oceans, rivers, mountains, deserts. The nationality principle was based on 'where you lived was who you are', logical enough when virtually all the world's peoples were dispersed through rural areas. As recently as 1800, for example, less than 3 per cent of the world's population was urban (Clark 1998), so that organizing scattered populations administratively into territorially based nation-states in the nineteenth and twentieth centuries had made sense.

Yet the expansion of nation-states in the twentieth century was, in the early decades of the new millennium, to be recognized as only a temporary solution to the problems of identity, territory and government. It had been an expected, and 'natural', outcome, the result of decades (sometimes centuries) of colonial rule that had given postcolonial peoples little option but to follow the example of their imperial European rulers – irrespective of the illogical ethnic or territorial basis on which such nation-states were built. Half a century of so-called independence from the 1950s, the increasing consciousness of their still postcolonial status at the millennium, made such states increasingly open to new forms of political, economic and territorial organization.

The shift to forms of city-states and city identities had resulted from five major developments, evident at the close of the twentieth century, which were to continue into the twenty-first. The first was a further destabilizing of the notion of fixed national identities resulting from the collapse of the Soviet empire in 1989 and the subsequent turmoil associated with the re-making of national identities in an increasingly globalized world. This collapse was only a sequel to the equally ambiguous identity situation, which had been created in many postcolonial states 30 years earlier – a situation, for example, where people could move through three or four national identities in a lifetime (e.g. British, Indian, Pakistani, Bangladeshi).

The second development was the massive increase in mobility and migration that had occurred in the twentieth and twenty-first centuries – some permanent, some temporary, some long-term, some short-term, though in total resulting in a massive diaspora of different peoples worldwide, with personal and kinship connections, property, business and personal interests diffused across different states. The effects on identity of such transmigrations (Glick Schiller et al. 1995) were never singular. People increasingly came to have multiple identities, deploying them to their advantage wherever they happened to be.

The third development came from the influence of the electronic media. Despite the fact that electronic communications – television, cell phones, Internet, the web – theoretically enabled people to make completely free decisions as to where they lived, because of the constant introduction of new, 'improved' products, and the need to constantly update software and other equipment, the demographic effect of these new technologies was to keep people close to sources of supply, in or near the cities. The effect of these developments was to loosen, or 'soften up', the attachment of people to singular national identities, to singular places of origin; not necessarily to erase or dismiss them, but rather to make people available for something else in addition.

The fourth development was demographic. Few world leaders (or indeed, the population at large) realized that 1996 was the year in which 50 per cent of the world's population had become urban. 'Despite its symbolic significance, this historical event went largely unrecognized and unnoticed' (Clark 1998: 85), even though reports in 1988 had already suggested that a figure of 60 per cent would be reached by 2025 (United Nations Center for Human Settlements 1988) and that cities of one million inhabitants, just over one hundred in 1960, would be nearing seven hundred in 2025, a figure that was roughly similar to that for cities of half a million inhabitants. By 2015, many large cities with over ten million inhabitants (almost thirty by this date) were already much larger than many small states. In this situation, it was hardly surprising that many visionaries had already seen the nation-state as an increasingly obsolescent form of social, spatial and political organization.

The fifth development was to take place in East and Southeast Asia, which had rapidly overcome the temporary economic crisis of the 1990s. In some postcolonial states (Korea, Hong Kong, Taiwan, Malaysia, Indonesia, Singapore) the high rates of economic development and growth had, by the early twenty-first century, pushed what was often a rural population into cities, cities themselves built to the very highest standards, 'modernized', offering an opportunity not simply to be like others in the Western world but, in fact, to be much better off in every way. In this context, Shanghai had long since overtaken Manhattan as the paradigmatic example of a certain version of 1930s 'modernity' and was to occupy this somewhat obsolescent role for many decades.

The real model of global living came to be Hong Kong. The citizens of this city, by far the wealthiest in the world by the year 2020, had, through an act of unprecedented collective self-reflexivity not unconnected to the inter-action between capitalist and socialist values, come to realize two foundational truths. The first was a realization of the essentially mimetic nature of its first strivings for modernity which, in following the (Western) example of New York, had resulted in an imitative version of Manhattan. However, now (2020) that Manhattan was itself largely a heap of ruins following the gradual decline and then collapse of its financial trading function (taken over by Kuala Lumpur and Hong Kong), the people of Hong Kong had come to realize the false values on which their first 'global city' had been built – a total commitment to profit-hungry capitalism and a way of manifesting this, in the skyscraper skyline, that was totally dependent on Western, especially American, forms of design.

By 2020 such values had gone through a 180-degree turn. While it was still the richest city in the world, the citizens of Hong Kong had become committed to the ideas of an ecologically sound environment. The skyscrapers had been demolished, making way for low-rise, energy-efficient offices and apartment complexes. Parks, greenswards and commons were interspersed throughout the city where citizens could be seen daily practising the old discipline of Tai-chi, exercising minds and bodies. No longer confined to the cramped and obsolete colonial space of 'Victoria Island' and the so-called 'New Territories', the city with its 15 million inhabitants was evenly spread out over the mainland, with transportation provided by a highly efficient rapid transit system. In being thus encouraged to return to their cultural roots, the Chinese population (as well as the large proportion of cosmopolitan inhabitants) attained a new harmony of living, something previously dreamt of, but never attained, by earlier Utopian city planners. In terms of liveability indices – clean air, freedom from crime, longevity, social and spiritual happiness – it had the highest ranking in the world.

As the economic and political significance of the nation-state shrank as a result of economic globalization (already predicted in the 1980s and 1990s), and the worldwide system of cities came into its own, major alliances were formed, not only between cities in geopolitical blocs such as the European Community, NAFTA, SEATO and others, but also between groups of cities specializing in the production of particular services and products, and between those with similar ideological and political outlooks. No longer competing for the favour of investments from multinational companies, individual cities as well as city alliances regulated the conditions under which multinational companies were required to operate (not least as they also needed to compete with the highly efficient city corporations, each of which had largely specialized in terms of function, commodity production or the like). Multinational corporations, no longer footloose, yet with no other opportunities to exist, readily agreed to be taxed in order to pay for infrastructure. Alliances between workers in cities worldwide meant that it was no longer possible to threaten them with undisclosed plans to shift production to other sites.

In order to bring the system of city governments about, urban political infrastructure was strengthened and national levels scaled down. The culturally diverse populations that global capitalism had located in cities both encouraged diversity and difference there, and provided the popular support to sustain it. Because of this diversity, large parts of the (especially rural) world previously excluded from the world economy (ineffectively operated and administered through the competing and contradictory apparatus of private capital and the nation-state) were brought into the world economy, by a much larger, proactive policy run by the alliance of cities. What were, at the end of the twentieth century, single-issue parties – greens, ecologists, feminists, animal rights activists – began in the new millennium to target and win over particular cities. Subsequently, through these smaller social units rather than the state, they were able to diffuse their influence through city alliances.

National governments, while still continuing to exist, had their influence (as well as their costs) substantially reduced. Their task, however, was still considerable as they were responsible for those parts of the nation-states that did not come under the jurisdiction of cities, not least the vast areas of agricultural land and the production of food that goes with this. Quite early on they surrendered their responsibility to RRGs (rural regional governments) whose status and power equalled those of governments of the city. Jurisdiction of the seas, as well as concerns about fishing, marine recreation and the like, were the responsibility of coastal cities.

By the fourth decade of the twenty-first century, only 20 per cent or less of the populations of what, in the 1990s, were nation-states lived in non-urban areas, governed by RRGs. In their international capacity, national governments were also needed to oversee specific environmental, transportation and other matters. Security and defence, however, were transferred to alliances of city governments, logically enough, as here were the main centres of population.

The major shift in responsibility was at the supranational level where, from the late nineteenth to the end of the twentieth century, a myriad organizations had arisen to oversee, develop and provide economic and political relations and exchange between different nation-states at the level of the international. With the demise of the nation-state, and the replacement of the concept of national identity with city identity, a system of *intercity* relations was put into place. The world became an immense beehive of citizens, each one committed, on the one hand, as a Parisian, San Franciscan, Tokyan, Muscovite, Lahori, Delhiwallah, not only to her or his own city but to the idea of city government itself. The very innumerability of major cities in the world (well over three thousand), making it impossible for any one person (or government) to remember them all, was also a factor in the disappearance of the idea of nationality.

The United Nations, which had emerged in the middle of the twentieth century as the pinnacle of achievement in the era of the nation-state (even though there had been fewer than 25 of such units of social organization at the beginning of the previous century), though still continuing – at a level very much reduced in scale and cost – to deal with the semi-redundant apparatus of the nation-state, was eventually replaced by a new body, the United Cities Organization. As City Representatives were in constant electronic communication, there was much less need for a more permanent institution or building (the abandonment of which greatly reduced the influence of the United States, as well as New York, in world affairs). Instead, the United Cities Organization met in one of the world's largest cities every two years, moving round from one to the other. Building on the administrative and logistic structures developed during the era of nation-states, such as the Olympic Games and the World Cup, the UCO was therefore able, over the brief space of a century, to transform totally what, in the 1990s, had been the most over-crowded, dilapidated, polluted, unendowed, badly constructed and congested 50 cities in the world. Carefully pooling and deploying resources gathered on a global scale, combining these with taxes levied on multinational corporations and cooperating with the governments of individual cities, the UCO was able not only to eliminate global poverty but also gradually to even out the distribution of excesses and wants among the cities of the world. In addition, because of its relation to the grassroots of all urban problems and their solutions, the UCO was also able to eliminate the major environmental problems that had been of such concern in the previous century.

Having access to the bulk of the resources formally belonging to the United Nations, the UCO, in close touch with its individual members, was able to address, in a much more realistic and rational way, the principal social problems that had occurred in the world in the second half of the twentieth century, especially after the threat of the Cold War had disappeared in 1989. It had suddenly dawned on the Secretary-General of that august body (the UN) – at the stroke of midnight as the second millennium turned into the third – that by far the largest proportion of the world's problems were of an urban nature, and if not inherently 'urban', none the less erupting in cities: crime, drugs, pollution, poverty, ignorance, terrorism, disease, riots, racism, sexism, global warming, famine, traffic congestion, political corruption, social, racial and sexual oppression, and many more. With the active support of sympathizers worldwide, the creation of the UCO had taken only 20 years. By 2020, as all one-time 'national' as well as 'international' politicians were elected by their urban constituencies, lived in their cities, and so were immediately accessible to the inhabitants, urban conditions rapidly improved. Particular administrative, technical or social ideas to improve the quality of urban life, found to be effective in one or more particular cities, were quickly disseminated round the world (Perlman 1995).

With populations largely located in well-planned yet also architecturally and spatially immensely varied cities, systems of public transport were much improved and developed. By this time, the vast majority of the population lived in a form of accommodation and settlement that had slowly evolved through the nineteenth and twentieth centuries. Just as the interaction of social, architectural and spatial developments had given rise to the neologism 'suburbia' in 1895 (*Oxford English Dictionary* 1989), and the multi-ethnic transmigration of populations had, a century later, spawned 'ethnoburbs' (Li 1998) so, by the 2040s, the total multicultural diversity of massive major cities worldwide, created by total global mobility, had given rise to the metropolitan 'globurb'.

As the problems of poverty and starvation had, by this time, been largely resolved, leading politicians recognized that the main life-threatening disease was overeating and obesity, brought about by a combination of the consumption of industrialized food, marketed by multinational corporations, and irrational forms of individualized, city-polluting transport. By 2030, so committed were people to eradicating obesity worldwide, creating immense strain on hospital facilities and health-maintenance organizations, that in addition to laying down intricate webs of cycle routes in all the world's cities, most people walked between their various destinations. The 415 million automobiles worldwide that had fouled the air of cities in the declining decades of the twentieth century, the oil and gas fuelling of which had not only endangered the future of the planet but led to the loss of millions of lives in futile wars (fought around the oil-producing states of the Middle East), were now recycled and put to better use. The millions of people previously employed in their production – especially in the cities of Japan, the United States, Britain and Germany – were in this way released to be engaged in more satisfying and socially useful work.

Early on the morning of 6 July 2036, in the crystal clear air of east

London's Tower Hill, the silence broken only by the cry of seagulls above and the lapping of the waves against the shore of the River Thames below, two hundred tourists from every corner of the world, waiting to visit the Tower of London, were suddenly startled, and then amazed, to see a clear, bright, technicolour vision of a figure they quickly recognized as Sir Thomas More – head intact, and with what appeared to be a smile of satisfaction. Five hundred years after his execution, his image rose over their heads, moved slowly into the sky and floated off towards the celestial city ...

Acknowledgements

This is a revised version of a paper given at the Institute of Social Studies forty-fifth Anniversary Conference 'Global Futures', The Hague, 8–10 October 1998. I am indebted to participants for their valuable comments, not all of which I have been able to accommodate on this occasion. My thanks to Michael Ma for references.

Note

1. Thanks to Ursula King for this comment.

References

Ashcroft, B., G. Griffiths and H. Tiffin (eds) (1995) *The Post-Colonial Studies Reader*, Routledge, London.

Atlas of the World (1996) Oxford University Press, Oxford.

Benjamin, W. (1986) 'Paris, capital of the nineteenth century', in W. Benjamin, *Reflections: Essays, Aphorisms, Autobiographical Writings*, Schocken, New York.

Birch, A. (1989) *Nationalism and National Integration*, Unwin Hyman, London.

Chakrabarty, D. (1992) 'Postcoloniality and the artifice of history: who speaks of Indian pasts?', *Representations*, 37 (winter): 1–27.

Certeau, Michel de (1988) *The Practice of Everyday Life*, University of California Press, Berkeley.

Clark, D. (1998) 'Interdependent urbanization in an urban world: an historical overview', *Geographical Journal*, 164 (1): 85–95.

Dirlik, A. (1994) 'The postcolonial aura: third world criticism in the age of global capitalism', *Critical Inquiry*, 20 (2): 328–56.

Donald, J. (1992) 'Metropolis. The city as text', in R. Bocock and K. Thompson (eds), *Social and Cultural Forms of Modernity*, Polity (in association with the Open University), Cambridge.

Durrschmidt (1997) 'The delinking of locale and milieu: on the situatedness of extended milieux in a global environment', in Eade, (ed.) (1997).

Eade, J. (ed.) (1997) *Living the Global City*, Routledge, London.

Ellin, N. (ed.) (1997) *Architecture of Fear*, Princeton Architectural Press, New York.

Fisher, J. (ed) (1995) *Global Visions: Towards a New Internationalism in the Visual Arts*, Kala Press, London.

Friedmann, J. (1995) 'Where we stand: a decade of world city research', in Knox and Taylor (eds) (1995).

Glick Schiller, N., L. Basch, and C. Blanc-Szanton (1995) 'From immigrant to transmigrant: theorizing transnational migration', *Anthropological Quarterly*, 68 (1): 48–63.

Hall, S. (1991) 'The local and the global: globalization and ethnicity', in King (ed.) (1991, 1997a).

— (ed.) (1997) *Representation. Cultural Representation and Signifying Practices*, Sage, London.

Harvey, D. (1973) *Social Justice and the City*, Arnold, London.

— (1989) *The Conditions of Postmodernity*, Blackwell, Cambridge.

Kapur, G. (1995) 'A critique of "internationalism"', in Fisher (ed.) (1995).

King, A. D. (1976) *Colonial Urban Development*, Routledge and Kegan Paul, London and Boston.

— (1990) *Global Cities. Postimperialism and the Internationalization of London*, Routledge, London.

— (1994) 'Terminologies and types: making sense of some types of buildings and cities', in K. Franck and L. Schneekloth (eds), *Ordering Space: Types in Architecture and Design*, Van Nostrand Reinhold, New York.

— (ed.) (1996) *Re-Presenting the City: Ethnicity, Capital and Culture in the 21st Century Metropolis*, Macmillan and New York University Press, London.

— (ed.) (1991, 1997a) *Culture, Globalization and the World-System. Contemporary Conditions for the Representation of Identity*, Macmillan, London; 2nd North American edn University of Minnesota Press.

— (1997b) 'The problem of global culture and the internationalization of architecture', in Eva Barlosius et al. (eds), *Distanzierte Verstrickungen: Die ambivalente Bindung soziologisch Forschender an ihren Gegenstand*, Sigma Verlag, Berlin (in German).

— (1997c) 'Locution and location: positioning the postcolonial', in Vikram Prakash, *Theatres of Decolonization: Architecture/Agency/Urbanism* II, College of Architecture and Urban Planning, University of Washington, Seattle.

Kirby, A. and S. Marston (1995) 'World cities and global communities: the municipal foreign policy movement and new roles for cities', in Knox and Taylor (eds) (1995).

Knox, P. L. and P. J. Taylor (eds) (1995) *World Cities in a World-System*, Cambridge University Press, Cambridge.

Li, W. (1998) 'Anatomy of a new ethnic settlement: the Chinese *ethnoburb* in Los Angeles', *Urban Studies*, 35 (3): 479–501.

McGrew, A. (1992) 'A global society?', in R. Bocock and K. Thompson (eds), *Social and Cultural Forms of Modernity*, Polity, Open University Press, Milton Keynes.

Miles, M. (1997) *Art, Space and the City: Public Art and Urban Futures*, Routledge, London.

Nalbantoglu, G. B. and Wong Chai Thai (eds) (1997) *Postcolonial Space(s)*, Princeton University Press, Princeton, NJ.

Nederveen Pieterse, J. (1996) 'Globalization and culture: three paradigms', *Economic and Political Weekly*, 8 June: 1389–93.

O'Byrne, D. (1997) 'Working class culture: local community and global conditions', in Eade (ed.) (1997).

Penguin English Dictionary (The) (1982) Penguin, Harmondsworth.

Perlman, J. (1995) 'The Megacities Project', paper presented at a conference on World Cities in a World System, Washington, DC.

Prakash, G. (1990) 'Writing post-orientalist histories of the Third World: perspectives from Indian historiography', *Comparative Studies in Society and History*, 32 (2): 383–408.

Robertson, R. (1992) *Globalization: Social Theory and Global Culture*, Sage, London.

Rushdie, S. (1988) *Satanic Verses*, Viking, London.

Said, E. (1978) *Orientalism*, Pantheon, New York.

— (1993) *Culture and Imperialism*, Chatto and Windus, London.

Sassen, S. (1991) *The Global City: London, New York, Tokyo*, Princeton University Press, New York.

Scott, A. (ed.) (1997) *The Limits to Globalization*, Routledge, London.

Smith, N. (1984) *Uneven Development: Nature, Capitalism and the Production of Space*, Blackwell, Oxford.

Spivak, G. C. (1992) 'Can the subaltern speak?', in L. Grossberg, C. Nelson and P. Treicher (eds), *Cultural Studies*, Routledge, London.

— (1997) 'City, country, agency', in Vikram Prakash (ed.), *Theatres of Decolonization: Architecture/Agency/Urbanism*, College of Architecture and Urban Planning, University of Washington, Seattle.

United Nations Center for Human Settlements (Habitat) (1988) *Global Report on Human Settlements*, Oxford University Press, Oxford.

United Nations Center for Human Settlements (Habitat) (1996) *An Urbanising World. Global Report on Human Settlements*, Oxford University Press, Oxford.

Wager, W. W. (1989) *A Short History of the Future*, University of Chicago Press, Chicago.

Walker, J. and S. Chaplin (1997) *Visual Culture: An Introduction*, Manchester University Press, Manchester.

Watson, S. and K. Gibson (1995) *Postmodern Cities and Spaces*, Blackwell, Oxford.

Williams, P. and L. Chrisman (eds) (1993) *Colonial Discourse and Postcolonial Theory: A Reader*, Harvester, Brighton.

Yeoh, B. (1996) *Contesting Space: Power Relations and the Urban Built Environment in Colonial Singapore*, Oxford University Press, Oxford.

Index